W9-DIM-540

WITHDRAWN

PRAISE FROM OUR READERS

Mastering Access 97

"I read this book from cover to cover and found each page loaded with very practical information and explicit examples. I commend the authors for their ability to communicate otherwise very technical detail in understandable 'user friendly' language. I highly recommend this book."
Jim Shannon, Montana

Mastering FrontPage 98

"Best of the 9 FrontPage 98 books I own. Sybex does it again! I have been reading computer books for the last 10 years and Sybex has been a great publisher—putting out excellent books. After reading 3/4 of the book so far, I know that the publisher and the authors take pride in their product. It's a wonderful book!"
Mike Perry, New Jersey

"This is THE book for mastering FrontPage 98! I skimmed through 4 other books before deciding to buy this one. Every other book seemed like a larger version of the weak documentation that comes with the software. This book provided the insight on advanced subjects necessary for administering a web. A must buy for FrontPage users."
Richard Hartsell, Utah

Mastering Windows 98

"The first book I've read that does what it says it will do! I learned more about Windows 98 in the first one hundred pages of this book than in all of the previous books I had read. My copy lies, dog-eared, beside my computer as a constantly ready source of easy to understand information. It really does show you how to Master Windows 98."
Steven Dean, Arizona

SYBEX

www.sybex.com

MASTERING
POWERPOINT
2000

MASTERING™
POWERPOINT® 2000

Katherine Murray

SYBEX®

San Francisco • Paris • Düsseldorf • Soest • London

Associate Publisher: Amy Romanoff
Acquisitions Manager: Kristine O'Callaghan
Acquisitions & Developmental Editor: Sherry Bonelli
Editors: Elizabeth Hurley-Clevenger, Diane Lowery
Technical Editor: Susan Glinert
Book Designers: Patrick Dintino, Catalin Dulfu
Electronic Publishing Specialist: Kris Warrenburg
Project Team Leader: Shannon Murphy
Proofreaders: Bonnie Hart, Sandy Young
Indexer: Lynnzee Elze
Cover Designer: Design Site
Cover Photographer: Sergie Loobkoff

Screen reproductions produced with Collage Complete. Collage Complete is a trademark of Inner Media Inc.

SYBEX is a registered trademark of SYBEX Inc.

Mastering is a trademark of SYBEX Inc.

TRADEMARKS: SYBEX has attempted throughout this book to distinguish proprietary trademarks from descriptive terms by following the capitalization style used by the manufacturer.

The author and publisher have made their best efforts to prepare this book, and the content is based upon final release software whenever possible. Portions of the manuscript may be based upon pre-release versions supplied by software manufacturer(s). The author and the publisher make no representation or warranties of any kind with regard to the completeness or accuracy of the contents herein and accept no liability of any kind including but not limited to performance, mer- chantability, fitness for any particular purpose, or any losses or damages of any kind caused or alleged to be caused directly or indirectly from this book.

Library of Congress Card Number: 99-61296
ISBN: 0-7821-2356-2

Manufactured in the United States of America

10 9 8 7 6 5 4 3 2 1

To Kelly, Christopher,
and Cameron—
Love, Mom

ACKNOWLEDGMENTS

Thanks to all the great and talented people at Sybex for shepherding this book through the publishing process, netting out the bugs, and putting it in a layout both inviting and useful for our readers. In particular I'd like to thank Development and Acquisitions Editor Sherry Bonelli, Editors Elizabeth Hurley-Clevenger, Diane Lowery, Brianne Agatep, Lisa Duran, Malka Geffen, and Rebecca Rider for all their work on this book. Many thanks should go to the production team: Project Team Leader Shannon Murphy, Electronic Publishing Specialist Kris Warrenburg, and Proofreaders Bonnie Hart and Sandy Young. Their behind-the-scenes work of marrying art with text (and lots of project management!) makes for a beautifully illustrated book.

CONTENTS AT A GLANCE

TABLE OF CONTENTS

PART III • QUINTESSENTIAL POWERPOINT   237

9   Coloring Your Presentation   239

10   Printing Slides and Handouts   261

INTRODUCTION

Two things are certain about that next presentation you're going to give: (1) It's going to include the best ideas you can come up with and (2) it will be better than your last one, because this time you're using Microsoft Power-Point 2000.

If you're a professional who doesn't have much time to devote to learning new programs, PowerPoint is the program you need. This popular presentation graphics program has been designed with one thing in mind: to help *you*, the harried professional, assemble all the pieces that comprise an effective presentation, with minimum time and trouble.

Whether you want a simple presentation with no-nonsense bulleted lists, or an entertainment feature with built-in narrations, sound, video, and special slide-show effects, PowerPoint 2000 can help you create the biggest effect for the least hassle, making sure your message is communicated in the clearest possible way.

How to Use This Book

Mastering PowerPoint 2000 introduces you to the kernels of knowledge all users need when exploring a program for the first time. Like the software it presents, this book takes you through the process of creating presentations in a sequence of logical, "What-do-I-do-next?" steps.

Beyond the basics, however, *Mastering PowerPoint 2000* adds depth and breadth by providing tips for creating both quick and more detailed presentations. Additionally, Part II includes side discussions that give a professional spin to the topic at hand. For example, in Chapter 4, "Creating and Enhancing Graphs," the discussion "The Four Most Effective Charts" tells you which charts professional presenters use most often when displaying different types of information.

Pictures of what you should expect to see on your computer's monitor illustrate important steps within each section. Additionally, tables are used to organize and highlight information in a quick-look format. Bulleted lists call attention to items in each section, and each chapter begins with a list of the major topics covered in that chapter.

Throughout the book, you'll find tips, notes, and warnings, as well as sidebars that give you information above and beyond the basic procedures and examples.

Feel free to use this book in the most logical way for you. If you're pressed for time or need a simple reminder on a task you've tried before, look up the task you need in the index or in the table of contents, and use the book as a reference. When you have a few minutes to spare and want to experiment with some of PowerPoint's new features, use this book as a guide and follow along with some of the examples. You will learn the hows and whys behind different operations, and you'll find that you've sped through the learning curve in no time at all.

Who Should Read This Book?

This book will help you concentrate on the process of creating your presentations as quickly and cleanly as possible. You'll find the organization, examples, and illustrations of this book helpful if you fit any of these descriptions:

- You are responsible for creating weekly production charts used in the departmental meeting.
- You are new to presentation graphics and need a straightforward, no-frills guide to creating effective slides and going a few steps beyond the ordinary.
- You hope to learn more about multimedia and want to master PowerPoint in order to produce professional-looking slide shows.
- You are looking for a way to make professional-looking presentations easily.
- You are working as part of a group and want to work on a presentation collaboratively while you are online.
- You want to create and publish Web pages using PowerPoint for your company or personal use.
- You want to be able to open and work with HTML files in PowerPoint.
- You have a lot of work to fit into an already filled-to-bursting day and you want a guide that will help you cut the time and effort you would usually need to invest in learning a new program.

Highlights of Microsoft PowerPoint

You'll see one of the biggest benefits of Microsoft PowerPoint 2000 from the first moment you start the program. Recognize the general layout? If you've worked with other Microsoft programs, you'll be able to find your way through PowerPoint easily. Other features that help you create your presentations include the following:

- Professionally designed templates, some with animation, that you can use to create presentations quickly.

- An AutoContent Wizard that actually helps you write the content of your presentation (it doesn't just proffer advice).

- A new Normal View which displays the slide, the outline, and a notes area. The slide changes dynamically as you add to the outline and make modifications.

- An Outline view in which you can enter the text for your presentation and organize your thoughts before adding artwork.

- A wide array of charting features (including the ability to create 3-D charts in a variety of styles), which gives you almost unlimited capacity to display data.

- A large palette of preset color schemes that are consistent with Office color palettes, providing you with color sets that work effectively together (or you can create your own).

- Full drawing capabilities, which give you the freedom to either add hand-drawn art to your slide show or use one of the many clip art files included with PowerPoint.

- Six different views—Normal, Slide, Outline, Notes Pages, Slide Sorter, and Slide Show—that allow you to see your presentation in all possible perspectives.

- Full text support, including such enhancement options as font, size, style, and color selections, as well as special effects like shading and shadowing.

- The ability to print collateral materials—handouts, speaker notes, slide printouts—in either full color or black and white.

- The option of easily publishing your presentation to the World Wide Web.

- Seamless compatibility with other Microsoft Office programs so that you can use data from other programs in your presentations with a minimum of hassle.

The designers of Microsoft PowerPoint had a two-pronged goal: to create an easy-to-use presentation graphics program that gives you all the help you want and to give you the freedom to be creative. PowerPoint's flexibility and wide variety of features will help you make your points powerfully—right from the first time you use the program.

What's New in Microsoft PowerPoint 2000?

PowerPoint 2000 builds on the easy-to-use features of its predecessor and, as you might expect, adds more Web capability and online features. PowerPoint 2000 introduces these additional or enhanced items:

- **HTML to your heart's content.** Now you can save your presentation as a Web page and open it and work with it again in its HTML format.

- **Browser big display.** Now that everything works so seamlessly with Internet Explorer, you can choose to give your presentation in full-window view with only the Explorer interface showing.

- **The Office Assistant.** This interactive help utility "watches" what you're trying to do and offers help when you need it; it now has a cute new companion, a little hound that scratches, taps his toes, stretches and yawns—oh, and offers you help when he thinks you need it. (I always *suspected* my dog Edgar knew more about computers than I do.)

- **The Office Assistant morphs into the Presentation Assistant at show-time.** The Presentation Assistant gives you tips and suggestions as you practice your slide show.

- **A new Normal View.** Normal View incorporates three of the other Power-Point views: Slide, Outline, and Notes Pages. All three elements display in individual windows within the work area. This reduces the time you spend clicking back and forth among views you use often.

- **Become a broadcaster.** Are you into push technology? Did you always want to be a Web broadcaster? PowerPoint enables you to broadcast your presentation over the Web. You arrange for the audience, set up the show, and Power-Point does the work.

- **Resize slides on the fly.** Now you can automatically resize slides when you are giving a presentation in Internet Explorer 4. Simply drag the window border and the slides resize proportionately to the window.

- **Present online, now.** You can easily have online meetings and show your PowerPoint presentation. This enables you to collaborate with others online and create the presentation your department—or company—is looking for.

- **Artsy buttons.** Now you can turn any graphic image into a bullet.

How This Book Is Organized

Mastering PowerPoint 2000 consists of three parts, and each will add to your repertoire of PowerPoint skills. If you have some experience with presentation graphics or with PowerPoint in particular, you may want to skip some of the early sections and go right to more complex operations. Overall, this book is presented in a sequential, process-oriented manner to ensure that you'll learn everything you need to know about PowerPoint from the ground up. Information is provided for both the exploring beginner and the stretching enthusiast. The following sections explain each of the parts of *Mastering PowerPoint 2000*.

Part I: PowerPoint Essentials

This first part sets up the groundwork for the rest of your PowerPoint experience:

- *Chapter 1* tells you what's possible with PowerPoint. You'll find out what you need to present effectively and explore the variety of features that PowerPoint includes to help you get going quickly on your first presentation. This chapter gives you the basics of all the important PowerPoint elements you'll encounter throughout the program and finishes up with tips for creating effective presentations.

- *Chapter 2* gives you a quick PowerPoint once-over. If you're in a hurry ("The meeting starts in 20 minutes. Can you whip up a quick presentation?"), you can use the techniques in this chapter to help you quickly produce a professional presentation. You'll learn about all the basic facets of the program and see how it all fits together in this fast, bird's-eye-view of program features.

Part II: The Right Tools for the Job

Part II gives you the information you need for working with the various components in your PowerPoint presentations:

- *Chapter 3* lets you jump right in and start on the text of your presentation. Whether you choose to let PowerPoint direct you (the AutoContent Wizard will walk you through the process of creating the slide text) or go solo, you'll quickly discover how simple text entry, editing, and enhancement is in PowerPoint. You will learn about the new editing features in PowerPoint 2000 and discover additional features like AutoCorrect that can help you make sure you've got the right word in the right place. Finally, Outline view gives you an easy way to scan the content of your presentation at a glance.

- *Chapter 4* explains the ins and outs of creating and working with graphs. From learning what graph type best represents what data to working with the datasheet, modifying entries, adding labels, and enhancing the graph, you'll uncover ways to display your information graphically using the best of Power-Point's graphing capabilities.

- *Chapter 5* takes you into the world of graphic arts—PowerPoint style. Whether you choose to use the new AutoClipArt feature PowerPoint offers (the program will suggest what pieces of clip art fit the text in your presentation), make your selection from the ClipArt Gallery, or draw it yourself, you'll find the information you need to add art to your slides.

- *Chapter 6* is all about sound. From beeps to soundtracks, sound adds an element unavailable just a few years ago on most PCs. Today, you can easily add sound to your PowerPoint presentation. This chapter helps you add sound to single objects or slide transitions and play the sound either once or repeatedly to produce the desired effect.

- *Chapter 7* explores the basics of adding video to your multimedia presentation. Where can you find video and how do you set it up to run in your PowerPoint presentation? Learn how to add video objects to your PowerPoint presentation and use the Windows 95 Media Player to select, edit, and save the video you want without ever leaving PowerPoint.

- *Chapter 8* takes you one step closer to presenting by helping you add the finishing touches to your presentation. This chapter focuses on things like setting automatic or manual timing, choosing slide transitions, and working with build and hidden slides. You'll also learn to start a slide show, rehearse the timing of your presentation, and use PowerPoint's special presentation features like the Slide Navigator, the Meeting Minder, and Presentation Conferencing.

Part III: Quintessential PowerPoint

Now that you've got the basics (and then some), this part concentrates on those features of PowerPoint that go above and beyond creating the traditional presentation:

- *Chapter 9* explores the wealth of color options available in Microsoft Power-Point. Professional designers have created a large number of color schemes that work together effectively; you can use their expertise to help you design the best presentation possible. Or, if you prefer, you can mix and match your own colors—whether you're re-coloring a single item or an entire presentation.

- *Chapter 10* shows you how to best print the slides you've created. You can print a variety of other materials as well, including audience handouts, speaker notes, and slide printouts. Also in this chapter, you'll learn to add headers and footers to your slides and evaluate the printouts you produce.

- *Chapter 11* tells you about another output option for your presentation files: the Internet. You can become an Internet or intranet publisher simply by preparing Web pages from your presentations. You can use animations, ActiveX controls, and more, to make your site interesting and functional. And now PowerPoint 2000 gives you the ability to collaborate with your peers online—working with Net-Meeting to review, mark up, and comment on your blossoming presentation. You can also use the HTML features to save and open HTML files. A final cool Internet feature is broadcasting your presentation—now you can schedule a time and broadcast your presentation over the Web, complete with video and audio files.

- *Chapter 12* gives you information on working with multimedia files—which ones you're most likely to be working with, how to store them, and what you can do to manage them most effectively.

- *Chapter 13* completes the book by opening the curtain on your actual presentation. Are you ready? Tips for presenting, practicing advice, evaluation sheets, and practical considerations in this chapter are included to help you make the best statement possible. The chapter concludes with case studies of presentations used in different settings.

- *Appendix A* may turn out to be the first resource you need, because it covers the procedures for installing PowerPoint. *Appendix B* tells you how to change some of the program defaults once you are comfortable with the basic workings of the program. *Appendix C* provides a number of tips for the first-time presenter. Look here before you get up in front of that crowd.

Now that you know the overall game plan for the book, it's time we got started. In just a few short minutes, you could be making points—powerfully—with PowerPoint.

PART I

PowerPoint Essentials

LEARN TO:

- *Getting started*

- *Discover presentation possibilities with PowerPoint*

- *Learning important elements*

- *Create your first presentation*

- *Using templates*

- *Save your presentation file*

CHAPTER 1

PowerPoint Possibilities

ommunication is everything. Whether you are trying to win board approval for that new product you're designing, getting up in front of a group of potential clients for the first time, or preparing to broadcast your presentation over the Web, the way that you present your message—and yourself—is the most important factor determining whether or not you hit your mark.

PowerPoint 2000 is a presentation graphics program that helps you create simple, yet slick, and even stunning presentations that are limited only by the capability of the computer equipment you use and your imagination.

Why Presentations? And Why PowerPoint?

If you're a Microsoft Office user, you may have stumbled across PowerPoint on your way from Word to Excel. PowerPoint is the presentation part of the Microsoft Office suite of programs, giving you the ability to present data created in the other applications in your PowerPoint presentations.

For example, suppose that you've been writing an annual report for a client. You use Microsoft Word and create a professional, four-color report with photos and a sophisticated layout. The client is pleased. "You know," he says, "Our annual meeting is coming up. Do you think you could do a presentation to go along with the report?"

"Sure," you answer, and then think to yourself, "But *how?*"

PowerPoint gives you the answer. With PowerPoint, you can easily adapt the text from your Word document to fit your PowerPoint presentation. You can use the photos; you can design a similar layout. And then you can go several steps farther and add multimedia, including elements like a video of the CEO talking about his vision for the future, sound capsules of happy employees, or even animation showing the changes in the production line. When you're through with the presentation, you can save the file in HTML format and post it as a page on the World Wide Web, or even make the presentation in cyberspace to a group of invited guests.

As new technological standards become the norm, people are creating presentations in more varied settings and with better tools than ever before. Never again must you face a roomful of 20 expressionless faces, armed only with two weak visual aids and note-cards dog-eared from hours of nervous practice. Now the small business owner trying to drum up financial support for his endeavors can take a laptop into the potential investor's office, fire up PowerPoint, and show the investor an animated slide show with striking color and design and even music—a hard thing to resist if you're accustomed to an open hand and an apologetic gaze. PowerPoint helps you make a strong statement, even when making statements isn't your strong point.

How Are Presentations Used?

Presentations are used in all kinds of settings, all over the globe. In corporations large and small, one-person businesses, and volunteer organizations, presentations are used to inspire ("Look what a great job we did this quarter! Let's do it again next time!"), educate ("Here's how you apply for financial aid..."), and inform ("Statistics show that 38 percent of all households currently own computers equipped with CD-ROM drives...").

What Do I Need to Present?

Before you begin exploring PowerPoint on your own, you may be wondering what type of system you'll need in order to present these eye-opening, pulse-quickening presentations you'll be creating.

Years ago, a presentation was a pretty bland affair. An instructor-type person stood in front of the room with a wax pencil and an overhead projector. A typesetter may have created the acetate sheets, if you were lucky and got a "professional" presentation; otherwise, you may have seen hand-written slides or images dummied up with press-on letters.

When the PC came into the picture, the support for on-screen display was minimal. Presentation programs need lots of memory, lots of RAM, and lots of pieces like sound cards, video cards, and interfaces that must be compatible for everything to work together smoothly. In the old days, this was a rare thing.

With the introduction of Windows 3.1, multimedia—the mixing of a variety of media to create a presentation that includes music, video, graphics, text, and sound effects—was officially recognized. That version of Windows included multimedia capabilities, acknowledging to the world that multimedia was here to stay.

Windows 95 brought support for multi-media features. Plug-and-Play, which was touted as one of the big benefits of Windows 95, means that you can easily add components to expand your system's capabilities. With a range of CD-ROM titles and multimedia experiences available to us today (even America Online says "Hello!" when you log on), we are riding the wave into an ever-more interactive future. In the 97 generation of programs (such as Office 97 and PowerPoint 97), the focus was on ease of use, seamless Internet access, and point-and-click Web page creation. PowerPoint 2000 takes this approach a step further by pushing powerful presenting to the edge of the Net and beyond: now we can make our presentations online to groups (using a feature called *broadcasting*), prepare sophisticated Web sites from PowerPoint presentations, and use the simple and elegant tools to create the impact we want and need.

Windows 98 continued the ease-of-use trend and made the operating system even more fully integrated with the Web. Now you are just a click away from the Internet, no matter which Windows application you are using. And increased performance shows up in your PowerPoint presentations, which load and run faster and more smoothly than previous versions allowed.

Hardware-wise, to run presentations you need a computer capable of running Windows 98 comfortably, including at least 16MB of RAM (32 or more is better), plenty of hard disk space, a sound system, a fast modem if you intend to run Web presentations or upload presentation files, and a good video system.

For presenters, this embracing of multimedia means that the choices you have available in terms of how you will present have greatly improved. You might make your presentation on your laptop that you position on a client's desk. You may stand in front of a crowd of 200 people, projecting the presentation on a screen. You may send your presentation over the airwaves as part of an infomercial, upload it to an online service to be accessed by thousands of interested potential clients, or incorporate it into a shareware CD-ROM given to subscribers of industry magazines.

When you use the technology and the tools available to you, each presentation you create is a potential masterpiece—you are limited only by your own imagination and your willingness to use it.

Getting Started with PowerPoint

No matter who you are or what you work with, chances are that PowerPoint will not be something you'll use every day. Your need for it will come and go. You'll use it every day for a week while you prepare a special presentation, and then perhaps not use it again until the following month—or year.

Foreseeing this, Microsoft created PowerPoint to be easy to use in a short period of time. You won't need lengthy refresher courses or spend hours retaking tutorials or scanning the documentation. The features in the following list are part of this easy-to-return-to design:

- When you first start PowerPoint, you can access the AutoContent Wizard shown in Figure 1.1, which will actually create the basic content of your presentation for you. If words aren't your strong point, you can choose the type of message you've got to convey and let PowerPoint assemble the outline for you. Then just plug in your text, add sound and video if you like, and present.

FIGURE 1.1

PowerPoint includes an AutoContent Wizard that will suggest topics for your presentation's content.

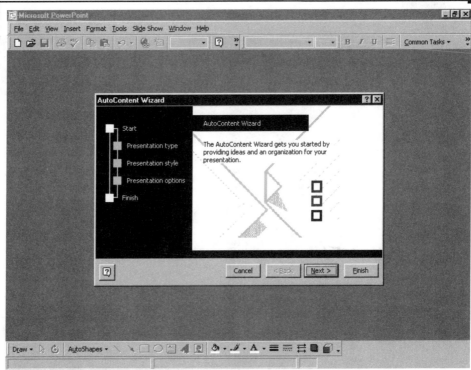

- PowerPoint Presentations are templates that have been designed, from start to finish, with all the necessary colors, text choices, and slide layouts. As you'll see in Chapter 2, they have their own tab in the New Presentation dialog box. You simply choose the presentation you want and enter your own information.

- Presentation Designs are slides that contain basic color, style, text, and alignment choices for your presentation. You choose the look you want and then create the rest of the presentation—slide layouts and all—the way you want it.

- A new tab for Web Pages lets you keep your Web designs separate from traditional presentations. And you can use the two samples as the basis for your own Web pages.

- The PowerPoint screen is organized so that everything you need is visible at all times (see Figure 1.2). Once you've had a few minutes to get oriented, you won't have any trouble remembering where things are and how you move from one view to the next. From the Window-style toolbars and on-screen buttons to the status bar and work area, everything will become familiar quickly.

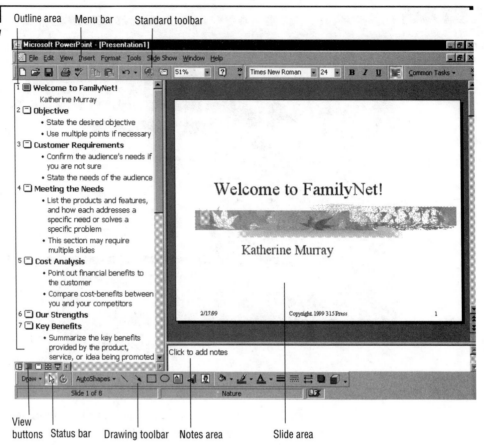

- ToolTips appear when you position the mouse pointer above specific tools, telling you the name of the tool you're about to select. This way, you don't need to remember which tool does what, because PowerPoint will tell you what you need to know when you need to know it. Automated features—special tools such as AutoCorrect and Style Checker—keep an eye on you as you create the presentation and provide additional tips and suggestions to help you stay on track.

- Without prompting, AutoCorrect automatically changes things like mistakes in capitalization (two capitalized letters in a row or days of the week in lowercase letters). AutoCorrect can also be used to change your "shorthand" into longer phrases you don't want to spend the time typing out (see Figure 1.3). For more information on using AutoCorrect, see Chapter 5, "Entering and Editing Text."

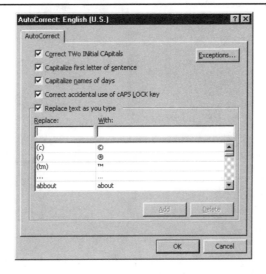

FIGURE 1.3

AutoCorrect changes capitalization and can substitute your short-hand for longer words that you teach it.

- The Office Assistant sits in the upper right corner of your screen, ready to help when you seem stuck in the middle of a procedure (see Figure 1.4). You may see a paperclip character (called Clipit) who offers you help or, depending on which Assistant is set up to be the default on your computer, you may see a dog instead. When you are first learning PowerPoint, you may find the tips and help your Assistant offers invaluable, but as your experience grows you will probably want to turn the Assistant off to free up the screen space and memory he uses. (To turn off the Assistant, select Help ➢ Hide the Office Assistant.)

- For more information about working with PowerPoint Help, see Chapter 2, "The Quick and Easy Presentation."

FIGURE 1.4

The Office Assistant watches your every move and presents help options when you seem to need them.

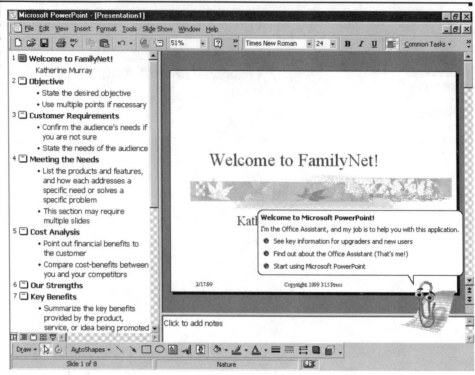

Important PowerPoint Elements

Before you start creating your first presentation with PowerPoint, you need to know a little more about the tools that are available to you. This section gives you a basic introduction to some of the features and tools unique to PowerPoint, like the choices you have for displaying slides and the various toolbars, templates, palettes, and such. Table 1.1 introduces the new highlights of PowerPoint 2000, giving you an overview of the features newest to the program.

TABLE 1.1: POWERPOINT 2000 HIGHLIGHTS	
Feature	**Description**
Office Assistant	Not brand-spanking new in this version, but new-and-improved, the Office Assistant offers animated interactive help when you need it most. Once you get comfortable with the program, you can disable the Assistant if you want to.

Continued ▶

TABLE 1.1: POWERPOINT 2000 HIGHLIGHTS (CONTINUED)

New HTML features	Now you can save various file formats in HTML and you can open, modify, and save them again once you're done.
Browser display	Windows 98 brought the Web to everything; now you can present in Explorer mode, so your presentation looks like an interactive Web site for your viewers to peruse.
Online collaboration	Work teams are all the rage, and PowerPoint 2000 enables you to work collaboratively with team members literally all over the globe. Set up an online meeting to review your presentation and incorporate notes, suggestions, and action items as you go.
Broadcast features	Now you can broadcast your presentation on the Web—you bring the audience, and PowerPoint does the work.
Normal view	Slide view, which once upon a time just displayed the full slide, now incorporates both outline and notes view so that you do less switching among views. PowerPoint 2000 now calls this new variation of Slide view: Normal view.
Graphic bullets	Now you can use any piece of art as a bullet character in your presentation. This means you can use your company logo, a special symbol you create, or something else that is unique to your company, your message, or your audience.

PowerPoint Views

With PowerPoint, you can look at your presentation six different ways. Depending on what you're doing, different views will be helpful at different times. Table 1.2 explains the different views and gives you an idea of when you might use each.

TABLE 1.2: POWERPOINT 2000 VIEWS

View	Description	Use To
Normal view	Shows a combination of Slide, Outline, and Notes Pages view	Work in multiple areas at once; add text in Outline and see it appear on the slide. Type in notes that will remain with the current slide.
Slide view	Displays the current slide—in the work area	Add text or objects to a single slide or format only one slide.

Continued

TABLE 1.2: POWERPOINT 2000 VIEWS (CONTINUED)

Outline view	Displays the presentation text in outline form, in a thumbnail slide, and in the Notes area	Enter text quickly, following a format provided by PowerPoint or your own; move, copy, or cut text; spell-check text; read through for consistency; or print a script for your presentation.
Slide Sorter view	Displays multiple slides in reduced size on the screen	Add transitional effects, set timing, move or delete slides, or check presentation continuity.
Notes Pages view	Displays the current slide in a reduced size with room for notes at the bottom of the page	Add a memo, notation, or instruction for a slide or slides. You can also use Notes Pages view to design explanatory handouts for your audience.
Slide Show	Presents the slides in a slide show, using the entire screen	Check the timing, transition, and multimedia effects of a show before you present it, see what you've done so far, or show a client the presentation you've been working on.

After you make your initial choices about your presentation in the New Slide dialog box (such as do you want to use the AutoContent Wizard or a Design Template, start from scratch, etc.), you can choose the layout of the first slide you want. After you click on OK, the first slide of your presentation appears in the work area, displayed in what's known as Normal view (see Figure 1.5).

 TIP In subsequent work sessions, PowerPoint will open an existing file to wherever you were when you saved and closed the file. If you were working in another view, for example, or had used the Zoom command to enlarge the display, those settings will be in effect the next time you open the file.

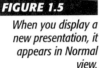

FIGURE 1.5

When you display a new presentation, it appears in Normal view.

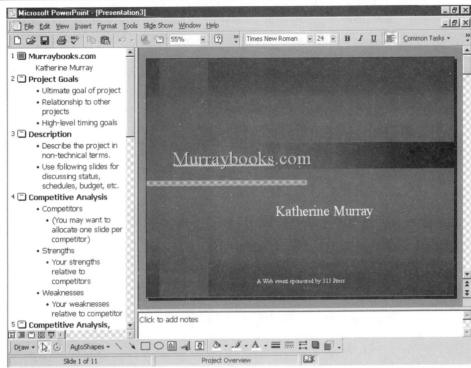

Normal View

Normal view is a new look for PowerPoint 2000. Taking the best of three of Power-Point's other views—Slide view, Outline view, and Notes Page view (which has been deleted as a stand-alone view in the new version—Normal view puts all the different perspectives together so you can do less switching on-screen. You can see at a glance how changes you make in the outline affect the actual look of the slide; you can add notes in the Notes area that will stay with the current slide.

You work with one slide at a time in Normal view. When you change to one of the other views, you can return to Normal view by choosing View ➢ Normal view or by clicking the leftmost button in the View buttons row in the lower-left corner of the work area.

Slide View

Slide view shows you the slide you're creating as it will appear in final display. Years ago, Slide view would have been comparable to the desktop, where you put together this piece of text, that clip art (manually clipped out of an art set), and that piece of acetate to come up with the most professional slide you possibly could.

In Slide view, you work on slides one at a time, adding the various elements of your presentation. You will do most of your up-close work here. While in Slide view, you'll also choose colors, perhaps add text, create charts, add clip art, insert movies, add sound, and copy, cut, and paste slides. To select Slide view, click on the Slide view button.

MASTERING THE OPPORTUNITIES

A Matter of Perspective

Different views appeal to different people, and as your experience with PowerPoint grows, you'll settle into using the views you like best. Here's a general idea of the different ways in which you will use the views:

1. Start in Slide view to design the basic look of the page. Here you can choose colors, add background elements, and make decisions about text color, font, and alignment.

2. Next, go to Normal view. Here you can brainstorm ideas for the content of the presentation, jotting down roughly what you plan to cover and then cleaning it up into a recognizable outline. It's a nice perk that you can see the way the individual slides are affected by the additions you make in the outline area.

3. You can go back to Slide view to look at each page individually, change formats, move text, and add charts and clip art.

4. If you need to edit the outline, switch to Outline mode, where you can see and deal only with text.

5. When you have the basic elements in place, go to Slide Sorter view and take a look at the whole presentation in thumbnail size. Here you can see whether you've been consistent with certain elements and varied enough with others. Did you use the same headline font all the way through? Did you break up the slides so you don't have four charts in a row? Slide Sorter view helps you see patterns you might not see in Slide view.

6. Next practice the presentation in Slide Show view. Make notes of anything you need to remember at the point of presentation and add those notes in Notes area of Normal view.

7. Then, after practicing a few times, you're ready to give the presentation to your best and most helpfully critical friends, so they can help you identify spots you still need to work on.

Outline View

Outline view looks like a scrap of paper on which you might jot down ideas between meetings, in addition to a Notes area and a miniature slide display. Instead of scribbling notes and using them (or losing them), you can enter the notes directly into Power-Point's Outline view, using them as the basis for your presentation.

To select Outline view, click the Outline view button in the bottom left corner of the work area. Your presentation appears in outline form, as shown in Figure 1.6. Note that an existing presentation is displayed in the figure; if you are creating a new presentation from scratch, the page will be blank when you display Outline view. However, if you are creating a presentation based on one of PowerPoint's templates, sample text appears in the outline.

FIGURE 1.6

Outline view makes it easy for you to write down your thoughts quickly and coherently.

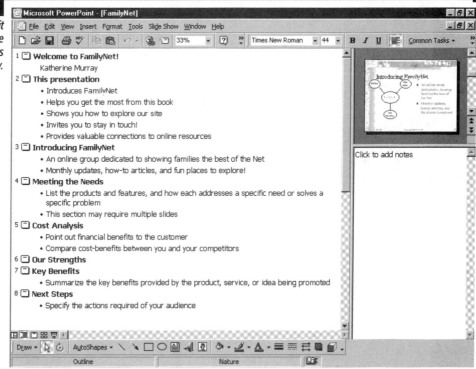

Entering the text for your presentation in Outline view is simple; just position the text cursor and start typing. Commands in the toolbar let you start new slides and indent points easily, and text control settings help you get the look you want. A new feature in PowerPoint 2000 is a miniature image of the current page shown in Slide view in the upper-right corner of Outline view.

TIP You can do anything—except add art—in Outline view. If you think better on paper, you'll find the Outline view comforting, as you can just type in your thoughts and worry about the graphics later.

Slide Sorter View

Have you ever spent an afternoon arranging scraps of paper on your desk, trying to decide the order in which you should present your information? We all know there's more than one way to present a good idea—but searching for the best way is sometimes an exhausting experience.

Slide Sorter view lets you experiment with different page orders by moving pages around on the screen. While you're at it, you can check out the way your colors look and decide whether you like the overall effect of the text, transition, and timing settings you've chosen. Slide Sorter view itself resembles a big light table (remember those?) on which you can arrange a number of slides (see Figure 1.7). Using the Summary Slide tool, you can create a slide that provides a summary of your presentation, including only those slides you select.

FIGURE 1.7

Slide Sorter view displays a number of slides on the screen at one time so you can rearrange them and change their settings if necessary.

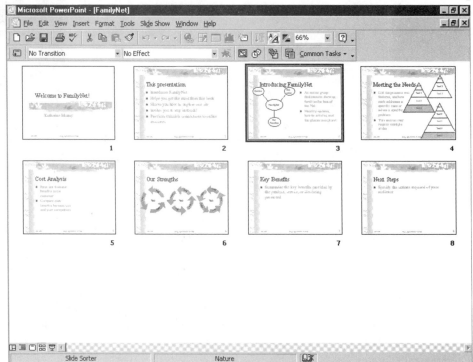

Notes Page View

Trying to use ordinary notes while giving a presentation can be pretty risky. Papers get shuffled and fall out of your folder or even get stuck to the back of other documents.

PowerPoint helps you create notes that will stay with your presentation—and with you. To display the view, open the View menu, click the Expand button at the bottom of the menu, and select Notes Page. This view provides you with an area for speaker notes, along with a reduced picture of the slide. You enter the notes in a text box beneath the slide so that when you print the page, the slide and your notes are printed on the same sheet.

Figure 1.8 shows an example of Notes Page view. The small image of the slide appears in the top half of the page; your notes go in the bottom half. You can type—or add artwork if you like—in the notes section.

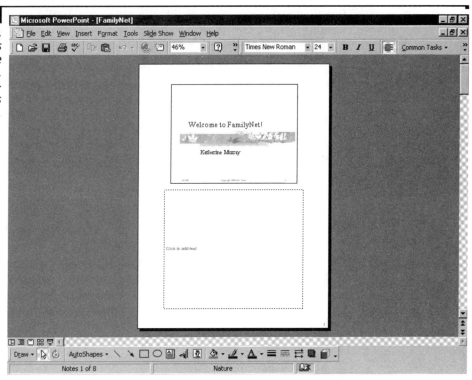

FIGURE 1.8

In Notes Page view, you can enter notes that correspond to the displayed slide, producing self-documenting slides and handouts.

The AutoContent Wizard

A *wizard* is an automated utility that walks you through a particular process so you don't have to figure it out from scratch. By asking you a series of questions, the wizard interactively assembles the presentation for you. The AutoContent Wizard that appears when you first start PowerPoint will, if you like, help you develop the basic content of your presentation. In Chapter 2, *"The Quick and Easy Presentation,"* you'll use the AutoContent Wizard to create a fast presentation of your own. Although PowerPoint 95 first introduced the AutoContent Wizard, PowerPoint 2000 gives it a new level of helpfulness. Now you'll find new ideas, more content, and suggestions from the experts on how to make your presentations the best they can be.

Masters

One of the keys to a good presentation is consistency—you want your presentation to have a certain look and feel so readers or viewers can follow your ideas easily.

PowerPoint *masters* can help you get and keep that consistency throughout your presentation. A master is like a piece of your company's letterhead—it has the same basic information on every sheet. On the Slide Master, for example, which serves as the background for all slides in your presentation, you might want to include the following things:

- Your company's logo
- Your company's name
- Your department
- The date the presentation was prepared

PowerPoint includes masters for slides, titles, handouts, and notes. In addition to adding different objects to masters, you can control the way the text appears by choosing a certain typeface, size, and style for text. The master "remembers" your text selections and displays the text in your slides in the specified style. The same thing applies to color—you can assign a certain color scheme to the master and PowerPoint will apply the color you've chosen to your developing presentation.

Templates

PowerPoint knows that you aren't always sure how you want your presentation to look before you start. For that reason, the developers included a number of presentation templates you can use as the basis for the presentations you create. PowerPoint divides its templates into two groups, both of which are available when you choose New from the File menu.

In the New Presentation dialog box, you can choose templates from either the Design Templates tab or the Presentations tab (see Figure 1.9). Both include a number of templates. The difference is that a Design Template includes only a single slide with all the color, background, and text options already set; you then build the rest of your presentation based on those choices. The Presentations tab, on the other hand, displays templates of entire presentations, complete with various slide layouts, as well as color, background, and text choices.

Choose the template you want in the Design Templates or Presentations tab of the New Presentation dialog box.

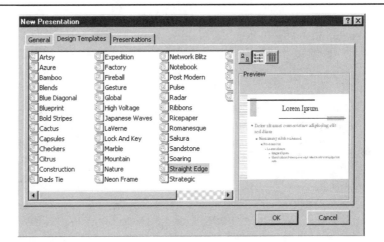

 NOTE If you want a presentation in which you need only plug in text and art, select the Presentations tab. If you want to make your own slide layout selections and build the presentation based on preset color and design choices, click on the Design Templates tab instead.

MASTERING TROUBLESHOOTING

Help! I'm Webless!

Do you need Internet access to use PowerPoint 2000? No. But you'll find that the capabilities of the program and the resources you can tap into to make your presentations the best they can be will be limited if you don't have access to the World Wide Web. Several of the new features—include saving to and using HTML formats, working with online collaboration, and Web broadcasting your presentation—involve working with the Net.

How do you get Web access? First you need a modem, of course. A fast modem. 56K KBPS is currently the fastest standard modem, but 33.6 or 28.8 will do. (The numbers refer to the speed at which the modem sends and receives data—the higher the number, the faster the transmission.)

Next, you need an account with an Internet Service Provider (ISP) or an online service that offers Internet access. Information services like CompuServe, America Online, and The Microsoft Network all offer general Internet access in addition to their own offerings. Internet Service Providers are available in your local area (check your phone book or call a local library or university to find out where).

Finally, you need a *Web browser*, which is a program that enables you to "surf" or browse the World Wide Web. Your Internet Service Provider may provide you with one, or you can download Internet Explorer 5.0 from Microsoft's Web site at www.microsoft.com or Netscape Communicator from www.netscape.com. Not only will having Internet access expand your computer horizons, but it will add ideas to your storehouse of things you'd like to try, and significantly increase your resources for doing new and unusual presentations. And who knows? You might wind up becoming a Web publisher yourself. Publishing presentations to the Web is easy to do with PowerPoint. (See Chapter 11 for details.)

Color Schemes

Choosing the right color scheme often determines whether your presentation works or not. With effective color, you can turn a boring, no-one's-going-to-pay-attention-anyway presentation into something everybody talks about for weeks.

But many people have trouble mixing and matching colors. What looks good together, and why? What colors fit the tone of your presentation? What colors should you use under different lighting conditions?

Color-wise, PowerPoint knows what's hot and what's not. Simply select the Slide Color Scheme command from the Format menu and then choose the basic color scheme you want. You can choose from several preset palettes in the Standard tab or create your own by selecting the Custom tab. Figure 1.10 shows the Standard tab of the Color Scheme dialog box.

The color schemes are coordinated to work together on-screen, in print, and on slides. You control whether you want the color scheme applied only to the current slide or to every slide in the presentation. With over 16 million colors to choose from, this takes an enormous worry off the shoulders of graphics presentation neophytes.

FIGURE 1.10

PowerPoint makes choosing a collection of colors for your presentation a simple process.

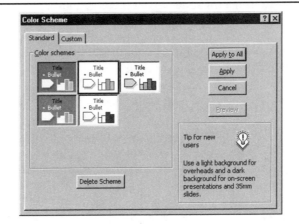

 TIP The color schemes you use in PowerPoint can be easily applied to other Office applications, as well. When you copy and paste shapes and text from one program to another, you can be sure that the color in one program will be consistent with the color in another.

In this section, you've seen some of the elements that make PowerPoint easy to use and master. Throughout the book, you'll find many more features to help you on your way through your PowerPoint experience.

Tips for Creating a Good Presentation

With some careful planning, adequate time, and the right tools, anyone using Power-Point can create a stunning presentation. But, especially if this is your first time creating a presentation, how do you know what makes a good presentation good? This section gives you some basic guidelines you can use while creating your own presentations. Remember, however, that you can always rely on the expertise in the templates to make design choices, and the AutoContent Wizard can lead you through the process of writing the text in an organized fashion.

When you are ready to create your own presentation without the help of a template or wizard, you can use these guidelines to help you hit the mark:

- Consider your audience
- Consider the tone of your presentation
- Consider your tools for presentation

Let's look at each of these considerations and ask some important questions as you begin planning your presentation.

Considering the Audience

Before you even start planning your project, you need to know about the audience that will be seeing your work. Are you going up before a board of directors for a large firm? A small non-profit organization? Stockholders? Advertising executives? Prospective clients?

Knowing the audience for your presentation will help you tailor the content and tone of your work. You wouldn't give an equipment training session to a group of high-level managers; similarly, you won't spend a large amount of time analyzing financial matters for personnel more involved with employee productivity.

The audience will also have some bearing on the type of presentation you create. Are you teaching a class? Title and bullet charts will help reinforce your points better than a series of complex charts. If you hope to motivate a roomful of salespeople by explaining sales trends, colorful attention-grabbing charts may convey in a glance what could take quite a bit longer verbally.

Before you actually begin creating your presentation, think about the best way to reach your audience. And remember that once you've reached them, you need to hold their attention.

Considering the Tone

The tone of your presentation is much like the personality of your work. After you've figured out who the audience is and what kind of presentation they may be expecting to see, think about the way you'll present the information. Is the meeting hurried, with only a few moments allotted to each presenter? Or do you have plenty of time, with more time left over for questions and answers? The answers to these questions will affect whether your presentation must be quick and to the point or can be more relaxed in style and content.

In a typical business, the corporate identity is important. Logos run rampant throughout presentations, and bulleted lists highlighting goals and productivity requirements are a staple. With PowerPoint, you can add some "serious" graphics by adding a picture of the world, international maps and flags, landmarks, or other far-reaching symbols that add a sense of importance to the background of your work. If you need to lighten things up a little, you can choose from PowerPoint's many cartoon illustrations to give your presentation a more relaxed look.

Considering the Tools

As you create your presentation, daydream a little about how you envision it being presented. Will you be standing before a large crowd? Sitting at a board room table? Will you have access to a large-screen monitor (or to a computer at all)? Will you be confined to a slide or overhead projector? Will you be giving the presentation over the Internet?

Think about the tools you'll have for delivering the presentation and how effective those tools will be, given the type of audience you're presenting to. If you are speaking to a large crowd and have only a small-screen monitor on which to display, you will either need to arm-wrestle the AV department for a data panel (a device that plugs into your computer and allows you to project the contents of your display onto a screen) or you'll have to make do with the small screen and print handouts for your audience. If you won't be present in person—for example, if you're giving the presentation on your company's Intranet or sending it via e-mail to a client in another country—think about the tools you'll need to get the file where it's going.

 TIP Giving members of the audience something to take with them after a presentation—notes or printed graphs—is good for reinforcing your message. Be careful not to simply repeat your presentation in print, however; that's a good way to make sure your printed materials wind up in the recycling bin.

The Big C: Continuity

When you get down to the nitty-gritty of on-screen composition, having a few simple design ideas in mind will help you create a usable and successful presentation.

This sounds like something out of fourth-grade English class, but it's important: Continuity makes sure your presentation hangs together as a whole, presents your message clearly, and gives that sense of "Aha!" that clicks inside people when they've just witnessed a well thought out and presented plan.

Continuity helps your audience understand the "big picture" of your presentation. Suppose, for example, that your presentation is about new products your toy company is manufacturing for the upcoming holiday season. The overall tone is one of excitement and anticipation, as your company has done very well in the last year. You put quite a bit of money into research and development and created a new line of top-quality toys. Hold onto that enthusiasm—it should carry through your entire presentation.

Continuity in tone is sometimes a difficult goal to achieve, especially when you've got both good and bad news to communicate to your audience. If you need to talk about both the phenomenal success of your new line of Slimeballs and the screeching halt of sales of Godzilla-tron, talk about Godzilla-tron first. That way, the good news washes the bad news off the palate.

Visual continuity is much easier to achieve. With visual continuity, your presentation holds together with the help of a series of design elements repeated from page to page or from section to section. Simple items you can use to add visual continuity to your presentation include the following:

- Company name and/or logo
- The project name
- Date and page information
- The background color used throughout
- A project symbol or logo
- Background design elements like custom art, shadows, maps, flags, etc.

Suppose, in a different example, you are creating a presentation that highlights the two best-selling products in your insurance agency. One, a life insurance policy, has been doing very well in sales to individuals and business owners. The other, a health policy, targets businesses and has seen a whopping increase in the last 12 months. For each of these products, you want to show three charts: last year's sales, this year's sales, and projected sales for the next 12 months.

A presentation without visual continuity might use a different chart type for each chart—leaving viewers unsure what you're saying and wondering why you chose the charts you did. A visually continuous presentation, on the other hand, would parallel the two products and use the same type of graph to show similar data relationships. The continuity helps viewers understand your points and remember more of your presentation later.

Chapter Summary

This chapter introduced you to PowerPoint 2000 and explored the benefits the program has to offer. You learned about many of the important elements you'll work with as you begin your hands-on experience with presentation graphics, and also picked up a few pointers that will help you create your own presentations. In the next chapter, you get to work creating a fast and easy PowerPoint presentation.

CHAPTER **2**

The Quick and Easy Presentation

f you, like many people, are responsible for putting together a presentation on short notice, you don't want to wade through lengthy academic descriptions of procedures you may never use just to find the few important pieces of information you need. Therefore, this chapter is designed around a "ready, set, go!" approach. You'll learn only what you need to start up PowerPoint; to make some choices for starting your presentation; to add text and graphics; and to save, show, and print the file. The procedures described in this chapter will walk you through your first presentation in 30 minutes or less.

NOTE If you have not yet installed PowerPoint 2000, take the time to do it now. Appendix A tells you how to install the program.

Starting PowerPoint

You can start PowerPoint two ways. One way is to Double-click the My Computer icon on your desktop, then navigate to the folder in which you installed PowerPoint 2000, and double-click the program icon, as shown in Figure 2.1.

FIGURE 2.1

You can start PowerPoint by navigating to the program icon and double-clicking it.

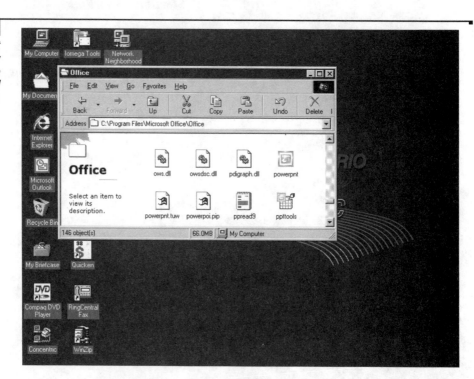

The other way to start PowerPoint is via a menu command. Choose Start ➤ Programs ➤ Microsoft PowerPoint. (Figure 2.2 shows the submenu that appears after you open the Programs menu.)

FIGURE 2.2

Choosing PowerPoint from the Programs menu

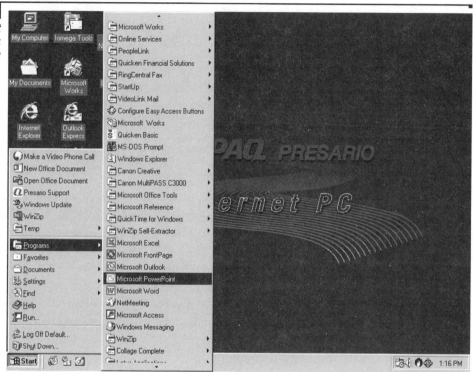

With either approach, after you click Microsoft PowerPoint to start the program, you'll see the screen shown in Figure 2.3.

In the center of the PowerPoint work area, the PowerPoint dialog box appears. This dialog box gives you the choice of starting a new presentation (several different ways) or opening an existing presentation. You can choose from the following options:

- AutoContent Wizard
- Design Template
- Blank presentation
- Open an existing presentation

FIGURE 2.3

The PowerPoint startup screen

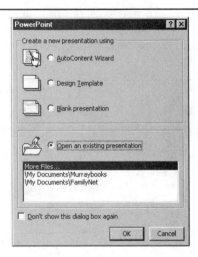

Choosing *AutoContent wizard* takes you to an automated utility that helps you create the content of your presentation. You'll learn how to create a simple presentation using this feature in the next section. If you choose *Template*, you will be given the option of choosing a basic presentation design on which you can build your own presentation. *Blank presentation* takes you to a blank presentation screen, where you can create all your own elements for your presentation. Finally, the *Open an existing presentation* option displays the Open dialog box so you can open a PowerPoint file you have already created. After you make your choice, click OK to start working with PowerPoint.

Getting Help

When you begin learning anything new, it's a good idea to know what tools are available to you in times of trouble. PowerPoint has a comprehensive help system that enables you to ask for and get help in whatever form is most comfortable for you. If you've worked with Windows programs before, you won't find any surprises in the PowerPoint help interface—the Help Topics dialog box enables you to search for help by topic or keyword, and the Answer Wizard enables you to enter plain-English questions and receive plain-English answers.

You'll also find help buttons in the upper-right corner of dialog boxes (click on the small question mark and then on any option or setting you don't understand).

Working with the Office Assistant

Changes have been made in Office 2000 to the Office Assistant, an animated little fellow who pops up in the upper right corner of your work area when you seem to be struggling with a particular operation (see Figure 2.4).

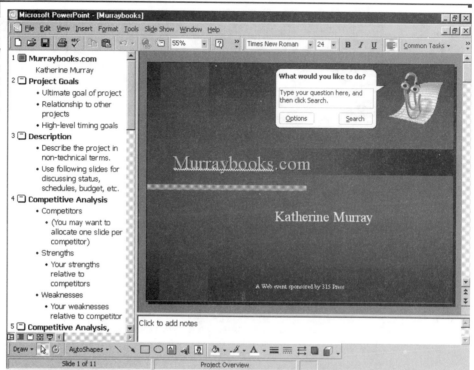

The purpose of the Office Assistant is to watch over your work and make suggestions when you seem to need it. You can also use the Assistant to help you search for information on specific PowerPoint topics. You can put the Office Assistant away if it annoys you, by right-clicking and choosing Hide. When you want its help again, simply open the Help menu and click Show the Office Assistant.

Microsoft on the Web

You can also get PowerPoint help surfing the World Wide Web. You'll find the *Office on the Web* option in the Help menu. After you click Connect and make the online connection, the Help menu lists the Office on the Web option, which you can click to move to the Microsoft Office Web site (see Figure 2.5).

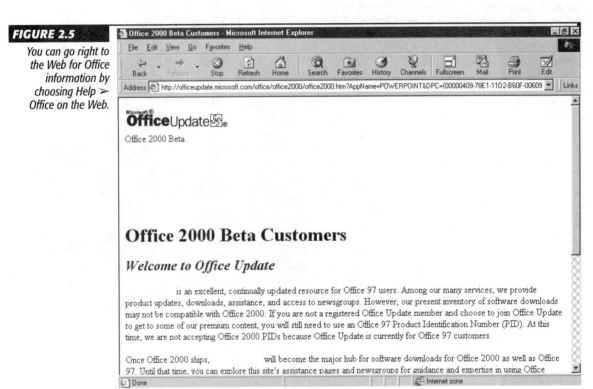

FIGURE 2.5

You can go right to the Web for Office information by choosing Help ➢ Office on the Web.

Creating a Simple Presentation

With PowerPoint's predesigned templates and the AutoContent Wizard, you have everything you need to assemble an on-the-fly presentation. You just need to plug in your own ideas and present. In this section, we'll take you on a quick tour of the steps involved in creating a simple presentation. Specifically, you'll learn how to do the following things:

- Work with the AutoContent Wizard
- Choose a template
- Add text
- Add a title
- Move text areas
- Resize text boxes
- Add art
- Resize art objects
- Start a new slide
- Start a slide show
- Save the presentation
- Print slides

Working with Wizards and Templates

We learn most things in our lives through imitation. If we see an office design that appeals to us, we try to design our office in a similar way. If we run across a particularly successful advertising gimmick, we might try to use the same approach in selling our product. Imitation can be a great teacher.

PowerPoint gives you two different ways of learning by imitation. The AutoContent Wizard interactively leads you through the process of creating a presentation by asking you a series of questions. Similarly, templates give you the bare bones of a presentation upon which you build using text and graphics. In both cases, you learn the process and basic design concepts while using the time-saving tools that PowerPoint provides.

Using the AutoContent Wizard

The AutoContent Wizard will lead you through a series of questions to help you construct the basic content of your presentation. From your answers, PowerPoint will assemble an outline to which you can add your own text, graphics, multimedia objects—whatever.

First, choose the AutoContent Wizard in the PowerPoint opening screen, which appears when you start PowerPoint (see Figure 2.6).

FIGURE 2.6

*Start the AutoContent
Wizard from
the PowerPoint
dialog box*

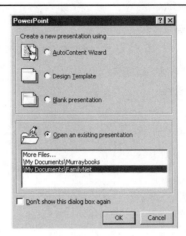

If you have been working in PowerPoint—that is, you're not just starting your work session—you can start a new presentation by opening the File menu and choosing New. The New Presentation dialog box, shown in Figure 2.7, appears.

FIGURE 2.7

*The New Presentation
dialog box*

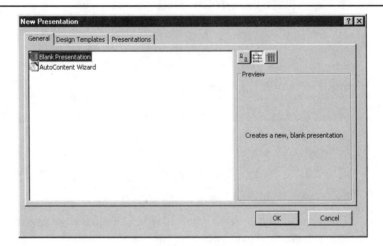

When the Presentations tab of the New Presentation dialog box is displayed, the AutoContent Wizard always appears in the upper-left corner of the window. To begin using the wizard, select it and click OK. The first screen of the wizard appears, as shown in Figure 2.8.

FIGURE 2.8

The opening screen of the AutoContent Wizard

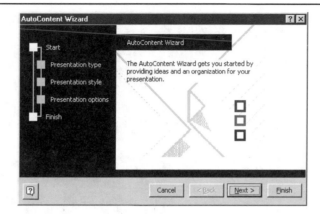

First you need to choose the type of presentation you want to create. A number of different presentation types are listed, because the All button is selected by default. If you want to see what's available for a particular type of presentation, such as Corporate, click the button in the center of the dialog box. The list shows only those presentation types that correspond to the category you selected.

If you click the Carnegie Coach button in the bottom center portion of the dialog box, you'll get a list of various presentations on how to run a presentation meeting. These choices will help you produce a presentation that can be used to teach others how to hold meetings, prepare presentations, introduce speakers, and more. Click your choice in the right column; then click Next.

Next you need to tell PowerPoint how you will give the presentation. Are you planning an onscreen presentation? A Web presentation? Will you be creating 35mm slides? The options on this page list your choices; click the one that is appropriate for your needs and click Next.

The next screen asks you for the presentation title and footer information. You can also elect to display the date and page number on slides. When you click Next on this page, the final screen tells you to click on Finish to complete the process. After you do so, PowerPoint puts all the information together and displays the presentation in Normal View (see Figure 2.9).

FIGURE 2.9

The AutoContent Wizard completes the basic presentation and displays it in Normal View.

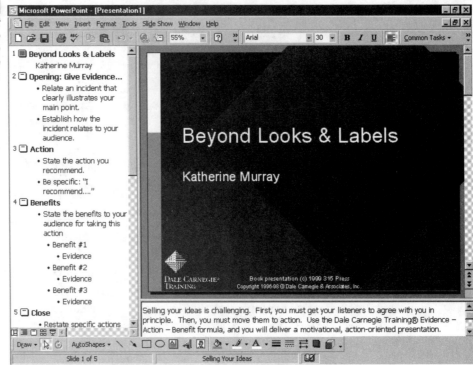

Now you need to add your own text, graphics, and multimedia objects. You can add text quickly here in Normal View. You just highlight the text you want to replace and type the new text. For more information about entering, editing, and enhancing text, see Chapter 3, "Entering, Editing, and Enhancing Text."

When you are ready to add graphics, charts, and multimedia objects, change to Slide view. To do that, click the Slide View button in the lower-left corner of the work area. Figure 2.10 shows the presentation in Slide view.

FIGURE 2.10

Display the AutoContent Wizard's creation in Slide view

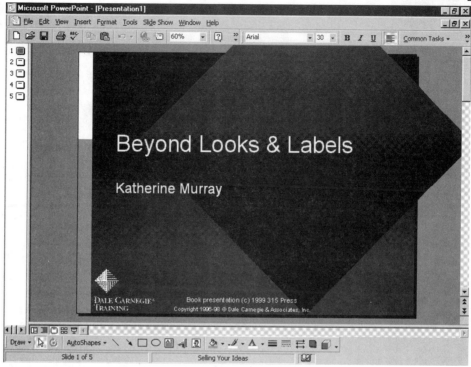

Using Design Templates

PowerPoint 2000 includes a number of new templates on which you can base your own presentations. Some include basic design elements for the background and text that are already set for you. Others include both these settings and sample text for your presentation.

To choose a template, either select the Design Template option in the PowerPoint dialog box which appears when you first start the program, or click on the Presentations tab or the Presentation Designs tab in the New Presentation dialog box. Figure 2.11 shows the Presentations tab with the Reporting Progress or Status template selected. Notice that a preview of the template appears to the right of the icon area.

FIGURE 2.11

Choosing a pre-designed presentation template

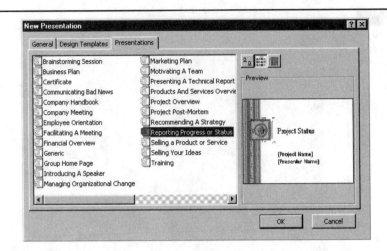

Here are the distinctions between the Presentations and Presentation Designs templates:

- A Presentation is a sample presentation that includes text prompts suggesting the topics to cover in a specific order in your presentation. Figure 2.12 shows the Reporting Progress or Status presentation displayed in Normal view, so you can see the text that has already been entered.

- A Presentation Design template includes background color selections, text settings, formatting specifications, and background graphics, but no text. When you choose a Design template and click on OK, PowerPoint prompts you to choose a page layout and then displays the first page you choose in Normal view, as shown in Figure 2.13. Notice that there are no text entries in the Outline pane.

FIGURE 2.12

The Reporting Progress or Status presentation template in Normal view

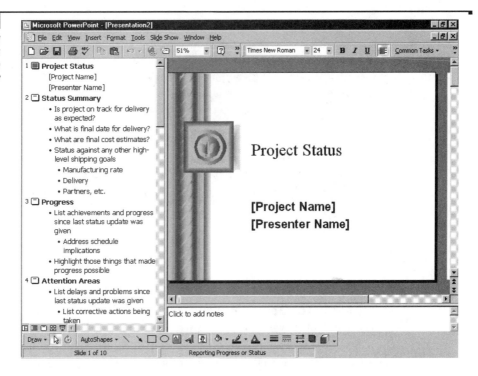

FIGURE 2.13

The first page of a presentation based on the Sumi Painting presentation design

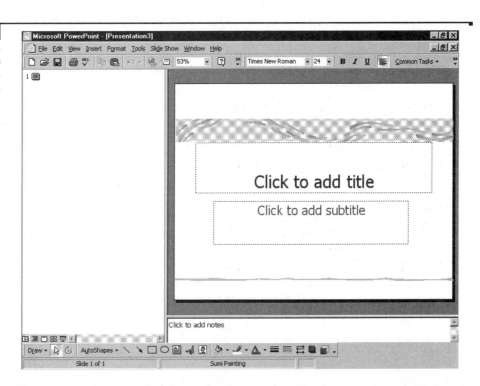

MASTERING THE OPPORTUNITIES

If you're new to presentation graphics, starting out with either the AutoContent Wizard or a template is your best bet. The AutoContent Wizard will help you create the content of your presentation, depending on what message you are communicating. Templates— either in the form of Presentation Designs, which give you only the basic design of the presentation, or Presentations, which provide complete multipage presentations you can use and then add your own text and graphics—show you how the experts put together presentations. You'll be able to see how the different elements of the presentation work together most effectively while you learn the basics of the program.

Exploring the PowerPoint Menus

PowerPoint uses nine different menus to house the commands you'll work with throughout your PowerPoint experience. You can also select commands by clicking the icons in the toolbar, just below the PowerPoint menu bar. You have the option of adding different tools to the existing toolbar and creating your own custom toolbars. For more about creating your own toolbars, see the "Understanding Toolbars" section later in this chapter. But let's start with a basic understanding of the menus.

As you become more familiar with PowerPoint's features and commands, you'll discover where the commands you use most often are stored. Each menu includes a group of commands related to a specific function. Table 2.1 explains the menus in more detail.

TABLE 2.1: AN OVERVIEW OF POWERPOINT MENUS

Menu	Description
File	Provides commands for creating new files; opening, saving, and printing files; setting up pages; preparing a file for the road.
Edit	Enables you to copy, cut, and paste objects; undo operations; establish hyperlinks; delete slides; and find and replace words or phrases.
View	Allows you to select the different PowerPoint views. Choose Normal, Slide Sorter, Notes Pages, or Slide Show, or display the Masters for selected page types on which you can add repeating background elements. You can also control the display of on-screen items like the toolbars, rulers, and guides. You can also magnify the screen up to 400 percent.

Continued

TABLE 2.1: AN OVERVIEW OF POWERPOINT MENUS (CONTINUED)

Menu	Description
Insert	Allows you to insert any of a number of elements into your slides and presentations. Specifically, you can insert a new slide, the date, time, or page number, slides from another file or outline, clip art, graphics, tables, graphs, or a sound clip or video piece. You can even insert an entire presentation into your presentation, if you like.
Format	Controls items like font, alignment, spacing, color, shadow, styles, and basic presentation characteristics such as layout, background, and color. You can also change the presentation design and replace fonts from this menu.
Tools	Provides add-on items that help you create effective presentations, including a spelling checker, AutoCorrect, a choice of transitions, and special effects. With the new Meeting Minder feature, you can take notes during a presentation or set up for presentation conferencing. Export allows you to prepare notes and slides you can use with Microsoft Word. Additionally, with commands in the Tools menu you can customize the displayed toolbar and control editing and general display options.
Slide Show	The commands in the Slide Show menu are concerned with displaying the show. You can choose to start the slide show, rehearse the timing of the show, create and set up animations, choose transitions, create custom shows, and more.
Window	Controls the look of your screen. New Window displays a new presentation window for you to work in, Arrange All tiles the slides on the screen, Fit to Page displays windows one at a time with no overlapping, and Cascade displays windows in overlapping style. Additionally, this menu shows you the names of any open presentation files.
Help	Includes commands for getting you out of tight places in PowerPoint. You can look through the Microsoft PowerPoint Help , show or hide the Office Assistant, use What's This? to find out about an object or item and get understandable answers and references; or go online with the Office on the Web option.

Understanding Toolbars

PowerPoint includes a number of toolbars that you can use to streamline your work. For example, when working with graphics, you may want to display the drawing toolbars (there are two) on the screen. When adding special effects to objects, you may want to display the Animation Effects toolbar.

A toolbar is a graphical representation of commands that exist in the PowerPoint menus. While you are working, it is often easier to click on a button than it is to find a particular command in one of PowerPoint's nine menus.

PowerPoint comes equipped with seven toolbars, each containing tools related to a specific function. Table 2.2 explains the different toolbars available in PowerPoint.

TABLE 2.2: UNDERSTANDING THE TOOLBARS

Toolbar	Description
Standard	Includes tools for working with files and cutting, copying, pasting, and undoing operations.
Formatting	Contains the font, size, style, alignment, spacing, and bullet options.
Animation Effects	Includes several tools you can use to add motion and sound effects to objects in your presentation.
Clipboard	Shows the contents of items you've placed there in cut and copy operations.
Control Toolbox	A set of controls from Microsoft Access that will enable you to create forms that readers can use for data entry.
Drawing	Contains commands for working with text used as a graphic element (i.e., logos, oversized first letters, etc.) and drawing shapes with various colors and fill patterns.
Outlining	The Outlining tool bar displays buttons that enable you to rearrange the levels of text in your presentation.
Picture	Gives you a variety of options for importing and then editing images in PowerPoint.
Reviewing	The Reviewing toolbar is a palette of seven tools you can use when you are reviewing a presentation— five for comments, one for Outlook tasks, and one for sending mail.
Tables and Borders	Displays various tools for creating and modifying tables.
Visual Basic	The Visual Basic toolbar includes tools that help you add programmability features to your presentation.
Web	Offers you standard browser buttons (like forward and back), the URL text box, and more.
WordArt	Displays a toolbar with the tool for creating WordArt and various tools for editing it.

You can display the toolbars available (and see which ones are enabled on your system) by choosing View and Toolbars. When you place the pointer on Toolbars, the drop-down menu shown in Figure 2.14 appears.

FIGURE 2.14

*Displaying the avail-
able toolbars in the
Toolbars cascading
menu*

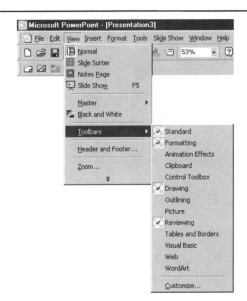

If you like to use a specific set of tools, you can create a custom toolbar. To do this, display the Toolbars cascading menu, then click on the Customize option. The Customize dialog box appears. Click the Toolbars tab. Click New. The New Toolbar dialog box appears, and you can enter the name for your new toolbar (see Figure 2.15). After you enter the name, click OK.

PowerPoint displays the new toolbar (here named Webtools in Figure 2.16) on top of the Customize dialog box. Click the Commands tab. In this tab, you will drag the commands you want to include in the new toolbar to the toolbar itself. As you add each tool, the toolbar grows. Figure 2.16 shows the Webtools toolbar after a number of tools have been added.

FIGURE 2.15

*Creating a custom
toolbar*

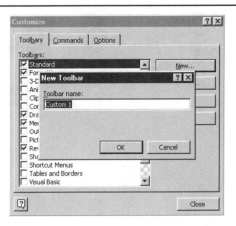

Creating a new
custom toolbar

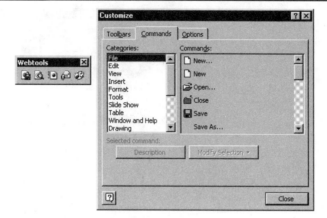

To close the Customize dialog box, click Close. If you want to close the toolbar
you've created, just click on the Close box in the upper-right corner of the box.

MASTERING TROUBLESHOOTING

Toolbars, Toolbars, Everywhere

PowerPoint includes many different toolbars you can use for various tasks as you
assemble your presentations. But what if your screen is cluttered with the multitude of
toolbars you display? Chances are that you use only a few tools from each toolbar for
the majority of your tasks. You can create a general toolbar that holds just the tools you
want to use, which reduces the toolbar clutter on your screen.

Create the new toolbar using the procedure described in this section. Then, if you want
to *move* tools from one toolbar to another, display the toolbar you want to move the
tools from and drag the tools to the new toolbar. Notice that the tools are removed
from the original toolbar. If you want to *copy* the tools from the original toolbar to the
new toolbar, press and hold Ctrl while you drag the tools from one toolbar to another.
When you're finished, click OK.

Adding Text

Thus far in the chapter, you've learned how to start a PowerPoint presentation with both the AutoContent Wizard and a template. Figure 2.17 shows the first page of a presentation based on the Bold Stripes design template displayed in Normal view.

As you can see, a PowerPoint Presentation doesn't leave any guesswork for you. Prompts on the screen tell you where to type the title and subtitle, and the color is already chosen. All you have to do is follow the instructions and enter your own text. We'll do this in the next few sections.

Adding a Title

To enter a title on the title page, position the mouse anywhere on the title box and click on the mouse button to highlight the text box (see Figure 2.18).

FIGURE 2.17

The first screen of the new PowerPoint presentation design

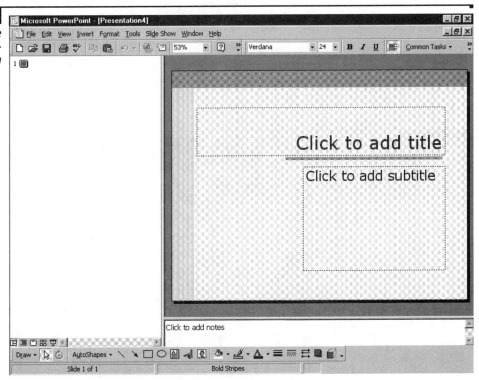

FIGURE 2.17

The first screen of the new PowerPoint presentation design

FIGURE 2.18

*Displaying the text box
for text entry*

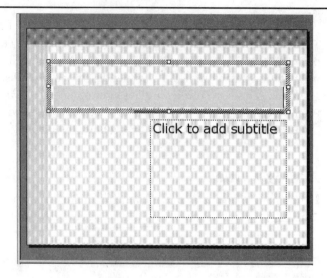

Few things in life are as simple as this next step: Type whatever title you want, and PowerPoint formats the text in the font, style, color, and alignment of the template.

When you click outside the text box, the edges of the text box disappear (see Figure 2.19).

FIGURE 2.19

An entered title

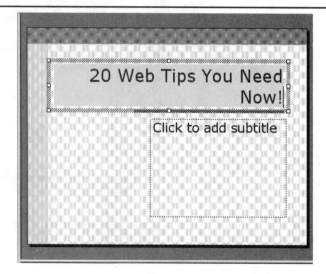

TIP After you add the title, you may decide that you want to change it. Simply click on the title. The text box will reappear and you can make your changes.

Adding a Subtitle

Adding a subtitle is just like adding a title, except that you click in the other text box and the text appears in a slightly different format, according to the template settings. Figure 2.20 shows the completed first slide.

FIGURE 2.20

The first slide with the title and subtitle entered

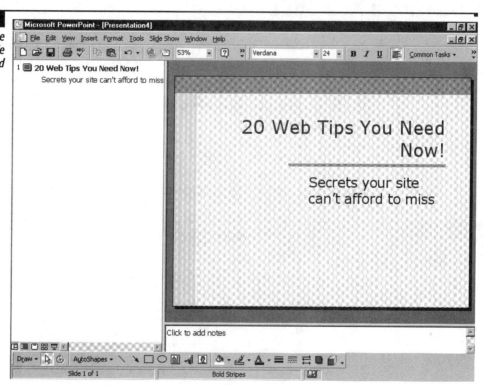

Moving Text Areas

Relocating a box of text is easy. For example, suppose that you want to move the subtitle down. Just move the pointer to the edge of the text box. When the pointer changes to an arrow, press and hold the mouse button while dragging the box downward. When the text box is where you want it, release the mouse button.

Resizing Text Boxes

It may be necessary to resize the text box so that it takes up less (or more) room on-screen. To do so, position the mouse pointer on the edge of the text box until you see a double-headed arrow, and then press the mouse button and drag the border, releasing the mouse button when the box is the size you want.

Starting a New Slide

Now that you've mastered the first slide, you're ready to tackle a few more. Let's add another slide so we've got room to work. You can add a slide one of four ways:

- Click on the New Slide button in the Standard toolbar
- Choose the New Slide button from the toolbar at the top of the screen
- Choose Insert ➤ New Slide
- Press Ctrl+M

Whichever you choose, the New Slide dialog box appears so you can choose the AutoLayout for the new slide (see Figure 2.21).

The New Slide dialog box

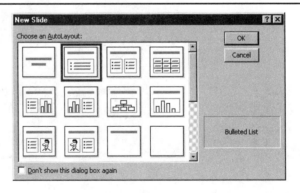

For example, select the layout in the bottom left corner of the dialog box and then click OK. A new slide with areas blocked out for title text, bullet text, and clip art appears, as shown in Figure 2.22. Notice that the status area tells you which slide you are looking at.

If you are working with one of the Presentations that PowerPoint provides, you already have other slides created in your file. You can select one of those slides or add a new one using the procedures described previously.

FIGURE 2.22

The new slide

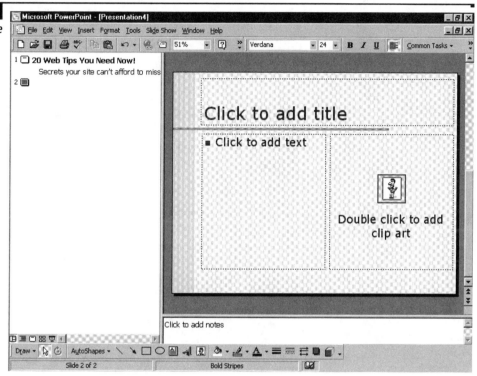

Before you add art to the slide, add the following text:

- In the title area, type **Know Your Visitor**
- In the bullet text area, type each of the following items, pressing Enter after each phrase:

    Who are you trying to reach?

    How will they find your site?

    What are they looking for?

Adding Art

The slide we just added has a spot included for clip art. You can add clip art anywhere on a slide you want; however, the clip art boxes designed into your PowerPoint slide enable you to add clip art easily. Double-click on the *Double-click to add Clip art* box, and the Microsoft ClipArt Gallery appears, as shown in Figure 2.23. You can move through the categories to display the different pieces of clip art and then choose the art you want from the Pictures box. After you've selected the art you want, click on Insert, and PowerPoint adds the art to the slide.

FIGURE 2.23

The Microsoft ClipArt Gallery dialog box

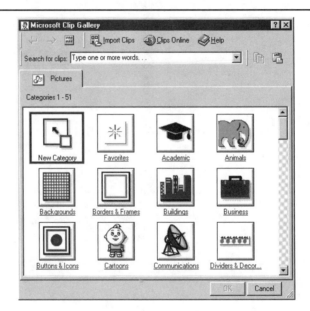

Resizing Art Objects

Resizing an art object in PowerPoint is the same basic process as resizing a text box. Click on the object you want to select, position the mouse pointer on one of the handles, and press and hold the mouse button while dragging the mouse in the direction you want to resize the object. When the object is the size you want, release the mouse button.

TIP You can add a variety of other art special effects to your presentations, including custom-drawn objects and shapes or color schemes, shading, and patterns. Now, in PowerPoint, you can also animate shapes and art on your slides. We'll talk more about custom artwork in Chapter 5 and about animating objects in Chapter 7.

Changing Views

So far, you've been working on your presentation in Slide view. By changing to different views, you can see how the content of your presentation—in terms of both text and slide design—is shaping up.

Display the presentation in Outline view by clicking the Outline button in the bottom left corner of the window. Figure 2.24 shows the presentation created up to this point in Outline view.

FIGURE 2.24

The two-slide presentation in Outline view

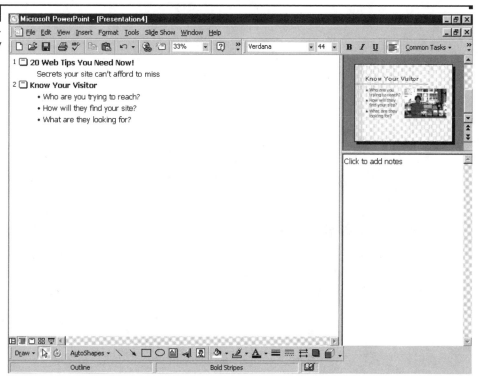

Slide Sorter view is helpful when you have several different slides and want to be able to compare and/or reorder them. Change to Slide Sorter view by clicking the Page Sorter button, which also lies in the bottom left corner of the window. Figure 2.25 shows the presentation in Slide Sorter view.

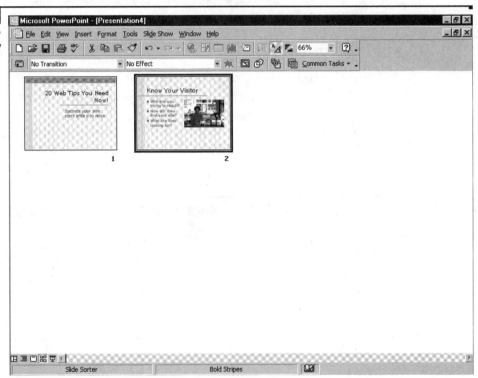

FIGURE 2.25

The presentation in Slide Sorter view

Starting a Slide Show

Although we're several pages short of what might be considered a real slide show, try out the slide show feature of PowerPoint. You can start a slide show four different ways:

- By clicking on the Slide Show tool (the display-board icon to the right of the view buttons)
- By opening the View menu and choosing Slide Show
- By opening the Slide Show menu and choosing View Show
- By pressing F5

When you choose the Slide Show command, the show begins. The slides appear one at a time, taking up the entire screen (see Figure 2.26). When you are ready to advance to the next slide, press Enter or click on the left mouse button. (To return to the previous view, press the Esc key.)

FIGURE 2.26

The Slide Show view

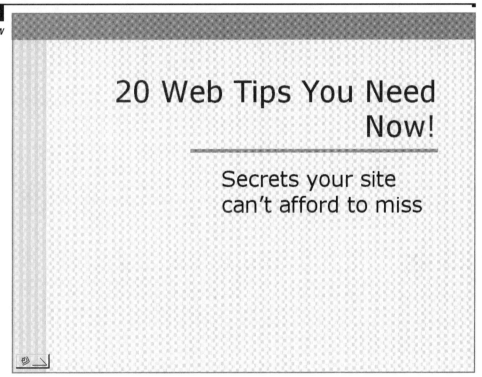

Saving Presentations

Periodically save the presentation you're working on. For best results, save regularly—don't wait until you're finished with the file. You never know when a badly timed thunderstorm or a trip over the power cord will interrupt power to your computer. Most people save their files after each major step in the creation process. In other words, you might pause to save the file the first time after you select the template and add the first slide of text; then again after adding subsequent pages; then again after adding art, charts, and so on.

The process of saving files in PowerPoint is the same as that of saving files in any other Windows application—just open the File menu and choose Save, navigate to the disk and folder where you want to store the file, enter the file name you want, and click on OK.

TIP The next time you save the file by selecting the Save command you will not be asked to enter a file name; PowerPoint will use the name you specified in the initial save procedure. From this point on you can save the file by pressing Ctrl+S.

Printing the Presentation

PowerPoint makes it easy to print multiple copies of presentations, to print only selected pages, and to choose a number of different formats for printing (Slides, Notes Pages, Handouts, or Outline view). You can also specify print quality, print to a file, omit the background color, resize to fit the page, and change the print order (see Figure 2.27).

FIGURE 2.27

The Print dialog box

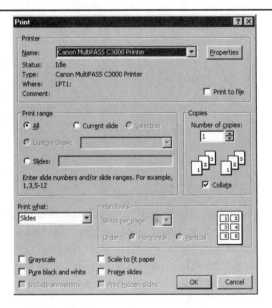

If you're having trouble getting pages to print, check to make sure you've got your printer set up to work with PowerPoint. (To do this, open the File menu, choose the Print command, and click on the Printer button.)

Chapter Summary

In this chapter, we've covered a lot of ground. From a basic understanding of the startup procedure for PowerPoint, you explored selecting templates and wizards and investigating each of the PowerPoint menus. Additionally, you learned the basic tasks for creating a presentation, getting help, adding text and clip art, resizing objects, adding new slides, displaying a slide show, and printing the presentation. In the next chapter, you begin Part Two of the book and start investigating each of the different tools that will help you create powerful PowerPoint presentations.

PART II

The Right Tool for the Job

LEARN TO:

- *Enter, edit, and enhance text in your presentation*

- *Add and modify charts*

- *Work with clip art*

- *Import graphics files*

- *Add sound*

- *Add and edit video clips*

- *Set transitions, timing, and navigation controls*

CHAPTER 3

Entering, Editing, and Enhancing Text

The text of your presentation carries a lot of weight. Even though you'll be presenting, which means you'll have notes or a script to narrate from as you go through the slides, viewers are further clued in to your message by the text and its meaning as they watch the story unfold on the slides. From the text you use—and the way you use it—your audience will understand:

- What's most important about your presentation
- What items you're covering
- Where they need to ask questions
- What response you hope to elicit

In this chapter, you'll learn to use text to its best advantage. We won't waste time proselytizing about the power of the printed word—you already understand that. The power you're working with here is a combination of platforms—multimedia—and the trick lies in knowing what to put on-screen and what to say. Where will text help and where will it detract from your presentation? You'll learn to make those types of judgments in this chapter.

Once you get the basic content of your presentation down, take a good long look at it. Proofread it carefully. Watch the punctuation. A good presentation can be blown out of the water by bad grammar or incorrect punctuation. This chapter will help you get a handle on the editing aspect of your presentation.

Finally, you need to think about the way your text looks. The text's appearance—although perhaps set by a wizard or a template—conveys quite a bit about your message. You may want to change the typeface, size, color, or other elements. Later in this chapter, you'll find out how to make these and other enhancements to your text.

Text Rules

This section gives you a few pointers for preparing the text content of your presentation. If writing is old hat to you, feel free to skip this section and move on to *"Using the AutoContent Wizard,"* later in this chapter.

Too Much Is Too Much

The temptation may be very great to pack too much text into your slides, especially if you are preparing slides that will also be printed as handouts (which means that they will go back to the office or home with audience members, so they remember what each slide was about). Fight it. Including too much text on a slide is overwhelming for audience members—they will read the first seven words of any bullet point or paragraph and then move on to the next item. Keep your blurbs succinct.

For example, consider this bullet entry, taken from a sample presentation:

- Before you can design an effective site, you need to think about who your audience is, how they will find you, and what they are looking for.

That sounds okay, but it's too long. By the time your audience gets to "effective" they've stopped reading. If you want to say clearly that you need to know your audience, you could rearrange the text (more succinctly and more powerfully, too) using the bullet points shown in Figure 3.1.

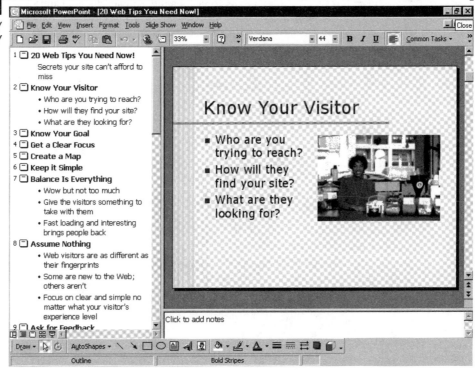

The Clearer, the Better

Whenever possible, be as specific as you can with the information you're presenting. Granted, being specific without being verbose is a difficult line to walk, but you should be as clear as possible about what's being shown. For example, although a slide titled "Projections vs. Actual Sales Results" sounds professional, your audience may better understand the content of the slide (and the charts on it) if the title is, "How Did We Do This Month?"

 TIP Tailor your presentation's tone to the audience you'll be speaking to. If conversational text won't fit their professional meeting, go with the flow and speak to them in a language they will understand.

Know Where You're Going

A presentation that wanders from topic to topic will seem disjointed and confusing to your audience. Make sure your text moves forward through a set series of topics—know where you want to go and then create the slides to get there. A good sense of direction will help your audience better understand your presentation.

Use Text to Highlight, Not Narrate

Keep text to its essential, most powerful minimum: resist the temptation to write captions for your charts, add notes to slides where they aren't completely necessary, or use titles of more than one line. The narration of your presentation should provide the bulk of the verbal communication. If you need to provide additional information, you can print handouts using Notes Pages view, which produces a reduced image of the slide plus any attached notes printed at the bottom of the page. Figure 3.2 shows an example of a page in Notes Page view.

FIGURE 3.2

An example of additional text entered in Notes Page view

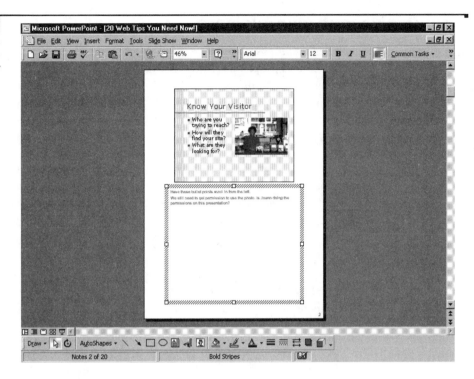

Color and Contrast Are Important

Even though the color of the background and text may have been selected by the template you chose or the wizard you used, you may need to make changes based on where you'll be presenting and how large your audience is. Make sure that you've got enough color contrast for your text to show up on-screen. Before you give the presentation, test the color combinations on co-workers. Check to see whether or not they have any trouble reading the display under lighting that's similar to where you'll be presenting. Generally, light text on a darker background is easiest to see, but you may need to test different color combinations to see what works best for your particular circumstance. If you're in doubt about what to use, try white or yellow text on a dark background. This combination is very legible in most presentation situations.

Think about Your Audience

Before you begin composing the text, think about your audience. Who are they? Are they engineers, sales people, managers? Are they support personnel, students, or prospective employees? The "who" will help you determine the tone of your presentation. Remember to speak the language your audience will readily understand.

Timing Is Everything

Consider carefully the amount of time you'll need in order to discuss everything you need to discuss about a particular slide. You can either use Manual timing and advance the slides by clicking the mouse button when you're ready to move on, or use Automatic timing to have PowerPoint advance the slides automatically after a preset period of time. Manual gives you more control, but Automatic helps you stay within a specified time frame.

 TIP For more about controlling the timing of slide display, see Chapter 8, "Finishing a Slide Show."

Before You Add Text...

Assuming that you've selected your presentation's template and are ready to start entering text, take a minute to write down the key points of your presentation. This will help you create a basic game plan from which to work.

Experienced presenters and writers often prefer the question-and-answer approach to outlining ideas. In this method, you brainstorm about the basic questions your presentation should answer and then answer each one.

For example, if you are creating a presentation to promote a new service your company is offering, you might come up with these questions:

- What is the name of our service?
- What does it offer?
- Who does it appeal to?
- What benefits does it offer?
- How much does it cost?

- When does it start?
- How do I find out more?

Then, to flesh out the basic progression of the presentation, you'd answer each question in turn:

- AsDec On-Site Training
- Corporate, individual, and group training on the AsDec 400
- Corporations and small businesses who have recently purchased or upgraded to an AsDec 400
- Professional trainers; on-going technical support; clear, useful manuals
- $1200 per three-day seminar, unlimited participants
- Seminars are scheduled on a bimonthly basis
- Call 1-800-55-ASDEC or write AsDec Industries, One Redfern Way, Sausalito, CA 94015

You can now build a presentation based on the answers you provided to your own questions. This gives you a basic plan for the presentation and makes sure that it moves logically from slide to slide.

Entering Text

In the previous chapter, you learned how to enter text quickly in the process of creating your first presentation. This section slows things down a bit and shows you the various ways you can enter and work with text in your presentation.

Once you've sketched out your ideas for the presentation, you're ready to get it on-screen. You can enter text in either Slide view or Outline view. The following sections explain how to do just that.

Adding Text in Slide View

When you first start PowerPoint and choose a Page Layout to begin a worksession, the first slide of your presentation appears on the screen. The text entry sections are already blocked out on the screen. Whether you start your presentation by choosing a template or opt to start with a blank publication, prompts on your screen tell you where to enter text (see Figure 3.3).

FIGURE 3.3

*Text sections on a
title page*

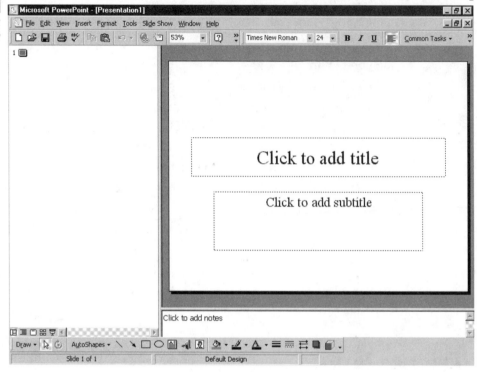

 TIP   Whether you choose to work with a template or start a file from scratch, PowerPoint applies certain default text settings to the words you type. You can change the text's typeface, size, style, and color at any time during your PowerPoint work session. For more about changing the font and enhancing your text, see "Enhancing Text," later in this chapter.

 TIP   What's a font? A font is a certain typeface in a particular size and style. For example, Times Roman 16-point italic is one font, and Times Roman 12-point bold is another.

To enter text, click on the text box you want to use. An entry box appears, as shown in Figure 3.4. Notice that your text cursor blinks in the center of the box This happens because the alignment setting chosen by PowerPoint (another default) is centered. Type the title for the presentation in the top text box, assuming that you've displayed a Title page layout and haven't already entered the title in the Autocontent Wizard.

As you type, the letters appear in the text box. After you finish typing the title, click outside the text area. PowerPoint closes the text box and the text is displayed in the title area at the top of the slide.

To enter the second section of text, repeat the same steps: double-click on the text box, and type the text you want to appear. If your text takes up more than one line, PowerPoint automatically wraps the text to the next line for you. You don't need to press Enter; in fact, doing so will tell PowerPoint that you are adding another item in a list (such as a bulleted list) and the text will show up as two separate items in Outline view. Now PowerPoint will underscore words it doesn't recognize or thinks you have misspelled; you can right-click on the word to see a list of possible spelling alternatives.

> **TIP** If PowerPoint wraps the line automatically for you and you don't like the way it breaks, you can re-size the box by positioning the mouse pointer on the corner and dragging the corner to re-shape the box.

FIGURE 3.4

The text entry box

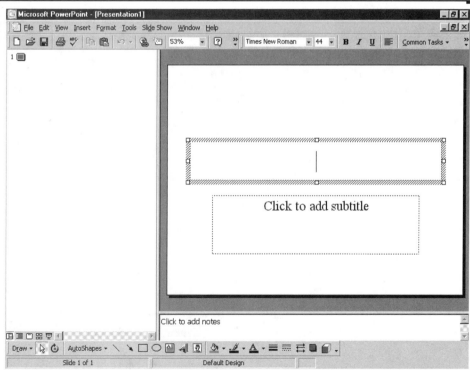

To add another item in the same text box, press Enter at the end of the first item and PowerPoint moves the cursor to the next line.

After you finish entering text, click outside the text box. Later, you can make any modifications you want by moving the text; changing the size of the text box; selecting a different font, size, or style; or even deleting the text at any time from Slide view.

Adding New Text Boxes

There will be times when you want to add more text than Slide view leaves room for. For example, suppose that on a particular slide, you want to add a line that shows the date the presentation was prepared.

Simply click the Text Box tool (it looks like a small document icon, and lies in the center of the drawing tools row, just below the work area) and move the cursor to the point on the slide where you want to add the box. (If the drawing toolbar is not displayed on your monitor, choose View ➤ Toolbars ➤ Drawing to display it.) Hold down the mouse button while dragging the mouse down and to the right, releasing it when the text box is the size you want. The data-entry area appears, as shown in Figure 3.5. You can move the text box around just like the original text boxes—by dragging it.

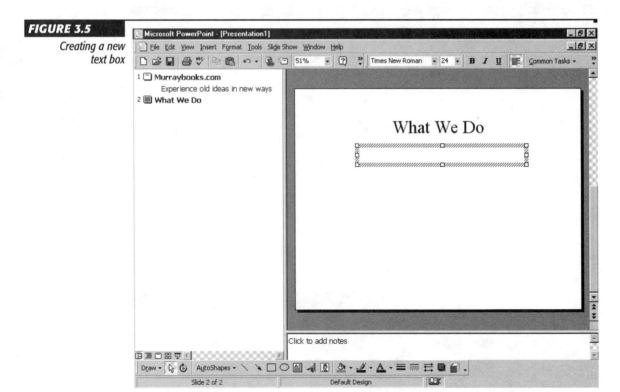

FIGURE 3.5

Creating a new text box

Adding Text in Outline View

Outline view gives you another perspective from which to view your text. This view shows you only the text in your presentation, organized to show the indention levels, in standard outline format.

To display the presentation in Outline view, click the Outline View button in the lower-left corner of the screen or choose View ➤ Outline. You'll see any text you've entered in the presentation, as shown in Figure 3.6.

FIGURE 3.6

Text displayed in Outline view

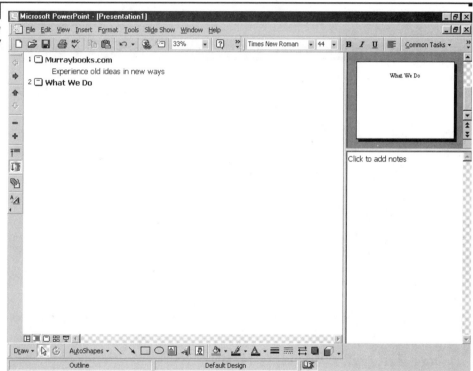

 TIP   If you don't see the Outline toolbar along the left side of your work area, choose View ➤ Toolbars ➤ Outlining to display it.

PART

II

The Right Tool for the Job

Outline Elements

The Outline screen looks quite a bit different from the Slide view screen. You see different tools along the left side of the window, and a different look in the work area itself. Table 3.1 explains each of the buttons in the Outline view toolbar.

 NOTE If your Outline toolbar does not appear automatically when you display Outline View, open the View menu, choose Toolbars, and click Outlining.

TABLE 3.1: OUTLINE BUTTONS

Button	Name	Description
	Promote (Indent less)	Moves selected text to the left
	Demote (Indent more)	Moves selected text to the right one level
	Move Up	Moves selected text up one slide in the presentation
	Move Down	Moves selected text down one slide in the presentation
	Collapse Selection	Hides all sublevels of the currently selected slide
	Expand Selection	Displays all sublevels of the currently selected slide
	Show Titles	Shows only slide titles
	Show All	Displays all text in the presentation
	Summary Slide	Creates a summary slide based on the highlighted text
	Show Formatting	Works as a toggle to display text in the selected font and size; click again to disable formatting display and show text in uniform size and style

TIP For more about working with the different tools in Outline view, see "Editing in Outline View," later in this chapter.

Adding, Indenting, and Outdenting Text on the Current Slide

To add text to the existing slide, use the arrow keys to move the cursor to the desired point. To begin a new line indented to the same point, simply press Enter, or press Tab to indent the line further. To "outdent" (that is, to move the insertion point to the left) the line, press Shift+Tab. Then type your text.

Creating a New Slide in the Outliner

To add a new slide, position the cursor in the slide where you want the new slide to follow. Then move the pointer to the New Slide button in the Standard toolbar and click the mouse button. Another number appears in the left column of the Outliner, indicating that you've started a new slide. The cursor is positioned so that you can add the title text for the slide (see Figure 3.7).

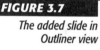

FIGURE 3.7

The added slide in Outliner view

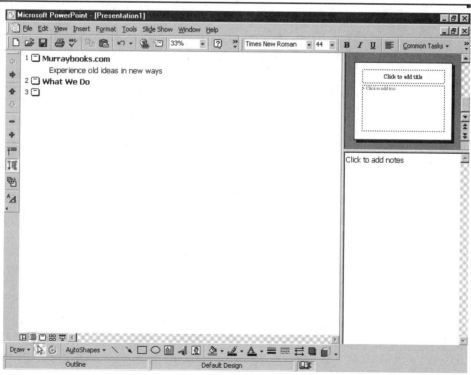

You can also add a new slide by pressing Enter after the preceding slide title or by "outdenting;" that is, press Shift+Tab to move the line of text to the left margin as a new slide entry.

Inserting Text from Microsoft Word

If you've previously created an outline in Microsoft Word and want to use it directly in your PowerPoint presentation, you can use PowerPoint's drag-and-drop feature to use the text as-is. Just minimize PowerPoint so that it appears only in the Taskbar; open the Windows Explorer, and locate the file containing the text you want to import.

Click on the file, and then, holding the mouse button down, drag the file to the PowerPoint tab in the Taskbar. After a moment, PowerPoint opens automatically, and you can drag the Word file's icon to the presentation. PowerPoint copies the information from the Word file directly into a new presentation file.

Working with Text Levels

Each of the text levels in PowerPoint is assigned a different text size so you can easily distinguish between them. Here's how it breaks down (the exact point size and appearance may vary depending on the template you use):

- The first level, shown in 44-point type, is the page title
- The second, displayed in 32-point type, is marked by a square bullet and indented two spaces
- The third, displayed in 28-point type, is marked by a dash and indented four spaces
- The fourth, shown in 24-point type, is marked by two greater-than symbols and indented six spaces
- The fifth, displayed in 20-point type, is a square bullet at eight spaces
- The sixth, also displayed in 20-point type, is a dash at ten spaces

To indent text to a new level, you can either position the cursor at the beginning of the text and press Tab, or click the Demote button (the right-pointing arrow in the text settings row).

Figure 3.8 shows the different levels of indention. Notice that all the text in the Outline pane is the same size, but the text as it appears in the Slide view pane reduces in size with each level.

FIGURE 3.8

Outline view showing text indents

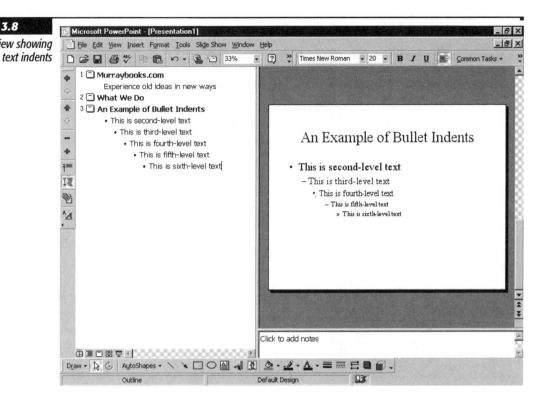

Editing Text

Now that you've got some text to work with, you may be tempted to move things around a bit. Perhaps the text on page three would work better on page five. What if you want to change the indent levels of text you've already entered or move a paragraph from one side of a slide to another?

This section explores the various aspects of editing your text. Editing includes many things: changing individual letters, replacing words, moving sentences or fragments, re-sizing text blocks, and running the spelling checker. We'll talk about enhancing text in the next section, but here, you'll make sure that the text is as accurate as possible.

Any program that lets you work with text must offer two different kinds of editing tasks: keystroke editing, in which you can correct a misspelling or a bad line break by typing a keystroke or two; and block editing, in which you mark a section of text as a block and move it, delete it, copy it, or paste it.

Simple Text Editing

Some typos don't even look like typos. How many times have you wondered how to spell the word "friend"? Is it I before E except after C, or what?

Luckily, the spelling checker can bail you out of spelling dead-ends where nothing looks right. There may be times, however (like when you're trying to spell your new boss's name), when a spelling checker can't help. Then you are on your own, with only your memory (or reference materials) and the backspace or Del key.

To edit text in a specific text block, your first step is to position the cursor at the point you want to edit the text. Click the text box and the border appears, indicating that you've selected the box. Now position the cursor where you want to make your changes.

PowerPoint keeps an eye on your typing and highlights the text when it thinks you have entered a word incorrectly. When this happens, right-click the word to see the suggestions that your spell checker has to offer.

 TIP If you're having trouble seeing what you're doing, use the Zoom controls in the toolbar at the top of the screen to enlarge the display. Click the down-arrow beside 50% and choose a larger percentage (100% is usually plenty). When you're finished with your close-up work, return to normal view.

When you're finished making the text changes, click outside the box.

Selecting Text for Editing

Some editing procedures require that you mark the text you want to edit as a block. A text block can be as small as a single character or as large as the entire presentation—PowerPoint recognizes whatever you highlight as the current block. For example, before you can copy text, you need to tell PowerPoint what block of text you want to work with. To do this, position the cursor and then highlight the block.

 TIP If you want to highlight all the text in your presentation, make sure the cursor is inside the outline and click Edit ➢ Select All. You might want to do this, for example, to make a global change such as changing the font, style, or color of all text in your presentation.

Click the mouse button when the pointer is placed at the beginning of the text you want to mark, then press the mouse button and drag the mouse over the section you want to highlight. If you're using the keyboard to highlight the text you want, move the cursor to the beginning of the text, and then press the right-arrow key while holding down the Shift key.

 TIP If you've marked a block and want to remove the highlight (deselect it) press the Esc key or move the pointer outside the text area and click the mouse button.

Cutting and Pasting Text

PowerPoint includes all the basic editing procedures you'll find in other programs—and they are in the same place, too (the Edit menu). The Copy, Cut, and Paste commands all enable you to work with blocks of text in your presentation. These commands use a special new Office Clipboard as a temporary storage place for the information you're working with. This clipboard holds up to 12 scraps and can be accessed from most Office applications, such as Word and PowerPoint (but not Outlook). To view the Clipboard, choose View ➢ Toolbars ➢ Clipboard. For example, if you're copying a block of text, PowerPoint puts the copy on the clipboard. Then, when you paste the text somewhere else, PowerPoint copies the text from the clipboard to the cursor position.

 TIP PowerPoint gives you two different kinds of Paste commands: the regular Paste puts whatever is stored on the clipboard at the cursor location, and Paste Special preserves the formatting style for the clipboard contents you insert.

Drag-and-Drop Text

If you're working in Outline view, you can drag and drop text to move it from one place to another. This procedure allows you to bypass Copy and Paste from the Edit menu. Just highlight the text you want to move, position the pointer on the text, and drag the text to the new location. A bar cursor shows you where the text will be positioned as you drag the mouse. When the bar cursor is placed at the point you want the text to be inserted, release the mouse button.

Undoing Editing Changes

For those times when you press a key and think "I really wish I hadn't done that," PowerPoint includes the Undo feature. You can customize Undo to reverse up to 150 (!) of your most recent operations; the default is 20. To change the number of operations Undo will reverse, select Tools ➢ Options, and then select the Edit tab. Change the setting in Maximum number of undos by clicking the up-arrow or down-arrow to increase or decrease the number.

Using the Spelling Checker to Catch Spelling Errors

Consider how many times you will have read the text of your presentation by the time you finish it, and you can see how easy it is to become blind to errors. By the end, you've read the text so many times that typos begin to look right.

PowerPoint reads through the presentation for you to ensure that all your words are spelled correctly. The spelling checker will check every word in your presentation, including additional material such as speaker notes and chart labels.

PowerPoint's spelling checker looks for three different kinds of possible errors:

- Any word not recognized in PowerPoint's dictionary

- Any word that includes numbers

- Any word that includes strange capitalization

Start the Spelling Checker one of three ways:

- Choose Tools ➢ Spelling

- Press F7

- Click the Spelling tool (sixth from the left, showing the letters ABC and a small checkmark) in the toolbar

When PowerPoint finds a word that's not in the dictionary, it displays a screen giving you a number of options. You can skip the word, correct it, add it to a personal dictionary, or choose a different word from a list of alternatives.

Using AutoCorrect

PowerPoint includes a feature shared with other Microsoft products: AutoCorrect. If you are like most people, there are certain words you always misspell. You can "teach" AutoCorrect to watch for those words and correct them dynamically when you type them. Additionally, you can use AutoCorrect as a kind of shorthand interpreter—if you must type a long word or phrase repeatedly, you can teach AutoCorrect to find the phrase you type and substitute the long phrase for you. For example, you could type the letters *ref* and have AutoCorrect automatically substitute *Biographical Reference of American Sports Heroes*. AutoCorrect is available in the Tools menu.

Five options—Correct TWo INitial CApitals, Capitalize the first letter of a sentence, Capitalize names of days, Correct accidental use of the caps LOCK key, and Replace Text as You Type—are selected by default. You can disable each of those options by clicking the appropriate checkbox.

Enter the words you want to substitute in the Replace: and With: text boxes. Before doing so, use the down-arrow to scroll through the word list in the bottom of the dialog box to make sure the word isn't already entered.

Using the Style Checker to Catch Style Inconsistencies and Problems

In PowerPoint 2000, the Style Checker is integrated in the program. This automated utility goes through your presentation and checks its consistency, visual clarity, and style, taking the guesswork out of whether your presentation is ready to be presented. When it finds something it doesn't like, PowerPoint underlines the phrase with a green wavy line. You can then right-click the underlined phrase and choose the option you want to use to correct it. PowerPoint will make suggestions on how you can improve the section of the text stylistically.

You control the Style Checker options by clicking Tools ➤ Options. Click the Spelling and Style tab (see Figure 3.9).

FIGURE 3.9

Turning on the Style Checker

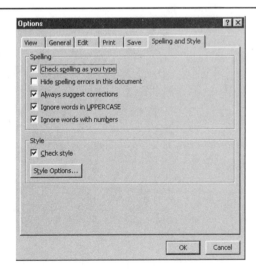

If you want to turn off the Style Checker, click the checkbox to the right of the Check style option to remove the X.

Click on the Style Options button. The Style Checker Options dialog box appears, with the *Case and End Punctuation* tab showing (see Figure 3.10).

Case and End Punctuation enables you to choose the punctuation method of your text. You may want to add or remove periods for your text items or watch for incorrect punctuation characters that may inadvertently slip into your text. Make your selections and then click the Visual Clarity tab (see Figure 3.11).

FIGURE 3.10

Setting up Case and End Punctuation in the Style Options dialog box

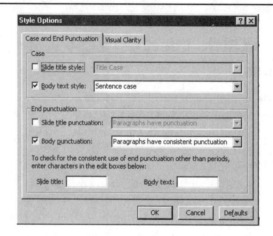

FIGURE 3.11

Making sure your presentation is visually clear

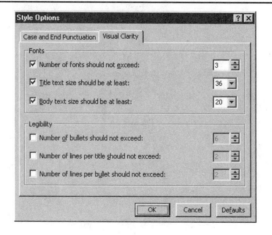

Visual Clarity refers to the way your text looks on the slide. The options in the Visual Clarity tab provide you with a number of choices regarding the number and sizes of different fonts; in addition, you can double-check the legibility of your text by making sure that you don't have too many bullets or lines on a slide.

When you're finished reviewing the options, click OK to close the tab and then close the dialog box.

Editing in Outline View

Up to this point, most of the editing tasks we've been talking about apply to both the Slide view and Outline view. You can do simple editing—like using the backspace or delete keys to make minor modifications—in Outline view; you can mark a text block and cut, copy, paste, or clear it, just as you can in Normal view.

You learned earlier that instead of using Cut and Paste to move a text block, you can use the drag-and-drop feature in the Outliner to move highlighted text from one point to another. But there are additional editing features available to you in Outline view that you *can't* accomplish in Slide view. In fact, an entirely new set of tools appears along the left edge of the outline, enabling you to collapse and expand outlines, check titles, and take a look at formatting changes. Earlier in this chapter, Table 3.1 provided a basic description of the different Outline tools.

Collapsing the Outline

PowerPoint gives you a way to determine easily whether your headings are parallel and your outline is balanced. The trick is known as collapsing the outline, and it turns the outline shown in Figure 3.12 to the outline shown Figure 3.13.

To fully collapse the outline, click the Show Titles button (fourth from the bottom) from the row of Outline tools. All sublevels of information disappear. PowerPoint shows you which slides have additional information, however, by including a gray underline on those slides that contain hidden sublevels. Now you can compare the titles of your presentation to see whether they are parallel and present topics in the clearest possible manner.

To display all levels of the outline again, click the Expand All button (third from the bottom) in the Outline tools row. The outline is displayed with all sublevels intact.

FIGURE 3.12

The outline before it is collapsed

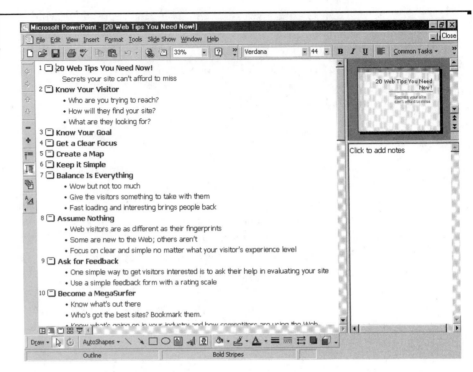

FIGURE 3.13

The outline after the collapse

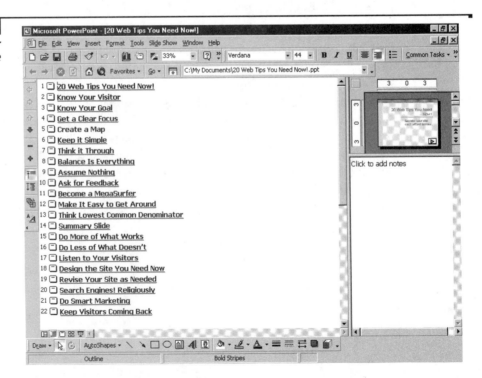

MASTERING THE OPPORTUNITIES

Creating a Balanced Outline

A significant part of creating a good presentation lies in making sure your concepts are organized in an orderly way. In fact, as an English teacher or two along the way has probably told you, there's a very definite process to creating a solid outline. PowerPoint won't make you stick to any particular rules when you're creating your outline, but you can make a good presentation better by making sure your outline works.

In a balanced outline, every A has a B, every 1 has a 2, etc.—there are two or more of everything. Here's an example of a balanced outline (on the left, you see the basic outline structure; on the right, you see how it can be applied to the AsDec 400 sample presentation):

Level One	We're AsDec Industries
Sublevel A	AsDec Yesterday and Today
Sublevel B	Building a Better Future
Level Two	We're a "People Company," offering
Sublevel A	Training Services
Sublevel B	Ongoing Technical Support

Levels One and Two supply the basic ideas—in this case, the slide titles—and the sublevels underneath supply the supporting ideas—in this case, bullet entries.

Many people find it helpful to go through and write the main points of their outlines first, before adding detail in the sublevels. As you become more experienced at writing and revising your own outlines, you'll learn what works best for you.

Collapsing and Expanding a Slide

In some cases, you may want to collapse only a single slide, rather than the entire outline. You can do this by positioning the cursor in the slide you want to collapse and clicking the Collapse Selection button (it resembles a minus sign). Only the collapsed slide's title will be displayed.

To expand a single slide, position the cursor in the title of the slide you want to expand and click the Expand Selection button (it looks like a plus sign).

Moving Text Items in Outline View

One additional feature available in Outline view that you won't find in Slide view is the ability to move a single line of text up or down through the presentation. Suppose, for example, that you want to move the fifth bullet item up to the third position. You would position the cursor on the line you want to move and then click the up-arrow (Move Up) button. The line exchanges places with the one above it. Click the Move Up button again, and the line is in the third position.

Similarly, you can move a line of text downward through the presentation by using the Move Down button. And you aren't limited to staying within the same slide; you can move text from slide to slide as necessary.

Creating a Summary Slide in Outline View

PowerPoint gives you the option of adding a summary slide—a slide that includes key points, slide titles, or important phrases—and enables you to show your audience at a glance what you plan to cover in your presentation.

You can create a summary slide from either Outline or Slide Sorter view by clicking the Summary Slide button. First highlight (in Outline view) or select (in Slide Sorter view) the slides you want to include on the summary slide (see Figure 3.14). Then click the Summary Slide button. The summary slide is then created for you (see Figure 3.15).

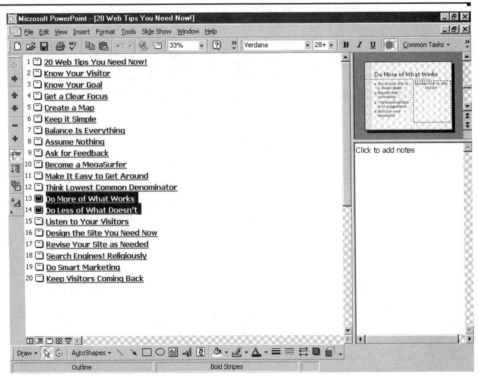

FIGURE 3.14

Highlight the slides you want to summarize and click the Summary Slide button to create a summary slide.

FIGURE 3.15

The summary slide is created automatically from the text you select.

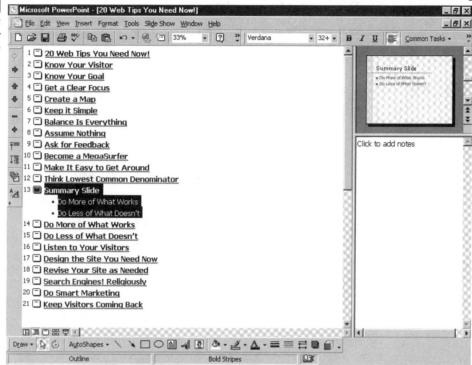

How will you use a summary slide? You might create a table of contents with hyperlinks that will take your audience—or individual users, if you're creating a self-directed presentation—to the slide covering the topic they select.

MASTERING THE OPPORTUNITIES

Hyperlinking the Easy Way

Hyperlinks are easy to add in PowerPoint. You simply highlight the text you want to use as a link and press Ctrl+K. The Insert Hyperlink dialog box appears, and you enter the URL for the Web page or select it from the displayed list. If you want to link to an existing page, an e-mail address, or another document, click the appropriate icon in the Link To pane. You can also link to a specific file by clicking the Browse button and choosing the file you want. Click OK when you've made your link.

PART

II

The Right Tool
for the Job

Editing in Slide Sorter View

Slide Sorter view, shown in Figure 3.16, doesn't look like a good place to edit text. After all, you can't see the text very well.

FIGURE 3.16

Displaying Slide Sorter view

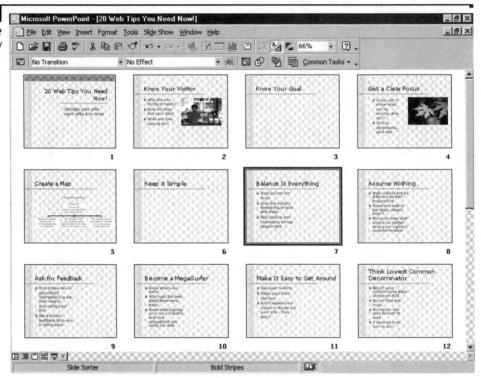

But there is one major editing task you can perform in Slide Sorter view—a task that has a great deal to do with how your presentation will be received. While all your slides are displayed on one screen, you can visually scan through them and determine how the overall presentation is shaping up.

 TIP Don't remember how to get to Slide Sorter view? Go to the row of View buttons at the bottom of the screen (the row with five small icons) and click the fourth button from the left, or choose View ➢ Slide Sorter.

Earlier you learned that the overall structure and clarity of your outline is important—you need balance and parallelism to help viewers know where you're going. Similarly, you need to make sure that the sequence of your slides makes sense.

By displaying your developing presentation in Slide Sorter view, you can keep an eye on the overall progression of your slides. Do they move logically from one to another? Are you missing a step? Should you vary the style of the slides you're creating? Slide after slide of bulleted text may present your idea, but it may also put your audience to sleep.

If you decide to re-arrange the slides, it's a simple job in Slide Sorter. Just click on the slide you want to move and drag it to its new location. The other slides move to accommodate the change.

TIP Remember to save your changes. After—and often before—every major change, take a few seconds to save the file. If you're preparing to make a sweeping change, like changing the color scheme, throwing out several slides, or selecting a set of off-the-wall fonts, back up the file first. Then, if you aren't happy with the new look, you can always go back to the original.

Formatting Text

What a presentation says—in words—is only part of its impact. How a presentation *looks* makes as loud a statement as the text itself. The way your text is positioned on a slide contributes to whether or not a viewer actually reads it. If the text is too small, in a font that's hard to read, or scrunched against other text, your audience may simply give up.

Once you get the text into your presentation, you may want to re-arrange it and try it in different formats to see what's most effective. The way you go about making format changes depends on how far-reaching you want the changes to be. You can do simple changes yourself, like changing indents, moving tabs, and modifying line spacing. Or, you can go all the way back to square one by letting PowerPoint apply a design template for you. This section describes the different ways in which you can change the format of your presentation:

- Apply a new design template to the entire presentation
- Choose a new page layout for the current slide

• Use the ruler, tabs, indents, and alignment options to change the way elements are positioned on the slide

Applying a New Design

The simplest and quickest way to change the look of your presentation uses the Apply Design Template command in the Format menu.

When you choose this command, the Apply Design Template dialog box appears. Choose one of the different templates (these are the same templates displayed in the New Presentation dialog box when you first choose a presentation design) and then click Apply. The new design is automatically applied to all slides in your presentation.

Changing Format with a New Layout

One of the easiest ways to change the format is to select a different layout for the current slide. Suppose you're working on a standard bullet slide in Current Slide view. You can choose a different layout—but keep the same text—by clicking the Slide Layout button in the Common Tasks list in the Standard toolbar. That opens the Slide Layout dialog box, shown in Figure 3.17.

FIGURE 3.17

The Slide Layout box

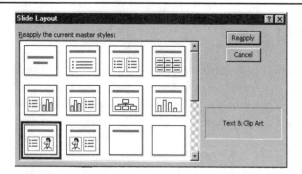

Click on the picture of the layout you want. Depending on the style you choose, you may have some additional work to do. For example, the new layout you choose may require that you add a chart or a table. When you click Reapply, the new layout is applied to the current slide.

 TIP   If you changed the layout and don't like it, choose Edit ➢ Undo. Your old layout reappears, good as new.

Displaying the Ruler

Many hands-on formatting issues—such as setting indents and tabs—involve using the ruler. If your ruler is not already displayed, choose View ➤ Ruler to show the two rulers along the top and left sides of the PowerPoint work area (see Figure 3.18).

FIGURE 3.18

The PowerPoint rulers

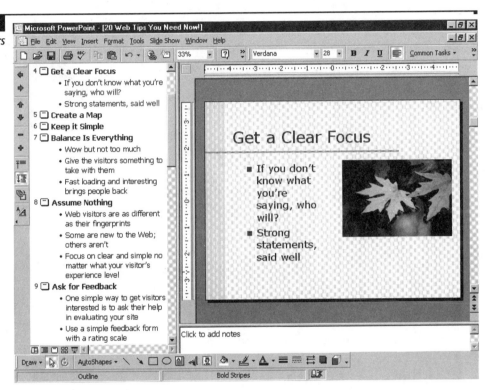

Notice that, unlike a typical ruler, the PowerPoint rulers show 0 (zero) as their center point. This enables you to measure from the vertical and horizontal center of the slide, which helps you position elements accurately.

When the ruler is displayed and you highlight text or click in a text box, the ruler changes (see Figure 3.19). Now the ruler reflects the width and height of the selected text box; the ruler is no longer vertically and horizontally centered to zero. Additionally, the white area narrows to show only the width and depth of the current text box.

FIGURE 3.19

When you click in a text box, the ruler changes to show text box position.

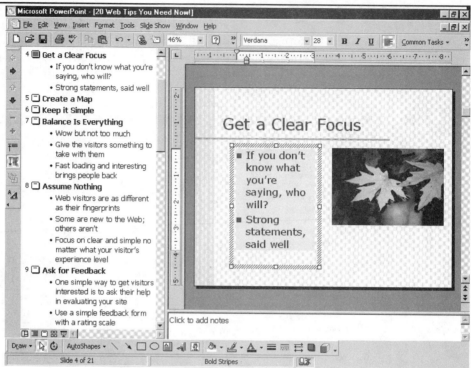

FIGURE 3.19

When you click in a text box, the ruler changes to show text box position.

In the small square in the upper-left corner of the PowerPoint work area, you see a tab symbol. To the left of the horizontal ruler, you see two markers—one pointing up and one pointing down. These are your indent markers.

Changing Indents

One of the first tasks you might perform using the ruler involves changing the indention of specific text. There are several types of indents you could apply to presentation text:

- All lines of text indented evenly

- Only the first line of text indented

- All lines except the first indented (used for bulleted and numbered lists)

To change the indent of a block of text, first select the block you want to change, then move the pointer to the indent marker you want to move. The top marker on the ruler controls the first-line indent, the bottom marker controls the indent of subsequent lines. Drag the marker to the new position on the ruler.

To move both markers but maintain their relative distance from each other (for example, suppose that you've created a hanging indent for a bullet and want to move all the text—just the way it is—to the right), click the small rectangle beneath the bottom indent marker. Both markers move together, preserving the space between them.

Working with Tabs

The primary function of a tab is to help you align text in your documents as painlessly as possible. The tab is a small marker that tells the text, "Stop here." PowerPoint gives you the option of choosing four different tab stops: left, right, center, and decimal tabs. (The first three types are pretty common; a decimal tab lines up the numeric values you enter according to the decimal point. It enables you to easily format columns of numbers in your presentations.)

Setting Tabs

You'll need the ruler and a selected text box to add tabs. After that, the steps are simple:

1. Choose the type of tab you want by clicking in the tab selection box at the left of the horizontal ruler until the tab type appears. Table 3.2 shows how the different tab icons appear.

2. Move the pointer to the ruler bar and click the point at which you want to add the tab.

TABLE 3.2: POWERPOINT TAB TYPES

Button	Tab Type	Description
L	Left tab	Left-aligns text at the tab
⌐	Right tab	Right-aligns text at the tab
⊥	Center tab	Centers text at the tab
⊥·	Decimal tab	Aligns text on decimal point

PART
II

The Right Tool
for the Job

Moving and Deleting Tabs

You can easily move or remove tabs you no longer need. First, you can simply slide them to a new location. Just move the pointer to the tab you want to move, press and hold the mouse button, and drag the tab to a new location.

Not good enough? Delete the tab by dragging it off the right end of the ruler. The tab just disappears, with no additional fanfare. Please note that Undo won't restore the tab.

Aligning Text

Another big part of formatting includes the position of the text on the slide. Depending on what other elements you include on the slide—such as a chart or other art items, or a table—you may want to experiment with different alignments. With PowerPoint, you can align your text in the following ways:

- Left aligned: the text is aligned with the left margin and is ragged along the right.
- Right aligned: the text is aligned with the right margin and is ragged along the left.
- Centered: the text is centered and ragged along both margins.
- Justified: the text is aligned with both the left and right margins.

How do you know which alignment to use? Table 3.3 provides ideas of when you might use the different alignment options.

TABLE 3.3: ALIGNMENT IDEAS

Alignment	Use For
Left	Bullet text Single paragraphs Chart legends Paragraph-style bullets
Right	Figure captions Data labels Special text effects Aligning against a chart or graphic item
Center	Titles Subtitles Chart titles
Justified	Two-column bullet slides Text along a chart or graphic item Text notes on a chart

If you are choosing either left, right, or centered alignment, you can do so by simply clicking in the text box you want to change and then clicking the appropriate button in the toolbar (see Figure 3.20). The text automatically changes to reflect your selection.

FIGURE 3.20

Choosing a different alignment

You can also change the alignment of text by opening the Format menu and choosing Alignment. A small pop-up box of different alignment choices appears.

Working with Line and Paragraph Spacing

PowerPoint takes care of the spacing of your text automatically. Type the text, and PowerPoint puts it where it needs to go. Sometimes, however, you may want to change the spacing PowerPoint has set for you. You might want to fit one more line of text on a slide, for example, or add space between lines.

You can modify the spacing between lines in your text box by choosing Format ➤ Line Spacing. The dialog box shown in Figure 3.21 appears.

FIGURE 3.21

Choosing the Line Spacing for your presentation

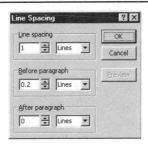

In the Line Spacing area, you can choose the number of lines you want separating text lines. You can select either Lines or Points as the spacing measurement. To change the value, click either the up-arrow or down-arrow to increase or decrease the number.

PART

II

The Right Tool for the Job

TIP A *point* is a standard typographical measurement, used in publishing and presentation projects. 72 points is roughly equal one inch. This means that if you set your title to 72-point Helvetica font, the letters will be one inch tall.

You can change the spacing increment point by point or in .01-line increments. This gives you precise control over the way your lines are spaced. Use the Preview button to see how the change will look before you click OK to accept it.

Selecting Paragraph Spacing

Also in the Line Spacing dialog box are the Before Paragraph and After Paragraph settings, which, respectively, control the amount of space before and after the current paragraph.

The only trick to using the Before and After Paragraph settings is that you must highlight the text you want to work with before you choose the Line Spacing command to display the dialog box, so PowerPoint knows which text to adjust. If you're not sure how your changes will affect the text, use the Preview button to get a glimpse before you return to the slide.

Enhancing Text

Now that you know how to enter, edit, and format the text in your presentation, you need to know how to change its font, size, style, and color. PowerPoint also makes it easy for you to add your own unique bullets to the presentation. This section introduces each of these text enhancements.

Changing Text Font and Size

Unless you have time to study typography and graphics design, you're going to rely on your own instincts when it comes to choosing fonts for your presentation slides. In most cases, you won't have to do much choosing: PowerPoint chooses the typefaces, text styles, colors, and sizes for you when you use a Presentation or Presentation Design as the basis for your file.

The text font you choose for your presentation is an important choice. The text should reflect whatever tone you are projecting. Is it a serious presentation? Stick with conventional-looking text. Is it a brainstorming session? Go for a font that gives you a little more creative freedom.

TIP When you're working with fonts, fight the temptation to overdo it—remember that *legibility* is your first goal.

To change the font, first select the text you want to change and then either:

- Click on the down-arrow beside the font box in the text settings row (see Figure 3.22).

  or

- Choose Format ➢ Font. The Font dialog box appears, as shown in Figure 3.23.

FIGURE 3.22

Displaying font options

PART

II

The Right Tool
for the Job

FIGURE 3.23

The Font dialog box

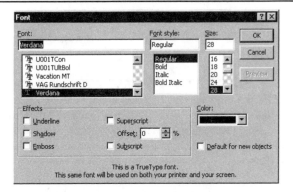

To choose a new font, select your font choice in the drop-down list. The text you selected appears in the new font.

TIP If you use one font in your presentation and then find something you like better, you can search for and replace the first font with another. Use the Replace Fonts command in the Format menu. Enter the name of the font to replace and the name of the font to replace it with. When you click OK, PowerPoint makes the change.

Changing the size of text is also a simple process. First highlight the text you want to change, then do one of the following:

- Click the down arrow to the right of the Size button in the Standard toolbar (see Figure 3.24).

- Click the Decrease Font Size or Increase Font Size button on the right side of the Formatting toolbar.

- Open the Format menu and choose Font; then select the size from the appropriate box.

Of these options, the easiest one is to highlight the text and click the down-arrow beside the size box in the Formatting toolbar.

FIGURE 3.24

Selecting a new text size

 TIP Some fonts work better in larger sizes. For example, some of the specialty fonts, such as Mistral and Gradl, are barely readable until you enlarge them. Experiment with font sizes until you get what you want. And remember to consider the slide from your audience's perspective: will everyone be able to read the words from several feet away?

Setting the Style

The style of text allows you to call attention to individual words or phrases. For example, you might want to boldface a new product name or italicize the name of a report you're quoting. PowerPoint offers Regular, Bold, Italic, and Bold Italic text styles. After you highlight the text you want to change, you can choose a new style by clicking one or more of the buttons on the Formatting toolbar (see Figure 3.25). If you prefer, you can choose the style by selecting Fonts from the Format menu and clicking the style you want in the Font dialog box.

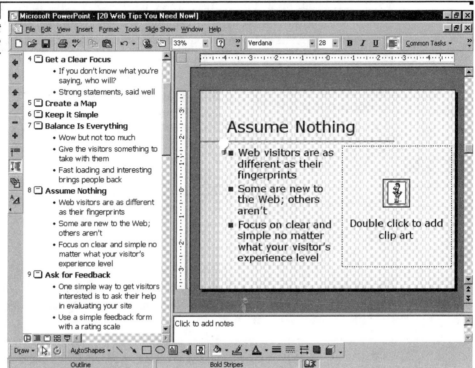

To select more than one item in the text settings row, just click the buttons you want. For example, if you want to make a word bold and italic, just highlight the word, click on B and then click on I.

Selecting Text Effects

Text effects are slightly different than text styles. Styles affect the text's appearance: regular, bold, or italic. Effects, on the other hand, include underlining, shadowing, embossing, superscript, and subscript.

You can select these effects in the Font dialog box, available by choosing Format ➤ Font. You can also choose two of the five effects (Underline and Shadow) from the toolbar.

Changing Text Color

If you started your presentation using the Design Template, Presentation, or Auto-Content Wizard, the colors of your background and text are already selected for you. The product designers at Microsoft put together effective color palettes that you can use as is or modify to suit your tastes.

To change the color of text on a particular slide, highlight the text, then click the Font Color button in the Drawing tools row at the bottom of the screen. (You can also use the Format/Font dialog box to set the color.) When you click the arrow beside the tool button, a small color pop-up box appears, as shown in Figure 3.26.

FIGURE 3.26

The color pop-up box

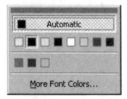

Click More Font Colors to see a larger palette of choices. For more information on mixing and matching color schemes, see Chapter 9, "The Dynamics of Color."

 TIP To change the text color for all similar slides in your presentation, change the slide's master, rather than the individual slides. For example, to change the color of all bullet text, choose View ➤ Master ➤ Slide Master to highlight the appropriate text level, and choose a different color.

PowerPoint shares a common palette with other Office applications. When you choose a color of blue in Word, you can be sure it's the same color blue when you copy the text to PowerPoint. This helps you create a consistent look among all your business applications.

Using Bullets

Even a small change like the type of bullet you use can change the look of your presentation. PowerPoint gives you an incredible choice of bullets.

PowerPoint 2000 knows you want to use customized images as bullets in your presentations. (You do, don't you? Oh come on—it's the latest thing.) Now you can use any graphical image as a bullet.

Before you start the process of selecting a different bullet character, highlight the bullet lines you want to change. If you want to change only one line, position the cursor in that line. Choose Format ➤ Bullets and Numbering, and the Bullet dialog box appears, as shown in Figure 3.27.

FIGURE 3.27

The Bullet dialog box

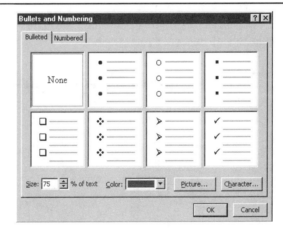

To select a different bullet, click the Character button. You can select a different set of bullets by clicking the Bullets From: down-arrow and choosing the font you want to work with. To choose a different bullet type, make sure the Use a Bullet checkbox is checked; then select the color, size, and the individual bullet character you want. When you click the bullet, it enlarges so you can get a better look at it (see Figure 3.28).

When you click OK, PowerPoint applies the bullet to all highlighted bullet points.

PART
II

The Right Tool
for the Job

FIGURE 3.28

Getting a closer look at a bullet

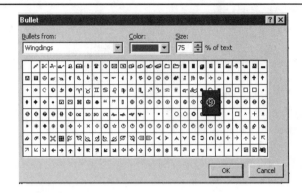

If you want to use a picture as a bullet, click the Picture button. The Picture Bullet dialog box appears, as Figure 3.29 shows. Navigate to the bullet picture you want to use, click it, and click OK to add the bullet.

FIGURE 3.29

Using a picture as a bullet

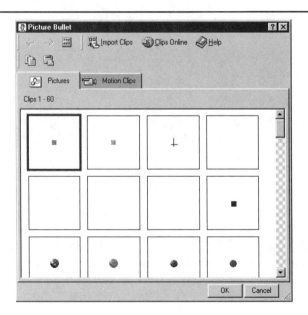

Chapter Summary

In this chapter, you learned how to enter, edit, format, and enhance the text in your presentation. You now know how to plan the basic text in your presentation, create an outline, use the Spelling and Style Checkers, work with the AutoCorrect feature, and perform a number of formatting and text-enhancement operations.

For the best results, take a few minutes and review your presentation after you've entered the basic text. Try printing the presentation in Outline view so you can show it to a few co-workers and get their input on the content you've got thus far. Making sure your text is the way you want it gives you a good basis for building the rest of your PowerPoint presentation. We'll start with the next step—creating and enhancing charts—in the next chapter.

PART

II

The Right Tool
for the Job

CHAPTER 4

Creating and Enhancing Graphs

FEATURING:

The text of your presentation is important, but it doesn't provide much in the way of visual instruction. You couldn't look at a printed page and know at a glance, for example, that sales in a particular area have increased dramatically or that your department has almost reached its productivity goal. A chart can call attention to that information immediately, letting you skip over the read-and-figure-it-out stage and see immediately what point the presenter is trying to make.

A Few Graph Ideas

How do you know what will work as a graph? Here are a few possibilities:

Comparisons   Graphs can help you illustrate relationships between data. For example, you can illustrate how the price reduction of an item increases or decreases sales, or show the hierarchy in your organization.

Processes   If you have several slides full of bullets, think about whether one could be converted into a graph. The change will break up the monotony of bullet lists and convey information in a new and interesting form.

Trends   When you need to show data trends, graphs can help you compare the progress of two data sets, whether or not those items are sales regions, products, or salaries.

 TIP   Certain types of graphs are better than others for showing certain kinds of information. For example, if you want to compare two or more items, you can use bar charts, bar-line charts, and area charts to help readers visually identify the differences between the contrasted data series.

Is This PowerPoint or Microsoft Graph?

The graph capability of PowerPoint is not PowerPoint's own—it is actually Microsoft Graph 2000, an embedded graph utility you can use to create graph objects in your presentation. You won't notice any difference when you move between PowerPoint and Microsoft Graph—you'll simply use the Graph datasheet to enter the data for the graph and then use various Graph options to choose the graph type, set options, change the format, and enhance the graphs you create.

Using Excel Graphs in Your PowerPoint Presentations

If you, as an Office aficionado, have already created Excel graphs, you may not need to worry about creating any PowerPoint ones. Instead, you'll paste the Excel charts directly onto the slide. Microsoft Graph is also used to create Excel's charts, although Excel actually leads you through the process of creating the chart by using the ChartWizard.

 NOTE Excel's ChartWizard is much like PowerPoint's AutoContent Wizard, in that it leads you through the process of creating the item by asking you a series of questions.

To use an already-created Excel graph in your PowerPoint presentation, you have several choices. You can copy the graph from Excel to PowerPoint, use Edit ➤ Paste Special to paste the graph on the slide while maintaining the link to Excel, or tile both the Excel and PowerPoint windows side-by-side and drag-and-drop the graph from Excel to PowerPoint.

The process of linking an object—a graph is considered an object—enables you to make sure the object is updated whenever the original file changes. This means that whenever you change the data in your Excel spreadsheet, the changes will automatically be reflected in your PowerPoint file.

An Overview of Graph Types

When you're creating two-dimensional or three-dimensional graphs from scratch with PowerPoint, you've got a number of different graph types to choose from, including these:

- *Area graphs* show one or more data trends over time
- *Bar graphs* show how data series "stack up" against each other
- *Column graphs* are similar to a bar graph, except that the bars are stacked on top of each other instead of side-by-side
- *Doughnut graphs* plot more than one data series as parts of a whole
- *Line graphs* compare data series over time
- *Pie graphs* show how individual data items relate to the whole
- *Radar graphs* compare data series
- *XY (scatter) graphs* plot data points according to x and y axes
- *Surface graphs* show data trends in a two-dimensional view

PART

II

The Right Tool
for the Job

- *Bubble charts* compare three sets of data
- *Stock charts* are actually high-low-close charts which show three numeric values along each bar
- *2-D and 3-D charts* offer cylinder, pyramid, and cone shapes

Each type of graph includes a number of subtypes. In addition, each of these graph types is available in 3-D (which means that the Line graph category becomes 3-D Line graph).

Once you choose a basic chart type, you select individual options to create the kind of graph you want. You might start with a bar chart, for example, and then select options that enable you to create a *stacked* bar chart—with data ranges stacked one on top of another.

Creating a Graph

First, you need a slide with a graph area. If your current slide doesn't have a graph area blocked out, click the New Slide button to display the New Slide dialog box (see Figure 4.1 and choose a slide with a graph area built in. When you've selected the file you want (click in the scroll bar to see more choices), click OK. The new slide appears on the screen with the graph area blocked out (see Figure 4.2).

FIGURE 4.1

*The New Slide
dialog box*

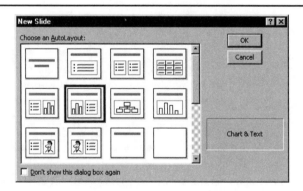

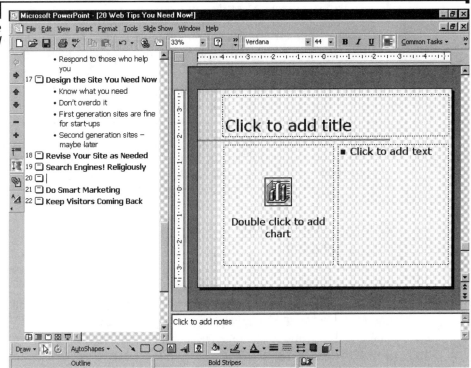

PART

II

The Right Tool
for the Job

FIGURE 4.02

The new slide with the graph area marked

Starting the Graph

When you double-click the graph area, PowerPoint churns away for a moment before displaying first a graph and then a datasheet. The datasheet already includes data, put there to provide an example of how PowerPoint's graphing capability works (see Figure 4.3). It is designed this way to prompt you to replace PowerPoint's data with your own, and choose the graph that best suits your needs.

FIGURE 4.3

PowerPoint puts data in the datasheet for you.

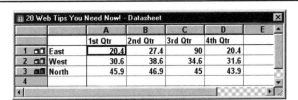

Working with the Datasheet

The datasheet contains the data PowerPoint uses to build your graph. You enter the labels for the data you want to graph across the top and left rows of the datasheet. Each row represents a single data series and shows what type of symbol—in this case, a 3-D bar—represents the data in the series.

 TIP Before you can enter anything of your own, you need to get PowerPoint's fake data off the datasheet. First highlight the data; then use Edit ➢ Clear ➢ All to remove all information on the datasheet so you can start with a blank slate.

Entering Data Labels

Your first step is to replace the labels in the datasheet with your labels. The datasheet looks a little like an Excel spreadsheet, organized in a row and column fashion. The intersection of each column and row is called a *cell*.

Each row is a single data series, and each column shows the data values compared in each data series. For example, if you are comparing the sales of two products, the labels Product A and Product B might be listed in the label area of rows 1 and 2, and the column labels might list the months (see Figure 4.4).

FIGURE 4.4

An example of row and column labels

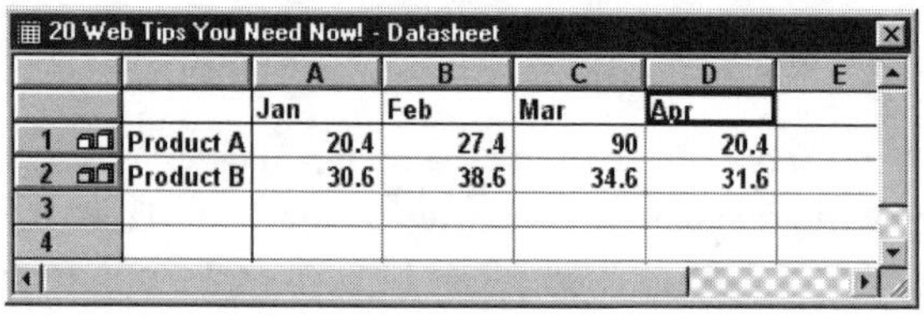

20 Web Tips You Need Now! - Datasheet		A	B	C	D	E
		Jan	Feb	Mar	Apr	
1	Product A	20.4	27.4	90	20.4	
2	Product B	30.6	38.6	34.6	31.6	
3						
4						

Entering Data

To enter new information in the datasheet, click in the cell where you want the data to go and type. The new data replaces the old data. To move to another cell, use the arrow keys or move the mouse pointer to the new cell and click.

Editing the Datasheet

Once you enter the data for the graph, it's likely that you'll want to make some changes. To modify the data you entered, just click in the cell and retype the data. You can also copy, cut, or undo data, using the commands in the Edit menu.

Deleting Datasheet Rows and Columns

To delete entire columns or rows on the datasheet, click the label area for the row or column to highlight it as shown in Figure 4.5. Press Del, and it's gone.

FIGURE 4.5

Removing an entire column in the datasheet

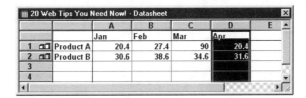

PART

II

The Right Tool for the Job

Resizing Datasheet Columns

When the data you need to enter is too wide for the cells in the datasheet, you can widen the column to accommodate the data. Position the cursor on the dividing line between two column labels so that the cursor changes to a double-arrow. To widen the column, drag the mouse in the direction you want and release the mouse button when the column is at the desired width. To have PowerPoint automatically adjust the column width to the text, double-click the dividing line. The column width will close to the widest data entry in the column.

Closing the Datasheet

After you've entered your own data labels and data, you are ready to close the datasheet and begin experimenting with graph types. Close the datasheet in one of these three ways:

- Double-click the control-menu box in the upper left corner of the datasheet
- Click the X in the upper-right corner of the datasheet. Click the View Datasheet tool
- Select View ➢ Datasheet

TIP At some point, you may want to redisplay that datasheet to make additional changes. Click the View Datasheet button or choose   View ➤ Datasheet to display the datasheet again.

Choosing the Graph Type

Now that you've entered the data you're going to work with, the next step is to choose the type of chart you want. You can select a chart type in one of two different ways:

- Click on the Chart Type button on the Standard toolbar to display the drop-down chart box (see Figure 4.6).

- *Or* choose Chart ➤ Chart Type.

 TIP If you don't see a Chart Type command in your Chart menu, you haven't selected the graph.

FIGURE 4.6

Choosing the type of graph you want

MASTERING THE OPPORTUNITIES

The Four Most Effective Graphs

When you are displaying information visually, you want to show data in the clearest form possible. For that reason, if you have only a short amount of time to spend on each graph that you create, be sure to choose a graph type that will be recognized by your audience and will suit the type of data you are presenting.

One of the most common types of graphs is the bar graph. A *bar graph* is used to depict a particular data series. For example, suppose you are tracking the sales of four different regions. Each region would be represented by a bar on the graph. By looking at the height of the bars, audience members could easily tell which region had the highest sales, which had the lowest, etc. PowerPoint enables you to create both 2-D and 3-D bar graphs for different looks. You can enhance the appearance of bar graphs in other ways, too: for example, you can add a grid or labels and titles, or create a stacked bar graph where the data series are stacked one atop another.

A *pie graph* is another popular graph, used to show how portions of a data series relate to the whole. Suppose that you're doing a cost analysis of a recent project you've completed. What portion of your investment went to research and which portion went to development? What portion went to production? How much was spent on marketing and distribution? By plugging these numbers into the datasheet and then creating a pie graph based on the data, you can show what percentage of the total expenditure was allotted to each of these categories. Each of the categories are a data series, each getting one slice of the pie. Like bar graphs, you can enhance the appearance of a pie graph in many ways: you can make either 2-D or 3-D pies, create multiple pies, make pie slices explode out from the body of the pie, and add or change labels and titles.

Line graphs are popular for showing the progression of data over a specific period of time. You might be watching the development of a particular industry trend (How does the number of computers sold with CD-ROMs in 1994 compare to the number sold during each quarter of 1995?), tracking the expenses of a department (How much did Marketing spend on Federal Express charges over a 12-month period? How does that relate to the number of projects published?), or comparing projected and actual sales over a fiscal year. Again, line graphs can be flexible in appearance: you can choose 2-D or 3-D lines, change colors, add or remove gridlines, modify the legend, and more.

Continued

> ### MASTERING THE OPPORTUNITIES CONTINUED
>
> Another type of graph used to show a data progression is an ***area graph***. An area graph allows you to compare two or more data series over time, representing the totals with a colored area assigned to the data series. For instance, if you are comparing how well two products sold over a quarter, you could show the different data series cumulatively in an area chart. One colored area represents the first product; the other colored area represents the second. At a glance, viewers can see the total amount sold of both products and tell which product fared the best in the marketplace.

If you choose the chart by selecting the one you want from the list, PowerPoint automatically changes the chart in the selected box. If you select a chart with the Chart Type command, the Chart Type dialog box appears (see Figure 4.7).

FIGURE 4.7

The Chart Type dialog box

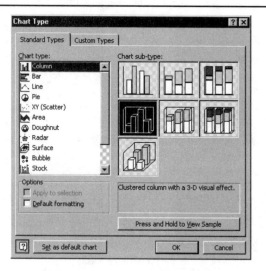

The first set of options in the Chart Type dialog box allows you to specify the type of chart you want. The second set enables you to choose the chart subtype. When you make your choice of chart type, the subtypes you can select appear in the display area on the left side of the dialog box. Click the type you want and then click OK to return to the slide.

Choosing Custom Options   PowerPoint 2000 also gives you the option of creating custom charts. Click the Custom Types tab in the Chart Type dialog box to see additional choices (see Figure 4.8). Then click on the type of chart in the column on the left side of the dialog box; subtypes appear on the right. You can now click the chart that best fits the type of data you're presenting. Click OK when you're through.

You can choose additional chart types by selecting the Custom Types tab

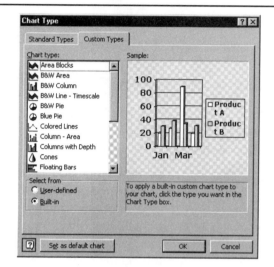

PART

II

The Right Tool
for the Job

Setting Chart Options   Once you've selected the chart type, you can modify chart options. Open the Chart menu and choose Chart Options. The dialog box shown in Figure 4.9 appears.

The dialog box includes as many as six different tabs, depending on the type of chart you've selected. Pie charts, for instance, will offer only three of the following tabs, most of the others will show all six: Titles, Axes, Gridlines, Legend, Data Labels, and Data Table. The Titles tab gives you the space to enter chart titles and axis labels; the Axes tab lets you choose the measurement and type of the axes; the Gridlines tab controls where the gridlines are placed; the Legend tab enables you to choose the placement of the legend; the Data Labels tab lets you make selections about the data labels; and the Data Table tab helps you choose options for any data tables you display. In every tab, make your selections; when you are finished, click OK to close the dialog box.

FIGURE 4.9

The Chart Options dialog box gives you up to six different tabs of choices

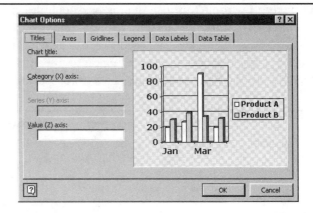

Importing Chart Data

Microsoft Office is built on the enter-it-once, use-it-many-times concept. You can write an outline in Word, for example, and use it as the basis for a PowerPoint presentation. You can use a selected range from your Excel worksheet as the basis for your PowerPoint graph. You're not limited to importing from Microsoft products; PowerPoint lets you work with data from other applications as well. This section explores a few of the kinds of data you can use to create PowerPoint graphs.

What Data Can You Import?

In addition to Microsoft Excel files, PowerPoint directly supports several different text files and Lotus 1-2-3 files. If your spreadsheet file names end with any of these extensions, your data can be imported into PowerPoint:

- XL* (Microsoft Excel)
- PRN, TXT, CSV (Standard text format)
- WK* (Lotus 1-2-3)

(In the preceding list, the asterisk character (*) is a wildcard, meaning that any character can be substituted for the asterisk. An acceptable Lotus 1-2-3 extension, for example, is WK1.)

If you use a spreadsheet program other than Excel or 1-2-3, you may still be able to use your data files with PowerPoint. Save the spreadsheet file in Excel or 1-2-3 format and then choose Edit ➤ Import Data to bring the information into PowerPoint. The instructions in your spreadsheet program should tell you how to save files in those formats.

 TIP If you're drawing data from a Windows application—perhaps Microsoft Works or another Windows program with spreadsheet capability—you should be able to copy data into the PowerPoint datasheet using Edit ➢ Copy in the other application and Edit ➢ Paste in PowerPoint.

Importing Files

To import data as the basis for your graph, you must first display and clear the datasheet. Select the area to clear, choose Edit ➢ Clear All to erase the information in the datasheet, and then enter any labels necessary to describe the data that you're importing.

Position the cursor in the upper left corner of the datasheet work area and choose Edit ➢ Import File. The Import File dialog box appears, as shown in Figure 4.10.

FIGURE 4.10

*The Import File
dialog box*

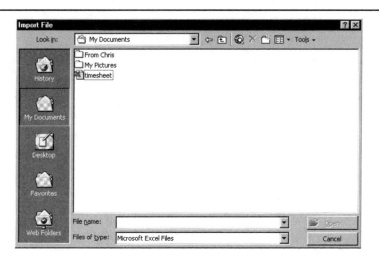

As a Windows user, you should be able to navigate this dialog box without any difficulty; it works much like File Open. Begin by navigating to the folder containing the file you want; then select it and click OK.

After you click OK, PowerPoint searches for the specified file, places the data in the datasheet, and updates the graph.

Editing Graphs

You may not know exactly what you want in a graph until you see it drawn on the screen. Then your ideas on how to improve it ("What if I added a title? Would those bars stand out better if they were a different color?") can help you fine-tune the basic graph into something ready for presentation.

Basic Procedures: Cutting, Copying, Pasting, and Resizing Graphs

Working with a graph frame is like working with any frame in PowerPoint—you can easily resize, cut, copy, or paste graphs just like you would any other item. To perform these basic editing procedures, click on the graph to select it. The graph frame appears, with handles around its outer edge.

To resize a graph:	Click a handle and drag the graph to resize it horizontally or vertically.
To cut a graph	Make sure the graph is selected; then press choose Edit ➤ Cut.
To delete a graph:	Make sure the graph is selected; then press Del or choose Edit ➤ Clear.
To copy a graph:	Select the graph; then choose Edit ➤ Copy.
To paste a graph:	Move to the slide on which you want to paste the graph and choose Edit ➤ Paste.

 TIP When resizing a graph, you can keep its original proportions by dragging the graph corner at a 45° angle inward or outward.

Modifying Graph Elements

When you double-click the graph to select it, several changes happen on the screen. First, the frame outline takes on a different look—instead of a thin outline with white handles, the outline becomes a thick white outline with black handles.

The toolbar also changes. Now a number of new tools appear, all having to do with importing, creating, displaying, and modifying graphs (see Figure 4.11). Table 4.1 shows the different tools in the graph toolbar. In PowerPoint 2000, some of the tools are tucked away in a tools palette until you use them for the first time (see Figure 4.11 for an example). Click the small down-arrow button to display the tools palette and select more graph tools. When you use one of the tools in the palette, it will automatically be added to the toolbar so you can use it in the future without going all the way back to the palette.

PART

II

The Right Tool
for the Job

FIGURE 4.11

When you select a graph for editing, the tools you need are displayed in the toolbar and the tools palette

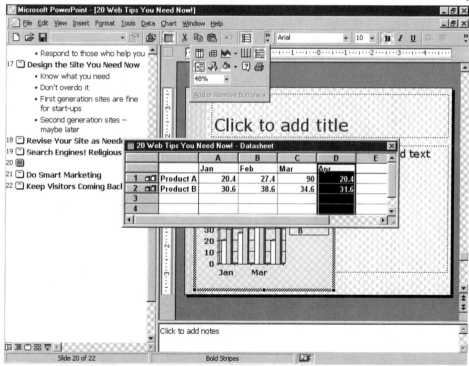

TABLE 4.1: TOOLS IN THE GRAPH TOOLBAR

Tool	Name	Description
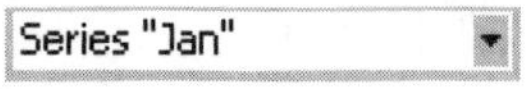 Series "Jan"	Chart Objects	Enables you to choose a chart element to modify
	Format	Displays the Format dialog box so you can change the way the selected element is displayed
	Import File	Imports an existing file from another application
	View Datasheet	Displays and hides datasheet
	Cut	Removes the selected item and places it on the clipboard
	Copy	Copies the selected item to the Clipboard
	Paste	Pastes Clipboard contents to selected area
	Undo	Reverses last action
	By Row	Associates data row-wise
	By Column	Associates data column-wise
	Data Table	Turns the selected chart into a data table
	Chart Type	Allows you to choose the chart type you want
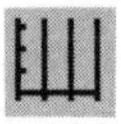	Category Axis Gridlines	Adds or removes the vertical gridlines on the graph
	Value Axis Gridlines	Adds or removes the horizontal gridlines on the graph
	Legend	Displays or hides the legend

Continued

TABLE 4.1: TOOLS IN THE GRAPH TOOLBAR (CONTINUED)		
Tool	Name	Description
	Drawing	Brings up the drawing tools
	Fill Color	Displays a color palette
	Office Assistant	Displays the Assistant so you can get help on the selected topic

TIP If you plan on doing up-close work—like changing data values, adding labels, or changing markers and gridlines—you may want to Zoom the display so you can see what's going on. Click the Zoom down arrow to display the list of possible percentages; choose the display you want. You need to do this *before* you double-click the graph to display the graph toolbar and put the graph in editing mode.

Changing the Data Arrangement

There's a method to PowerPoint's madness when it comes to the way data is displayed in your graph. When you enter data in the datasheet, PowerPoint graphs the information first by row, then by column. This means that if you're working with the datasheet in Figure 4.12, PowerPoint will show how Product A and Product B (rows) did over the first four months of the year (columns). The resulting chart is shown in an enlarged view in Figure 4.13.

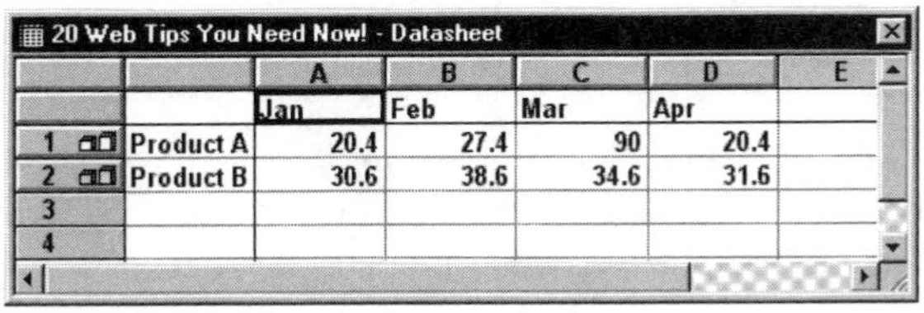

FIGURE 4.12

PowerPoint graphs the information in the datasheet first by row, then by column

20 Web Tips You Need Now! - Datasheet		A	B	C	D	E
		Jan	Feb	Mar	Apr	
1	Product A	20.4	27.4	90	20.4	
2	Product B	30.6	38.6	34.6	31.6	
3						
4						

FIGURE 4.13

PowerPoint creates a
default graph based
on the values you
enter in the datasheet

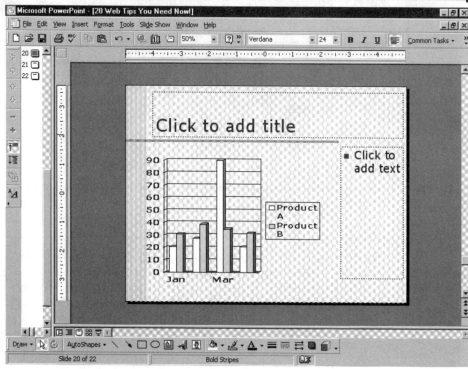

You can change the way PowerPoint displays the data—that is, you can put the row data where the column data is and the column data where the row data is—to display your graph another way. That way, instead of showing how Products A and B did over four months, you show how the months look for each of those products.

For instance, you can change the way the data is arranged (this is also called the association of the data) by clicking the By Column button in the toolbar. When you click By Column, PowerPoint graphs Product A and Product B separately, with each bar in the graph associated with a particular month (see Figure 4.14).

 TIP If you're having trouble displaying your data just the way you want it, try switching the association of the data. If the By Row button is clicked, try using By Column, or vice versa. Sometimes when data is arranged differently it makes more sense.

FIGURE 14.4

Changing the data association to By Column

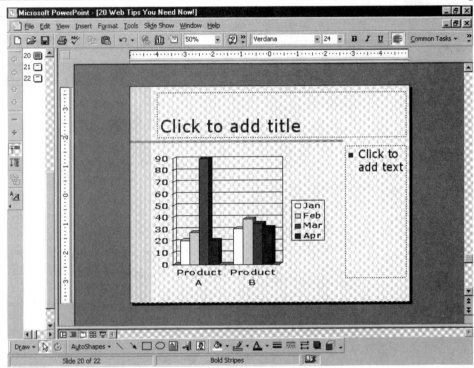

Creating a Data Table

Now you can easily turn a chart into a data table with the simple click of a button. When the chart is displayed on the screen, click the Data Table button, in the tools palette, unless you've used it before, and then it appears in the toolbar. The chart is redrawn as a data table (see Figure 4.15). If you want to change the data table back into a chart, click the Data Table button again.

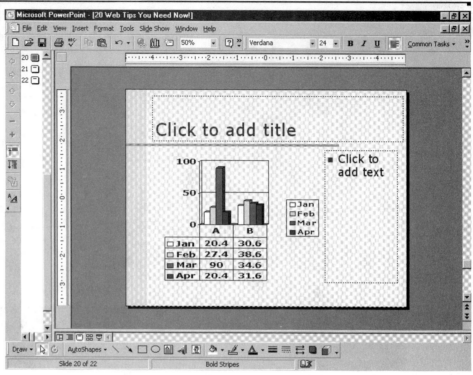

Changing the Appearance of the X and Y Axes

You may want to change the way the axes of your graph are displayed. In some cases, you might want to change their color or thickness, or you may want to change the tick marks and the way they appear.

NOTE The Y axis extends vertically; the X axis is horizontal. Tick marks are the small lines that mark off increments on the axes.

To modify the axes on your graph, double-click on the axis you want to change. Figure 4.16 shows the Format Axis dialog box that appears when you do this.

Like other Windows 95/98 dialog boxes, this one is divided into tabs. First and foremost in the Format Axis dialog box are aesthetic concerns. What color do you want the axis to be? How do you want the tick marks to appear? A sample line at the bottom of the Patterns screen shows you your selections.

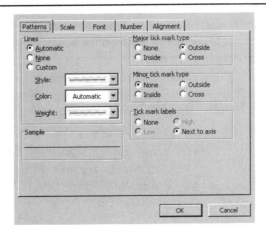

FIGURE 4.16

The Format Axis dialog box

Other tabs behind Patterns include Scale, which allows you to set the increment values between tick marks; Font, which controls the font of the axis labels; Number, which controls the numeric format of values displayed; and Alignment, which allows you to choose the basic layout of text.

You can modify these settings at any time during your work with PowerPoint. Simply make your selections and click OK to return to the graph.

Enhancing Graphs

Your graph is done. You've added and edited its data and arranged it to your liking. The only problem? It's boring. What might you do to spruce up a chart? Maybe add some color. Tack on a text note. Add a title or data labels. You could even change a font or style. To round out our discussion of graphs, we'll talk about how you can enhance their appearance.

Changeable Chart Elements

You can select and change any of the following elements by double-clicking on them:

- Individual data series
- The plot area
- The X and Y axes
- The legend
- The gridlines

TIP In most cases, you can also change chart element settings by using a menu command or a tool. Use whichever method is most convenient for you.

Working with Graph Text

You can change the appearance of chart text (the axis labels) by double-clicking on the axis you want to change and then choosing Font from the displayed screen. There are other types of text you might want to consider working with and/or adding. This section explains how you can add a graph title and data labels and shows how to make basic graph text changes.

Adding a Title

This graph needs a title. Make sure the graph is selected and then choose Chart ➤ Chart Options. The dialog box shown in Figure 4.17 appears.

If the Titles tab isn't already displayed, click it now. Type the text you want to use as the chart title and then click OK. A text box is added to the chart area where the title will go. Type the text for the title and click outside the Title box.

 TIP The best titles say it quickly and clearly. Make sure the graph title reflects in as few words as possible the basic concept of your graph. "December Sales Results" is much easier to understand than "Net Sales Based on December's Total Receipts."

The Chart Options dialog box

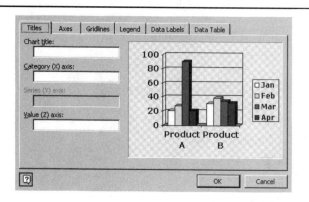

Rotating Chart Text

PowerPoint makes it possible for you to rotate chart titles, axis titles, or data labels. To rotate chart text, begin by selecting the text item you want to change. Right-click and choose Format Axis Title. The Alignment tab is already displayed. This tab gives you the option of choosing the alignment for the text (see Figure 4.18). Either enter the angle you want in the Degrees box, or drag the small red diamond up or down on the arc to angle the text. When you're finished, click OK.

FIGURE 4.18

You can rotate chart text by typing a value or by dragging the marker

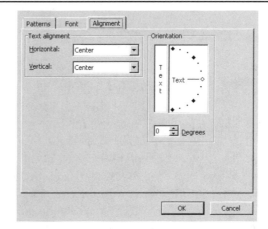

Adding Data Labels

Depending on the type of data you are displaying, you may find it helpful to show the data values or labels on or beside the bars, lines, or columns themselves. To add data values or labels, choose Chart ➤ Chart Options; then click the Data Labels tab (see Figure 4.19).

You can add either values or labels. If you add values, the numeric values appear beside the data series items. If you add labels, the names of the data series appear beside the graph elements. Some items in your dialog box may appear dimmed, depending on the type of graph you're working with.

After you make your selection, click OK.

 TIP Once you add the data labels to the graph, things may look too crowded. You can drag one of the graph frame handles outward to enlarge the graph and make more room for all the elements inside.

FIGURE 4.19

*The Data Labels tab of
the Chart Options dia-
log box*

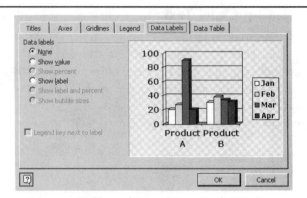

Changing Font, Size, and Style

The look of your text says a lot about your presentation. You may want to try using a different look—especially if you're worried about whether your data labels or graph titles will be legible to the people in the fourth row.

To change the font of something you've added, like a title or text note, click inside the text box and then open the Format menu in the menu bar. The first command there should reflect the item you've selected. So, if you've selected a chart title, the command is Selected Chart Title. (You can also double-click the item to display the dialog box.) If you've selected a legend, the command is Selected Legend. Click the command. The Format dialog box—either Format Legend or Format Title, depending on what you selected (see Figure 4.20)—will appear.

If you've been working with text in your PowerPoint slides, these options won't surprise you. In the Font screen, you choose the font, style, size, color, background, and effects of the text you've selected. The Sample box in the bottom of the screen shows you how your choices look. In the Alignment tab, you choose the alignment of text.

TIP If the x-axis labels on your graph bunch up and are difficult to read, you have three options: enlarge the graph, reduce the size of the label text, or change the orientation of the text so that the labels angle vertically instead of being spread horizontally below the graph.

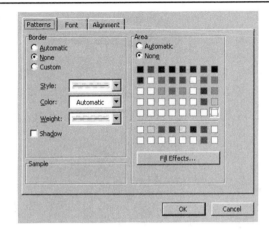

FIGURE 4.20

The Format Chart Title dialog box

Adding Gridlines

Gridlines can add a sense of proportion to the graphs in your presentation. If you've got a series of bar charts but no gridlines, it may be difficult for someone in the fourteenth row to tell how one data series compares to another. Gridlines help make it obvious which data series outreaches the other, even when it's a close call.

PowerPoint allows you to add two different kinds of gridlines: horizontal and vertical. The gridlines are tied to the major tick marks in the axes, so if you want to change the spacing of the gridlines, you'll need to make modifications on the X or Y axis of your graph. Figure 4.21 shows how the chart looks with both vertical and horizontal gridlines.

To change the gridlines settings, open the Chart menu and select Chart Options; then click the Gridlines tab. The dialog box appears with the Gridlines tab showing, as shown in Figure 4.22. If you want to attach the gridlines to the minor gridlines—which means you'll have more of them in your graph—click Minor Gridlines. You might want to do this, for example, if you are graphing data series with data points close together; the minor gridlines will help you read the placement of the data. When you've finished making changes, click OK.

FIGURE 4.21

Adding horizontal and vertical gridlines

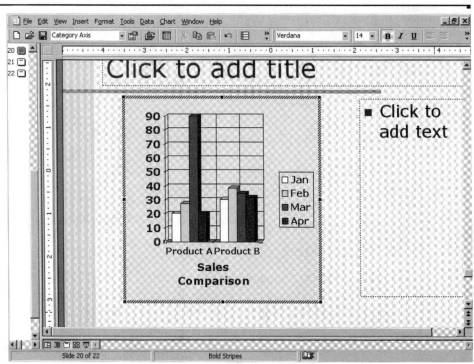

FIGURE 4.22

The Gridlines dialog box

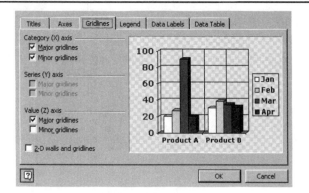

 TIP Remember that the actual tick marks and increments are part of the axis settings. To change the spacing between gridlines, double-click on the axis you want to change.

Hiding and Displaying the Legend

The legend of your graph is like the key to a map; it shows your viewers at a glance which data series is represented by which bar, color, line, or pie slice. By default, Power-Point adds a legend to your graph. In some instances, you may want to remove the graph legend from the display, if only temporarily. This could give you more room for other items or save you from unnecessarily cluttering your slide when the data speaks for itself.

To hide the graph legend, display the Chart Options dialog box and click the Legend tab. Next click the Show Legend checkbox to remove the X. When you click OK to close the dialog box, the legend is gone. To redisplay the legend, open the Chart Options dialog box again and click the Show Legend checkbox.

Adding a Text Box

Another tool in the graphics toolbar allows you to add text to your graph. You might do this to call attention to a certain feature or add a note to the presentation slide.

To add a text box, click the Text Box tool in the toolbar at the bottom of the screen and use the mouse to draw the box in the graph editing area. The cursor is positioned in the upper left corner of the new text box, ready to accept your text. Type the text for the note and click outside the box.

 TIP Once you add the text, you can change it easily: highlight the text and choose Format ➤ Font. Then make the necessary changes to font, style, color, size, and effect settings. Click OK when you're finished.

Specifying Color

Earlier you learned to choose the color of individual data items. Now you can use the Color tool to choose the background color of specific areas of your chart. For example, you might change the background color of the text note you just added.

Select the text box and then click the down-arrow beside the Fill Color tool in the More Buttons palette. A pop-up palette of colors appears below the toolbar (see Figure 4.23).

Click the color you want. Instantly, the palette disappears and the color is applied to the selected element—in this case, the text box.

TIP For more about which colors work best under which conditions, see Chapter 9, "The Dynamics of Color."

PowerPoint gives you some additional choices for the way you fill the bars of your charts. Now, in addition to choosing the color for chart elements, you can add a custom touch to your chart by using pictures, textures, or gradient fill patterns for the chart items.

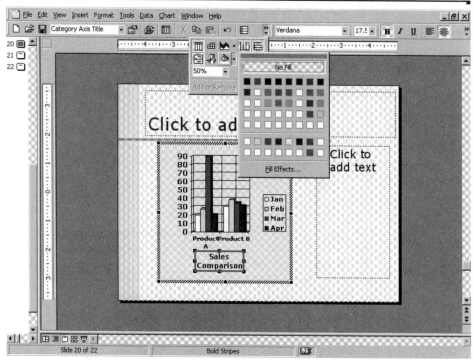

Changing Patterns

Like color, pattern also affects the background of elements in your chart. After you select the item you want to change, you can choose from a variety of patterns by clicking the Fill Effects option in the color palette. This displays a dialog box that enables you to make more choices about the textures and patterns used in the chart. To see the available patterns, click the Pattern tab (see Figure 4.24). When you make your selection, the palette closes and the new setting is applied to the selected element.

Choosing a different pattern

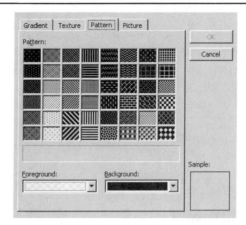

Animating Charts

Trying to think of new ways to keep your audience interested? How about having charts grow right before their eyes? PowerPoint enables you to animate charts so they change and grow as your audience watches.

To animate a chart, begin with the chart displayed on your screen. Make sure the regular toolbar is displayed; you don't want the Graph toolbar displayed. Click the chart one time so the handles appear. Then open the Slide Show menu and choose Custom Animation. The Custom Animation dialog box appears, as shown in Figure 4.25.

Notice that the Chart Effects tab is selected. To choose what you want animated, click the Introduce Chart Elements down arrow and select the option for the way you want the elements introduced: all at once, by Series, by Category, by Element in Series, or by Element in Category. Next, you can control the way the items appear and whether they are accompanied by a sound effect by choosing the options in the Entry animation and sound option boxes. Finally, if you want the element to be dimmed after it appears, you can set the After Animation option. Try out the effects you've selected by clicking Preview. When you are finished, click OK.

PART

II

The Right Tool
for the Job

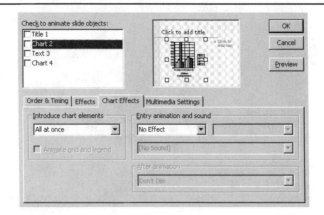

FIGURE 4.25

Animate a chart in the Custom Animation dialog box.

Chapter Summary

This chapter rounds out the discussion of graphs in your PowerPoint presentation. In this chapter, you've learned to create, edit, and enhance the appearance of your graphs. You found out how to choose a graph type, edit data values, add titles, labels, and legends, and make a variety of other changes. In the next chapter, you'll learn to add custom drawings to your PowerPoint slides.

CHAPTER **5**

Picture This! Custom and Clip Art

People love graphics. Sure, we can read text, but we've come to expect photos, graphs, drawings, logos, and special elements designed to keep our interest.

For presentations, though, text was about as exciting as it could get. When you made that presentation to the board about the new hummer motors for the pocket fans, you slapped a few acetate sheets on the overhead, full of bullet points on the projector, and read off your lines of text. Your audience approved or denied your ideas based on whether you held their attention long enough to get your points across.

Today, your presentations can dazzle your audience. PowerPoint makes it easy to add exciting graphics to your presentations. Even if you're not sure what will look right where, you can let PowerPoint suggest what art you should use, including art files created in another program, scanned images, or commercial clip art. You can even create your own art onscreen using PowerPoint's Drawing tools.

This chapter introduces you to your artistic possibilities and helps you make a graphic statement in your PowerPoint presentation.

Checking Out PowerPoint's Clip Art

PowerPoint strives to make things as simple as possible, so adding art to a slide can be as easy as point-and-click. This section explores working with clip art and all the options open to you. The tool you use for adding this art is called the Microsoft Clip Gallery, and it's an almost endless supply of art from within the Office 2000 suite and on the Web. This section shows you how to add, organize, and use clip art using the Clip Gallery.

Adding New Clip Art Slides

The first step to adding art is creating a slide to hold it. Begin by clicking the New Slide button and choosing one of the slides with a clip-art placeholder already mapped out for you (see Figure 5.1). Choose the slide you want, and click OK.

When the new slide appears, double-click the clip art area. The Microsoft Clip Gallery 3 appears, as shown in Figure 5.2.

FIGURE 5.1

The New Slide dialog box includes two slide placeholders with clip art blocked out.

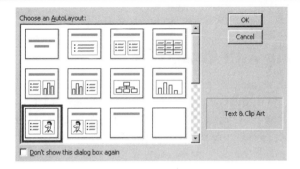

FIGURE 5.2

The Microsoft Clip Gallery stores and organizes all the clip art that comes with PowerPoint.

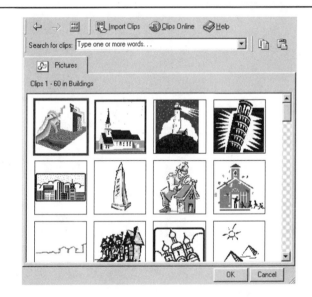

PART

II

The Right Tool for the Job

What's New in the Office 2000 Clip Gallery?

The slick new Clip Gallery replaces the old Category list of former versions of Power-Point. The Category list is now hidden behind a Categories button in the Clip Gallery toolbar. The Gallery also includes a Clips Online button that allows you to access the Web to find more pieces of art that suit your mood or your needs.

TIP You can also choose Insert ➢ Picture ➢ Clip Art to display the Clip Gallery so you can add clip art to a slide.

If you see the clip art you want, click it in the Pictures window, or click the down arrow at the end of the scroll bar in the Pictures window to see additional pictures.

Working with Categories

Chances are that at some point—if not immediately—you'll need to go looking around in the Gallery to find a specific piece of art. PowerPoint 2000 makes it easy because it organizes clip art into categories. You can display the different clip-art categories by clicking the Categories button in the Clip Gallery toolbar. The categories appear in the Gallery window, as shown in Figure 5.3.

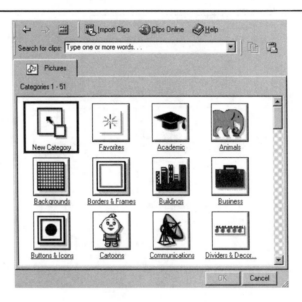

Next, click on the category you want to view, and the selection of clip art appears in the dialog box window. Once you locate the clip art you want, double-click it. Power-Point closes the Clip Gallery dialog box and adds the art to the slide (see Figure 5.4).

 TIP If you don't find the art you want, you can do a search on the Web for graphics that better match what you're looking for. Details on how to do this are covered in the next section.

FIGURE 5.4

The art you selected in the Clip Gallery is added to the slide.

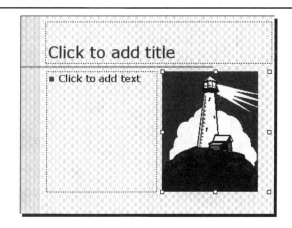

Finding Specific Clip Art

You can tell PowerPoint specifically what you're looking for by typing a word or phrase in the Search for Clips box just below the Clip Gallery toolbar. For example, if you want to show pictures of office furniture, you might type *office* or *furniture* or even *office furniture*. When I entered *office*, I got 60 matches. For *furniture*, I got 32 pieces of clip art returned. For office furniture (no big surprise here), the 60 matches were presented again (see Figure 5.5). Be as specific as you can with the descriptions you enter to narrow your search as much as possible.

Scroll through the list until you find the one you want, and double-click it. The art is then added to the slide.

 TIP Once you have entered a search string, you can use the same one again by clicking the down arrow to the right of the Search for Clips box and selecting it from the displayed list.

FIGURE 5.5

Searching for a specific piece of clip art

But what if you still can't find the art you want? At the end of the art PowerPoint found, a message appears: *Keep Looking*. You can click this button to have PowerPoint continue the search for your art. When PowerPoint has exhausted its own supply, the message is not shown at the bottom of the choices.

Taking It to the Web

Suppose that you were looking for a certain item and it didn't show up in your search of the Clip Gallery possibilities. You could, of course, launch out on your own, call all your friends, look through clip art CDs, begin a quest for the perfect art. Or you could simply click the Clips Online button and go to a special Microsoft site with additional clips to browse.

The Connect To dialog box is displayed so that you can connect to the Internet. You are taken to Microsoft Clip Gallery Live, an ever-changing database of clips, sounds, animation, and more. Before you can select art to use, you will be asked to accept Microsoft's end-user license agreement. After you read the information and click Accept, you will move to the Clip Gallery Live Web page (see Figure 5.6).

FIGURE 5.6

Finding clips online with Clip Gallery Live

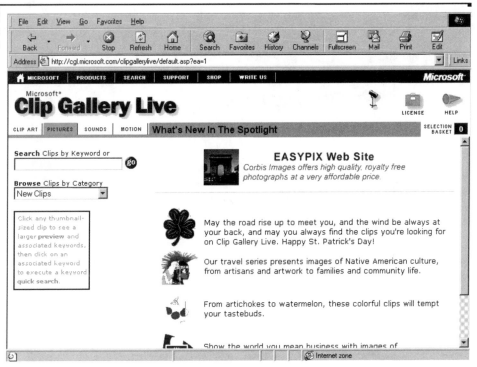

 NOTE   Because the Web is such a dynamic place, the Web page you see on your screen for Clip Gallery Live may be different from the one shown here.

You can click in the Search box and type a word describing the type of clip you'd like to find; you can browse the clips by category (click the down arrow to the right of the Browse text box); or you can click one of the category icons to see a displayed screen of images you can preview or download (see Figure 5.7).

PART

II

The Right Tool
for the Job

FIGURE 5.7

To choose one of the images for downloading, click it and Microsoft adds it to your Selection Basket.

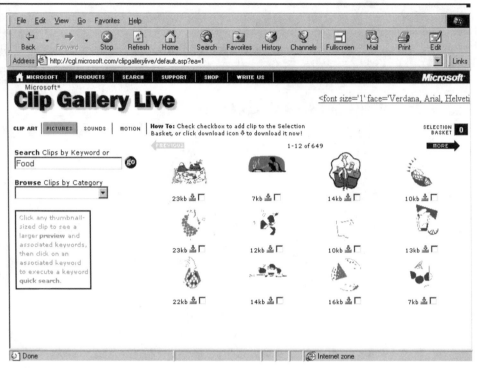

Organizing Clip Art

You can create a full library of clip art from all kinds of different sources: mail-order catalogs, other programs, magazine CD-ROMs, and online communications services. (We'll discuss *how* you accumulate these masses of clip art in the "Importing Clip Art" section later in this chapter.) If you get into the clip art–accumulation habit, you'll need a way of organizing the files you gather.

The Clip Gallery makes it easy for you to click your way through clip organizing by displaying a pop-up menu whenever you click a clip (see Figure 5.8). The set of four tools (shown in Table 5.1) enables you to find, add, and play (for motion or sound clips) the clip you are looking for.

Tool	Name	Description
CG1	![icon]	Allows you to insert a clip into your presentation.
CG2	![icon]	Previews the selected clip.
CG3	![icon]	Adds the selected clip to the current category in the Clip Gallery.
CG4	![icon]	Enables you to locate clips with the same basic theme.

TABLE 5.1 USING CLIP GALLERY TOOLS

FIGURE 5.8

*Organize your clip art
by using the Clip
Gallery tools, which
appear whenever you
click a clip.*

There are three things you can do to organize your clip art:

Create a new category   When you want to create a new category of your own, start by clicking the All Categories button. The New Category selection appears in the upper-left corner of the Gallery window. Click it. A small pop-up box appears, asking you to enter a category name. Enter a name that best reflects the type of clips you plan to store there. Click OK, or press Enter to add the category.

 TIP   You can also create a new category by displaying the Clip Properties dialog box, clicking the Categories tab, and clicking the New Category button.

Add a piece of clip art   When you find a piece of clip art you want to add to your new category (or any category, for that matter), click it. The pop-up tools appear. Click the Add Clip button. Another segment appears beside the toolbar, as shown in Figure 5.9. Click the down arrow, and choose the category to which you want to add the art; then click Add.

Delete clip art The procedure for deleting clip art is different depending on how much you want to delete. Do you want to remove a piece of clip art from all categories it appears in? If so, select the art, and press Delete. If you want to delete a piece of clip art from only the current category, right-click the art to display the pop-up menu (see Figure 5.10), choose Clip Properties, and in the Clip Properties dialog box, click the Categories tab (see Figure 5.11). When you see the categories in which your piece of clip art is displayed, click to remove the check mark from the one you want the art deleted from. Click OK to return to the Clip Gallery, and the art will be deleted from that category.

WARNING Be careful with Delete. Whether you press Del or right-click on a clip and choose Delete from the pop-up menu, this type of deletion removes all instances of that piece of clip art from the Clip Gallery.

FIGURE 5.10

Displaying the right-
click menu for working
with clip art

FIGURE 5.11

Remove the clip art
from selected cate-
gories by deselecting
them in the Clip
Properties dialog box.

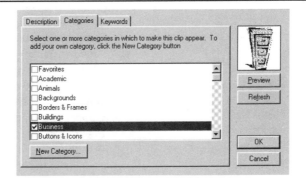

PART

II

The Right Tool
for the Job

Importing Art

You'll be able to get clip art from all kinds of places. Other programs—Microsoft's and otherwise—include clip-art libraries for use in word processing, desktop publishing, and multimedia applications. You can purchase clip-art collections from third-party manufacturers, and you can download countless clip-art files from the Internet. The PowerPoint CD-ROM includes additional clip art, as does Microsoft's Web site, which can be a source for graphics, sounds, templates, and more.

Another way to bring that creative flash to your presentations is to use art objects created in other programs, whether they're snazzy pop-art renderings that you created in another program or funky graphics from the Web or your favorite online service. You can import your art files using the Picture command in the Insert menu.

 NOTE Notice that now we're talking about art *objects,* as opposed to clip art. When you add clip art to PowerPoint, use the Import Clips button in the Clip Gallery. When you insert art objects into your PowerPoint slides, you import the art file with Insert ➢ Picture ➢ From File.

PowerPoint is flexible when it comes to art-file tolerance. PowerPoint will accept art files in any of the formats shown in Table 5.2.

TABLE 5.2: IMPORTING ART FILES

Extension	Full Name
BMP	Windows Bitmap
CDR	CorelDraw
CGM	Computer Graphics Metafile
DIB	Windows Bitmap
DRW	Micrograpfx Designer/Draw
EPS	Encapsulated Postscript
EMF	Enhanced Metafile
EMZ	Compressed Windows Enhanced Metafile
FPX	FPX Format
GIF, GFA	Graphics Interchange Format
JPEG, JPG, JFIF, JPE	Joint Photographics Expert Group
MIX	Picture It! Format
PCT, PCZ	Macintosh PICT
PCD	Kodak Photo CD
PCX	PC Paintbrush
PNG	Portable Network Graphics
TGA	Targa Format
TIF	Tag Image File Format
WPG	WordPerfect Image Format
WMF, WMZ	Windows Metafiles

If your graphics program won't save files in a PowerPoint accepted format, don't despair. There are several graphics file-conversion utilities available that will change an art file from one format to another so you can use it in different applications. GIF-Converter and Paint Shop Pro for Windows are two popular examples of graphics file-conversion utilities. Other file-conversion utilities are available as shareware on the major online services. The Multimedia and Graphics forums on CompuServe are good places to look for graphics utilities. There are also numerous newsgroups and communities online that are easily found by searching for *graphics, clip art,* and *graphics utilities.*

To import an art file into your presentation, choose Insert ➢ Picture ➢ From File to open the Insert Picture dialog box (see Figure 5.12). If you want to use an art file from another directory or drive, click the Look In down arrow, and choose the folder you want to see from the list. Choose the file type from the Files of Type box. When you've selected the file you want, click Insert.

FIGURE 5.12

The Insert Picture dialog box

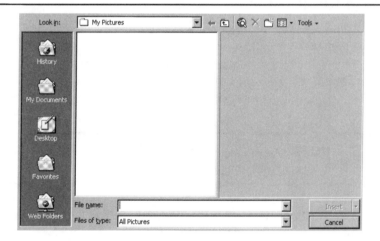

  TIP If the art you import doesn't look right, you may be able to clean it up using a few simple editing techniques. See the section "Modifying Art" later in the chapter for more on changing the art on your slides.

Drawing and Scanning Art

There's a blank spot in the middle of the first page of your presentation. The boss is looking over your shoulder. "Can't you just draw something in there real fast?" she asks. "Like our new logo or something?" Your pulse quickens. "It doesn't have to be anything perfect," she says.

Oh, good. *Now* you feel better. Thirty minutes until the corporate meeting and she wants you to draw the company logo. Lucky for you, PowerPoint's drawing tools are easy to use and make working with the objects you draw an easy task. So get a piece of company letterhead to use as a reference, and roll up your shirtsleeves. This section gives you the basics of drawing with PowerPoint—enough to get that logo done, hopefully, in thirty minutes or less.

Scanning: The Fast and Easy Way

The most logical and easiest way to get that logo into your presentation is to scan it. You can scan an image directly into PowerPoint and then modify it by changing color, brightness, contrast, and size. The only requirements are your scanner must be TWAIN-compatible and it must be set up to work within Windows. (If you haven't already done so, set up the scanner using Add New Hardware.)

 NOTE You can also use this basic procedure for capturing photos and importing them from your TWAIN-compatible digital camera.

Once you are set up to use your scanner with PowerPoint, you can follow these steps to scan your image:

1. Display the slide to which you want to add the image.

2. Put the logo in the scanner. Position it the way you want it.

3. Choose Insert ➢ Picture ➢ From Scanner or Camera. The dialog box displayed in Figure 5.13 appears.

4. Select your device from the drop-down Device list.

5. Choose Web Quality if you plan to display your presentation onscreen or Print Quality if you need to print your presentation.

6. Click Insert.

FIGURE 5.13

*The Insert Picture from
Scanner or Camera
dialog box*

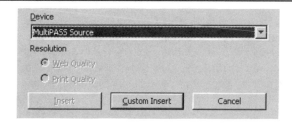

 NOTE Use the Custom Insert command if you are importing your image from a digital camera.

 TIP You may not have a scanner in your office, but that doesn't mean scanning is out of the question. Most quick-print places (such as Pip Printing or Kinko's) offer on-the-spot scanning. For a nominal fee, they will scan your logo and hand you back a file you can import into PowerPoint.

The Difference between Drawing and Painting

If you don't have a scanner or digital camera and can't get access to one, you may be stuck trying to draw the logo yourself. Luckily, PowerPoint has some pretty handy drawing tools. In the world of computer art, you'll find two different camps: drawing programs and painting programs. They may sound alike, but they're not.

- A *drawing program* creates illustrations by putting together a series of shapes, lines, and curves. The *objects,* as they are called, are then grouped together into an object you can move, resize, copy, paste, etc., without distorting it or losing any of the quality. This type of art is known as *object-oriented* graphics.

- A *painting program* creates illustrations by "painting" individual dots on the screen in the colors you select. These items are not shapes; they are just patterns of dots. That means that you *cannot* select them to resize or manipulate them. When you edit a paint graphic, you do so by changing the color of the individual dots in the picture. Painted graphics cannot be resized—especially enlarged—without a loss of quality. This type of art is often called *bitmapped,* or *raster,* graphics.

TIP If you are working with scanned photos in your presentations, you may want to touch them up with a paint program before you import them into PowerPoint. Scanned photos are saved as raster graphics, and in order to get the best possible quality and highest contrast, they may need some tweaking before you use them in your PowerPoint presentations. Popular paint programs with great bitmap-editing capabilities include Adobe Photoshop and Fractal Design Painter.

PowerPoint is a drawing (not painting) program. You use the various drawing tools to create shapes and lines and then combine or group them to make the complete object. You can change the color, pattern, rotation, and a variety of other object settings once you've grouped components into the object. If you later want to change the drawing, you can ungroup the object into its original pieces to make the modifications you want.

 NOTE Even though PowerPoint only has draw capabilities, you can import raster graphics files into PowerPoint for use in your slides. Common extensions for raster graphics files are PCX, TIF, BMP, JPEG, and GIF.

Planning the Art You Want

Taking a few minutes to think about what you want to accomplish with the art you create is a good investment of your creative time. Here are a few questions that may help you plan your illustrations:

- What is the tone of the art you're creating? It might be a technical illustration, a light-hearted cartoon, a businesslike graphic, or a dramatic logo.
- Will the art you create be used only on one slide or on every slide of your publication? If you want the art to appear on every slide, put the art on the Slide Master.
- Does the art need to be an exact size? If so, make sure you use the ruler when drawing or resizing.
- Is the art a file you've downloaded from an online service or borrowed from a clip-art collection? Be sure you check out any licensing regulations that apply. Some art is available for all to use, but there may be some regulations about

using the clip art for profit. An information file (.inf or .txt) or the collection's Help information will inform you of any restrictions on uses of the art.

• Do you want to create your own art from scratch or modify existing clip art?

TIP You can use the Edit ➤ Cut and Edit ➤ Paste commands to move art from the slide where you created it to its final location.

Displaying the Drawing Tools

Before you can begin drawing your own objects, you have to display PowerPoint's drawing tools and then create a workspace. First, click the New Slide button, and select the blank slide from the lower right corner of the New Slide dialog box. The blank slide appears in Normal View; notice the drawing tools along the bottom of the window (see Figure 5.14).

PART II
The Right Tool for the Job

FIGURE 5.14

The drawing tools in Normal View appear on the bottom of the screen.

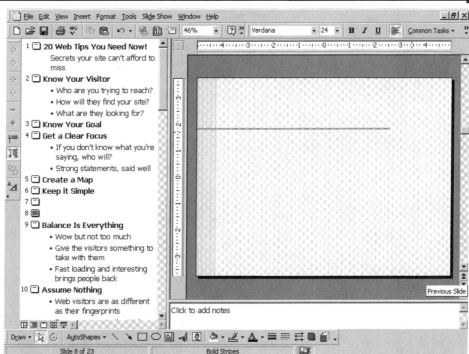

If you don't know what a certain tool in the Drawing toolbar does, put the pointer on it and the name of the tool appears. This is the ToolTips feature, an instant Help flashcard that tells you what you're looking at before you have time to ask.

Figure 5.15 shows a sample ToolTip when the pointer is positioned on the Rectangle tool.

FIGURE 5.15

When you position the pointer on a tool, a ToolTip is displayed that tells you the name of that tool.

Even with the information in the ToolTip, you may be left wondering how you'll use the various drawing tools. Table 5.3 lists all the drawing tools in Slide view and briefly describes each.

TABLE 5.3: DRAWING TOOLS

Tool	Name	Description
Draw ▾	Draw Menu	Displays a pop-up menu of drawing options.
	Select Objects	Chooses objects on the screen.
	Free Rotate Tool	Rotates the selected object.
AutoShapes ▾	AutoShapes menu	Displays a palette of shapes from which you can choose.
	Line Tool	Creates lines.
	Arrow Tool	Adds arrowheads to the line, arc, or polygon you select.
	Rectangle Tool	Creates rectangles.
	Oval Tool	Draws circles and ovals.

Continued ▸

TABLE 5.3: DRAWING TOOLS (CONTINUED)

Tool	Name	Description
	Text Box Tool	Creates text objects.
	Insert WordArt Tool	Allows you to draw a WordArt box.
	Insert Clip Art Tool	Displays the Clip Gallery so you can select a category and the clip art you want to use.
	Fill Color	Fills the selected object with the color and pattern selected.
	Line Color	Applies the selected line options to the current object.
	Font Color	Enables you to choose the color for selected text.
	Line Style	Allows you to choose the style of the line used in the selected object.
	Dash Style	Creates a dashed or dotted line for the current object.
	Arrow Style	Enables you to choose the type of arrowheads you want.
	Shadow	Adds (or removes) the default shadow to (from) a selected object.
	3D	Makes the selected item three-dimensional.

PART

II

The Right Tool
for the Job

Using Drawing Tools

Most basic drawing tools—Line, Rectangle, Oval, and Arrow—require the same steps to get objects on the screen:

1. Click the tool you want.

2. Move the pointer to the work area.

3. Hold down the mouse button while dragging the mouse in the direction you desire. This "draws" the object.

4. Release the mouse button when you are finished.

TIP   The Shift key is of special interest when you're using the basic drawing tools. If you are using the Oval tool, for example, pressing Shift while you draw gives you a perfectly round circle. If you press Shift while you use the Line tool, you get a perfectly straight line. In short, if you want a precise and symmetrical object, press Shift while drawing.

MASTERING THE OPPORTUNITIES

The Beginner's Guide to Electronic Drawing

If you're not formally trained in computer graphics, it may feel a little odd to use a mouse for drawing. If this is your first time working with drawing onscreen, take a few minutes to consider these rules:

Have a reference   For best results, sketch out what you want to draw, or work from a model, such as a photo or diagram. Having something to refer to helps you unlock any potential creative blocks you may run up against when you start drawing. (Remember that if you're using someone else's image as a reference, you may need to think about licensing permissions or credits.)

Know your tools   Before you start drawing, explore the tools you have available in PowerPoint. Display the drawing toolbars, and spend a few minutes playing around with the tools to see how they work. Check out the colors and line styles, and look for the patterns and textures. (More about this later in the chapter.) Learn what choices you have *before* you begin making choices—this can help you turn an ordinary drawing into something that really gets attention.

Don't draw unnecessarily   If you have something on file that will work for your purposes or you have a saved art file that will do with just a little tweaking, go for the shortcut, and save yourself some work. Do the leisurely onscreen doodling at home, not in a time-sensitive, pressured situation such as the workplace. Think about any options you have for acquiring the art before you try to create it yourself.

Create an art library   Once you begin creating your own art, be sure to store it in a library of art you can use again and again. You can add your art to the ClipArt Gallery (you found out how earlier in this chapter), or you can simply save the art to disk and file it away someplace safe. It's often helpful to print a copy of the art and label it with the filename so you can easily find it again later.

Continued

> ### MASTERING THE OPPORTUNITIES CONTINUED
>
> ***Changing is (usually) easier than starting again*** Especially at first, drawing on screen can be difficult; there's a definite learning curve involved in using the tools and options as expediently and accurately as possible. Even though you may be tempted to wipe out all you've done and start again when frustration strikes, remember that it's usually easier to modify what you've drawn than it is to start from scratch. Resize boxes and lines, relayer objects, change colors—but try to work with what you've done before you scrap it all and start over. It might save you minutes—or hours—recreating the basics of a drawing you could have recycled.

If you don't like what you just drew, press Del while the handles are still displayed to delete the object.

Using AutoShapes

Object-oriented drawing is the process of putting objects—lines and shapes—together to create an image. That means that many of the items you create with PowerPoint's drawing tools will be composed of shapes. To help you draw shapes quickly and accurately, PowerPoint includes AutoShapes. AutoShapes are predrawn shapes you can apply to your own drawings. When you click the AutoShapes button in the Drawing toolbar, a pop-up menu of AutoShapes palettes appears (see Figure 5.16).

FIGURE 5.16

Displaying the AutoShapes menu

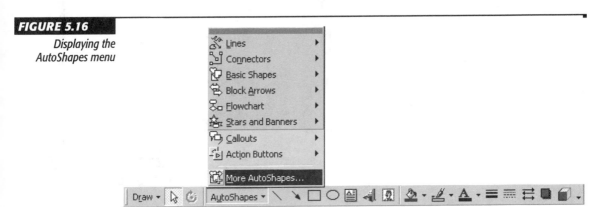

Choosing AutoShape Groups

PowerPoint organizes the AutoShapes into groups so you can make your selections from stars and banners, callouts, block arrows, connectors, flowchart elements, and action buttons. To see the individual shapes within each AutoShape group, click the AutoShape button, and position the pointer on the group you want to see. A palette of choices appears so you can make your choice.

 TIP You can "tear off" the AutoShapes palette and move it anywhere on screen. Click on the palette's title bar, and drag it to the new screen location.

Drawing one of the shapes from the AutoShapes palette is just like drawing a shape in the Drawing palette: click the tool you want, move the pointer to the work area, and click and drag the mouse to draw the shape. When the shape is the size and proportion you want, release the mouse button. Figure 5.17 shows a star drawn with an AutoShapes tool.

FIGURE 5.17

Adding a shape with an AutoShape tool

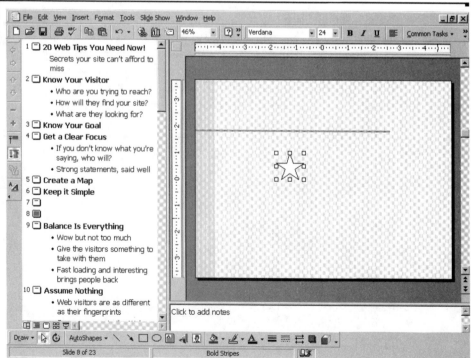

Setting AutoShape Options

Another new feature of PowerPoint 97 that impacts the AutoShapes is the ability to change 2-D objects into 3-D objects. You can control the way lighting reflects on the image—showing where the point of light hits the object—and you also have the option of adding shadows with different perspectives to AutoShape drawings.

To display the AutoShape options, select the AutoShape you want to modify, open the Format menu, and choose AutoShape. The Format AutoShape dialog box appears, as shown in Figure 5.18.

FIGURE 5.18

Setting AutoShape options in the Format AutoShape dialog box

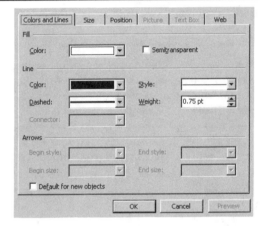

In the Format AutoShape dialog box, you can change the colors and lines, size, and position of the object. You can find options for making the object semitransparent or opaque. You can also create a shape that precisely matches the measurements you need or occupies a specific area of a slide. When you're finished making selections, click OK to close the dialog box, and return to your presentation.

TIP Once you draw a shape in PowerPoint, you can enter text inside it by clicking the text tool and then clicking the shape and typing the text. You can even rotate the object using the Free Rotate Tool, and the text stays put inside the shape—that is, the text is essentially glued to the shape and moves however the shape moves.

PART

II

The Right Tool
for the Job

TIP If you want to add artwork to a graph you've created, double-click the graph. This displays the graph in Graphics Editing mode, and you can easily access the drawing tools.

Modifying Art

You now know the basic ways of getting art into your presentation: draw from Power-Point's Clip Gallery, import it from another source, or create it yourself using the drawing tools. No matter how you bring the art to your PowerPoint slides, you have the option of changing the art to fit the image you've got in mind.

 NOTE One of the great things about multimedia is that no presentation is done until you say so. Just because you use a piece of PowerPoint's clip art doesn't mean you have to use it as-is. You can use PowerPoint's drawing tools and color and pattern palettes to change the look of the art until you get just the right effect.

You might want to group or ungroup objects, rotate or flip objects, change an object's line thickness, color, or pattern, or change the way objects are layered on the screen. This section gives you a quick overview of art editing techniques.

Basic Art Editing

The basics of resizing, copying, pasting, and cutting objects in PowerPoint are the same no matter what the content of the object. You resize an art object the same way you resize a text object: click it, and then drag its corner. (If you've added text to the object, as described earlier, the text is resized with the object.) Clip art is copied and pasted just like graphs are: use Edit ➢ Copy and Edit ➢ Paste, or drag-and-drop the item from slide to slide.

The fastest way to bring up the editing commands is to click the right mouse button while the pointer is positioned on the object. When you do that, the small pop-up menu shown in Figure 5.19 appears.

FIGURE 5.19

Display art editing options with a right mouse click.

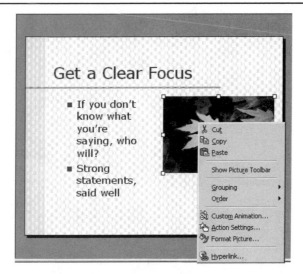

The editing menu contains the usual commands: Cut, Copy, and Paste. You also see a few new commands. Custom Animation enables you to animate the object you just drew. This gives you the freedom to perform some snazzy onscreen calisthenics and really grab your viewer's attention. Other options enable you to further customize the art object you have selected. When you are finished with the pop-up menu, click outside the area or press Escape to close the menu.

Editing an Image with Format Picture

You can also edit your images within PowerPoint by using the Format Picture command. Start by clicking the image, and then open the Format menu, and choose Picture. The Format Picture dialog box then appears, as Figure 5.20 shows. You can use Format Picture to change all sorts of things about your image—from the basic color of the fill or line to the size and position of the image on the slide.

The Right Tool
for the Job

FIGURE 5.20

You can edit graphics by using the Format Picture dialog box.

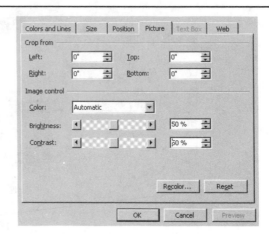

The Format Picture dialog box includes six tabs:

Colors and Lines Allows you to choose the line color, style, and arrows for the art.

Size Allows you to determine the size of the image.

Position Allows you to control cropping and brightness.

Picture Gives you control over cropping and color adjustments.

Text Box Disable for graphic images.

Web Allows you to enter text you want displayed in place of the graphic while the image is loading.

 TIP Search engines on the Web look for and read alternative text when scouring the Web for new sites. Use descriptive text that will be a big "hit" with visitors you want to come your way.

Make your selections and changes, and click OK to return to the slide.

 TIP For more about using Animation Effects, see "Animating Your Art Objects," later in this chapter.

Grouping and Ungrouping Objects

Once you learn to edit the individual shapes in your drawing, you may want to put them together to create a bigger effect. Because of the way object-oriented drawings go together—piece by piece—it would be difficult to move or resize several shapes at once without some means of lumping all the pieces together (grouping).

Even the clip art you use comprises a bunch of small shapes and lines. For example, consider the clip art in Figure 5.21. As you can see, the world graphic has been *ungrouped* (separated into its individual circles, rectangles, lines, and so on). It would be a nightmare to try to move each of these pieces individually.

FIGURE 5.21

Ungrouping a piece of clip art may result in dozens of small objects.

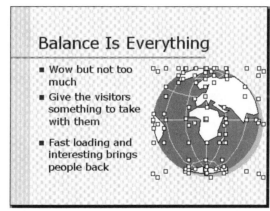

When you group objects, you combine them into one. This allows PowerPoint to treat the whole group as a single object so that when you cut, copy, paste, move, or resize the object, it is treated as one piece of art instead of a bunch of separate objects electronically glued together.

 WARNING When you try to ungroup some clip art, you may get a warning telling you that the art is an imported object and not a group. In order to ungroup the object and reduce it to its individual elements, the file must be converted to a PowerPoint object, or else any OLE links will be broken. If it's not important for you to maintain a link with the creating application (meaning that the object is not likely to change), click OK. Otherwise, click Cancel.

PART

II

The Right Tool
for the Job

To group a number of objects into one object, select the Select Objects tool and drag a rectangle around the objects. Then choose Draw ➤ Group from the Drawing toolbar. The objects are grouped into one and their individual handles replaced by four group handles, one at each corner of the newly grouped object (see Figure 5.22).

FIGURE 5.22

Grouping many objects into one enables you to move, resize, and copy items easily.

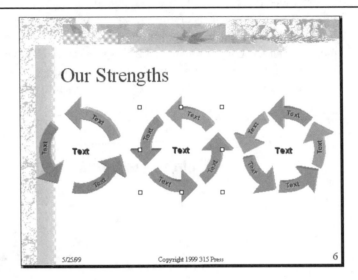

Layering Art Objects

Another concept along the lines of the grouping and ungrouping involves the use of layering. We've already established that PowerPoint's method of art—object-oriented drawing—enables you to produce drawings by combining shapes, lines, and curves. In order to get the right look, you need to be able to put some items in front of other items.

You can change layer arrangement of your objects in four different ways. Each operation starts with you displaying the Draw menu in the Drawing toolbar and choosing the Order option. Then select one of the following, depending on what you want to do with the selected item:

Bring to Front   Moves the selected object in front of all objects.

Send to Back   Sends the selected object behind all objects.

Bring Forward   Moves the object one layer forward.

Send Backward   Moves the object one layer backward.

Changing Object Layering

Before you can choose any of these commands or tools, you need to select the object you want to use. In Figure 5.23, one of the shapes has been moved to the front of the others using the Bring to Front command.

 TIP Before you use the Bring to Front command, ungroup the objects you're working with. Otherwise, Bring to Front will not be available.

Moving an object to the back of other objects is also easy. Just select the object and choose Draw ➤ Order ➤ Send to Back. If you're following along, you'll notice a small problem—sending the object to the back sends it too far back—so you need to click the Bring Forward tool to move the shape up one layer.

PART

II

The Right Tool
for the Job

FIGURE 5.23

*Moving an object to
the front of other
objects*

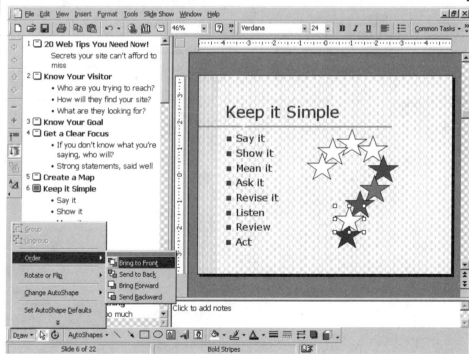

TIP To move an object all the way to the front or back of a stack of objects, use Bring to Front or Send to Back. To move an object forward or backward one layer at a time, use Bring Forward or Send Backward.

Changing Object Color and Fill Effects

Because so much of PowerPoint is done for you, you may wind up with a color you didn't expect the first time you draw a shape. You can change any object's color easily, however, by first selecting the object and then clicking the Fill Color tool (in the Drawing toolbar). When you click this tool, the pop-up box in Figure 5.24 appears.

Click one of the colors in the color scheme laid out for you at the top of the box, and the object is then displayed in the new color.

Other commands in the Fill Color pop-up menu include No Fill, Automatic, More Fill Colors, or Fill Effects, all of which allow you to choose additional options for the color of the object. No Fill removes all coloring inside the object, Automatic colors the object in whatever color is chosen as the default, More Fill Colors gives you a rainbow of options from which to choose, and Fill Effects enables you to choose a fill color that shows shading in a horizontal, vertical, or diagonal format. When you click Fill Effects, the Fill Effects dialog box appears, as shown in Figure 5.25.

FIGURE 5.24

Choosing a new color

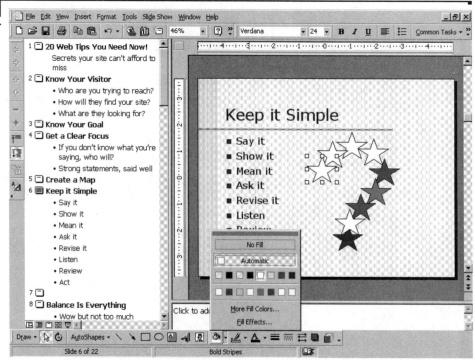

FIGURE 5.25

You can control the shading of a fill color by choosing the shade style and color balance.

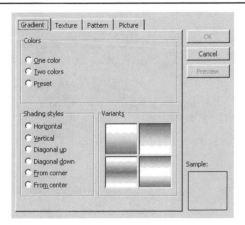

 TIP   If you try out the Fill Effects feature—and you should (it's cool)—be sure to click the Preview button to preview the art object before you click OK and return to the slide.

If you choose the Pattern tab in the Fill Effects dialog box, the Pattern fill dialog box shown in Figure 5.26 appears. Here you can choose a different pattern for the inside of the object.

FIGURE 5.26

Choosing a basic pattern for the object's fill area

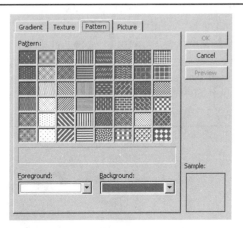

The Texture tab in the Fill Effects dialog box displays a large selection of textures (see Figure 5.27). You can select from woodgrain or marbled textures to create just the right effect for your graphics, backgrounds, or special text.

FIGURE 5.27

Special textures are available for art objects.

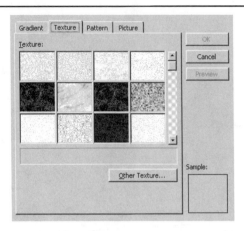

 TIP If you want to add textures from another source for special effects, click the Other button in the Texture dialog box to display the Add Texture dialog box. Now you can choose the drive and folder that stores the texture you want to use . You also can use a picture in an object you are recoloring. Display the Fill Effects dialog box, and click the Picture tab. Click Select Picture, and choose the picture file from the dialog box that appears. Click OK to add the picture to the object.

If you choose Automatic in the Fill Color pop-up menu, PowerPoint makes the object the same color as the currently selected Fill Color.

Finally, the More Fill Colors option lets you mix a color not displayed on the palette at the top of the pop-up menu. When you choose More Fill Colors, the Colors dialog box appears, as shown in Figure 5.28. You can choose the color you want or click Custom to create one of your own. For more about working with colors in PowerPoint, see Chapter 9, "The Dynamics of Color."

FIGURE 5.28

Choosing a different color for the selected object

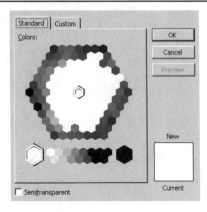

Changing Line Color and Style

The internal color and pattern of an object is not all you have to worry about. You might want to change the line color and style, as well. To do this, select the object and either choose Format ➢ Colors and Lines or position the mouse pointer on the object, click the right mouse button, and then choose Colors and Lines. Either way, the Colors and Lines tab of the Format AutoShape dialog box appears, as Figure 5.29 shows. (*Note*: If you selected an object that is *not* an AutoShape, the Format Objects dialog box will be displayed on your screen.)

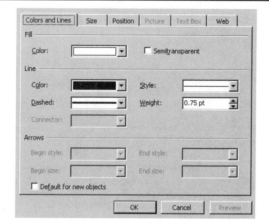

Although you made your color choices in the Fill Color pop-up menu, you can also change the fill color in Colors and Lines. You can also make four different choices about the way the selected line appears:

- The color of the line (now you can choose Semitransparent to give your lines a special look)
- The thickness and style of the line
- Whether the line is a dashed, dotted, or continuous line
- Whether the line has an arrowhead

Click the down arrow of the option you want to select, and make your choice from the displayed list. The lines in the selected objects are changed.

PowerPoint gives you the option of choosing a variety of arrowhead styles when you use the Arrow tool in the Drawing toolbar. You can change the width, height, and color of arrowheads used in the images you create.

PART

II

The Right Tool for the Job

Animating Art Objects

One of the neatest art features PowerPoint offers is the ability to animate objects. What is animation? The ability to move your objects—text, graphics, charts, logos—across, up, or down the slide. You can have text screeching into place, birds flying over the title, charts levitating from their places on slides, and hundreds of other effects you dream up yourself.

Start by selecting the object you want to animate; then click the right mouse button. When the pop-up menu appears, click Custom Animation. At first, all the options are dimmed, but click the down arrow in the Entry Animation and Sound area, and select any option other than No Effect. The dialog box then looks like the one displayed in Figure 5.30.

FIGURE 5.30

Using Custom Animation to animate art objects

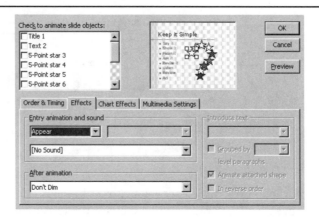

In the Effects area, click the first down arrow to the right of the Entry animation box to display the wide range of animation choices (see Figure 5.31). Click the one you want to select it.

PART

II

The Right Tool
for the Job

FIGURE 5.31

You can select the animation effect you want from the displayed list.

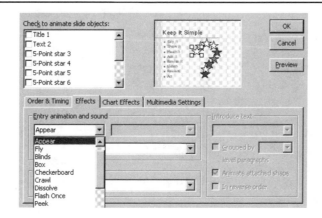

To add a sound to the animation, click the Sound down arrow to see your choices (see Figure 5.32). PowerPoint comes equipped with several special sound effects, and you can also get a number of other sounds from a variety of third-party sources. You can store the sounds you gather in the Clip Gallery. (For more about adding sound effects and sound objects to your presentations, see Chapter 6, "Adding Sound.")

You can make choices about the way in which text is animated on the slide. Do you want text items to fly in, one by one, or do you want all text to appear as a block? Your choices are in these areas.

To see how the animation effects work, click the Preview button. Then, when you're ready, click OK to return to the slide.

 TIP You can add more animation effects by displaying the Animation Effects toolbar and working with those tools. Display the toolbar by clicking Animation Effects in the Formatting toolbar at the top of the screen. To find out more about animating your slide objects, see Chapter 8, "Producing a Slide Show."

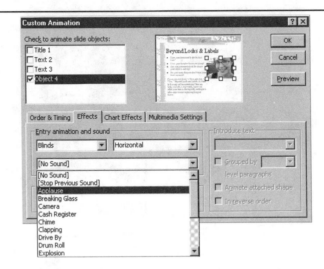

Chapter Summary

This chapter has introduced you to a number of artistic considerations, including possible sources of artwork and the most essential editing procedures.

The next chapter introduces you to the idea of adding sound to your PowerPoint presentations—putting the *multi* in multimedia and allowing you to capture and hold your audience's attention.

CHAPTER 6

Adding Sound

Have you ever watched television with the sound turned off? People gesture, move, make faces—and most of it escapes you. You may be able to tell roughly what the plot line is, but you'll lose the intricacies of the story without hearing what's going on. Similarly, a football game loses some of its excitement without the roar of the crowd, the speeding car seems slower without the squealing tires, and the poignant moment loses some of its poignancy without the lilting music in the background.

Music or sound effects in your presentations can make a big difference in the way your audience perceives what you're showing them. Just a few years ago, our simple presentations didn't incorporate sound—our own voices were the only sound we worried about. Multimedia has changed all that. Now you can add sound in the form of music or special effects to reinforce points, hold your audience's interest, add a spark of humor, or provide a smooth, sophisticated opening.

This chapter explores what adding sound to your presentations can mean in PowerPoint. After a brief exploration of sound basics, you'll learn to add PowerPoint sound effects to your slides, use sound files from other sources, and even record your own sounds for use in a presentation.

 TIP Many of the special sound effects you use in your presentation will be tied to other things; for example, you might play a sound when you advance a slide, build bullet text, or use a special text effect such as Fly From Left. This is just one example of the special effects discussed in Chapter 8, "Putting It All Together: Producing the Slide Show."

 MASTERING THE OPPORTUNITIES

What a Difference a Sound Makes

Sound can add a whole new dimension to your presentation. Here's how:

Support animations—When you have text "Fly From Left" to the center of the screen, you can make it screech to a halt with a sound effect.

Link sounds to actions—Assign a special click or other unusual sound effect (a bell ringing, a buzzer sounding, the click of a typewriter key being pressed, etc.) to play when you click the mouse on a particular button.

Continued ▎▶

MASTERING TROUBLESHOOTING CONTINUED

Provide instructions—You're designing a self-running presentation that customers can display at the upcoming trade show. You know that many of the potential customers may not be familiar or comfortable with computers, so you want to make the presentation as easy to use as possible. You can record and attach an instruction to a particular slide, such as "Click here to start our product demonstration!" so customers know exactly what to do when the slide appears.

Set the atmosphere—You want to open your presentation with a segment of a theme song affiliated with your company.

Add humor—You want to use an audio clip of Porky Pig's "Th-th-th-th-at's-all, folks!" at the end of your presentation. You even get to watch cartoons all afternoon so you can tape Porky signing off.

Sound Basics

If you are trying your hand at a multimedia presentation for the first time, sound may be a new issue for you to deal with. We'll start out this basic introduction with an introduction to some of the common terms and acronyms you'll find linked up to sound discussions.

A Sound Glossary

Sound file   A sound file is the synthesized or digital recording of music or a sound effect.

Sound object   When you add a sound element to a selected slide, Power-Point treats the sound as an object on the slide. You can have the sound play automatically or you can manually control the sound by clicking the object. See the section "Adding Sounds from Other Sources" to learn more about inserting and working with sound objects.

Sound card   A sound card is a special interface card that plugs into your computer to make it capable of high-quality sound reproduction. Having a sound card means you can play audio CDs, add full-score symphonic background to your presentations, or play cool sound effects for the games you play when work is done. Without a sound card, your sophisticated sound effects will be tinny noise.

PC speaker   All PCs come equipped with a PC speaker. The PC speaker is a small, bare-minimum device that broadcasts the beeps, squeaks, and dings affiliated with basic system functions. The PC speaker cannot produce the sound quality you need for a multimedia presentation, however. You'll need a sound card for more sophisticated sound capability.

Waveform file   A waveform file (*.WAV) is a digital recording of a sound—like something you might record on a cassette recorder or your answering machine. Sounds are actually waves in the air—the deeper the sound, the longer the wave. When you speak into a microphone to record a voice-over note or introduction, you are creating a waveform file. You can play waveform files with a basic PC speaker, although they won't sound very good.

MIDI file   MIDI (Musical Instrument Digital Interface) is a digital format for saving audio files. A MIDI file (*.MID) is not a representation of the sound waves (like a waveform file) but rather digital instructions of how to re-create the sounds. Think of a MIDI file as the sheet music your sound card uses to play a sound. MIDI files can be played only on a computer with a sound card and speakers.

Sampling   Sampling is the process of recording a sound as a computer file. For your presentations, you might want to sample sounds like footsteps, doors opening or closing, a car accelerating, a crowd cheering, or a number of other special effects. Or you might not—sampling is not for the faint-hearted, and bulletin boards and online services, as well as many vendors, can provide you with a wealth of sound effects and music clips. Exhaust these resources before trying to sample sounds yourself.

Sound Recorder   The Sound Recorder (choose Start ➤ Programs ➤ Accessories ➤ Entertainment ➤ Sound Recorder) is a special Windows applet that enables you to record sounds for use in multimedia projects (see Figure 6.1). Only use the Sound Recorder to record simple, short sounds—the sounds are saved in WAV format, which can be huge. For more about working with the Sound Recorder to add sound effects to your presentation, see "Recording Your Own Sounds," later in this chapter.

Voice-Over Narration   In PowerPoint, you can record your own narration for your presentations. Simply choose Slide Show ➤ Record Narration and make your recording.

FIGURE 6.1

*With the Sound
Recorder, you can eas-
ily record voice-over
notes and sound
effects*

Types of Sound Files: Which Do You Need?

As you learned in the last section, WAV files are waveform files that save the sound
you record in a format similar to the one in which the sounds exist: as sound waves.

WAV files give you good-quality sound, but because they store so much information,
WAV files grow to be enormous very quickly. A five-second sound clip—that's a full second shorter than the Microsoft Sound that plays when you start Windows 95/98—takes
up over 50KB. The longer your recording, the higher the storage considerations.
Depending on the amount of RAM in your computer, you may find yourself maxing
out with WAV files very quickly.

 NOTE A one-minute song-and-video clip—often saved in an AVI format (more about this
in Chapter 7)—can take up as much as 10 MB of space on your hard drive, or even more.

WAV recordings are high-quality, but their huge size makes them impractical for
sounds longer than a second or two. MIDI files are tightly compressed, so they take
up less room than WAV files. Although the compression reduces the quality of the
recording, MIDI files are the only practical way to store longer sound clips.

MIDI files are great for storing musical scores—especially when you have a long
piece of music, scoring what you want to run in the background, or music that inter-
acts with another action on the screen. But for sounds that must be clear, like a short
voice-over on an important slide of your presentation, a WAV file will give you better
quality.

MIDI and WAV files are available from a number of sources—as shareware, free-
ware, and purchased products. If you're using sound files from a third-party source, be
sure to find out about usage limitations and restrictions. Some original music pieces
may be protected as intellectual property, permitting you to use the music only as
part of a demonstration or for your personal use—they cannot be included in anything you charge revenues for. This includes a presentation you give as part of a training service or a product you create and sell to clients to present to their company.

As sound technology evolves, other sound formats come and go. The MOD format started out with Amiga computers years ago and offers users the flexibility of using a variety of sampled instruments. Newer file formats, like S3M (Screamtracker 3 Module) and XM (eXtended Module), offer high quality and CD-like sound. MP3, the newest offering in sound, is an audio standard that enables you to capture, play, and create your own sound files on the Internet.

 TIP No matter what sound format you are working in, you can get a sound file converter that will enable you to turn your compositions into something PowerPoint can use. A number of sound file conversion utilities are available on the Web; check out Awave 5.0, Audio Suite, Gold Wave, and WAVmaker.

The Media-Ready PC

Most computers sold today are media-ready, meaning that they are equipped to play the sounds, run the animations, and display the high-resolution graphics today's user is becoming accustomed to on the Web and in applications. Chances are the computer you're using—or the system you will use to give the presentation—is equipped with a sound card and enough memory to adequately support the media objects you want to use.

Today you need the following basic items for a bare-bones media-ready PC:

- A Pentium computer
- 32 megabytes of memory
- At least a 1.5 gigabyte hard drive
- A sound card (at least 16-bit, but 32-bit is better)
- A fast CD-ROM drive
- Good external speakers
- A microphone, if you plan to do your own recording

 NOTE What's the bit in 32-bit? The terms *16-bit* and *32-bit* reflect the size of the path between the sound card and the motherboard it's plugged into. The wider the path, the more data can travel to the motherboard at one time and the higher the sound quality. 32-bit sound does not automatically sound twice as good as 16-bit sound, however—many other factors can come into play.

The following short sections review what you need in order to get sound out of your PC for presentation purposes.

What You Need for Sound

Even in your basic, no-frills PC (that is, not media-ready), the PC speaker does the job of playing WAV files. This means you can get bells, whistles, and other special effects no matter what kind of equipment you've got.

For presentations, you'll need a sound card that can do more than grunt and beep. You need a system that can keep up with anything from an opening gong to Beethoven's Fifth Symphony. Popular sound cards are offered by a variety of manufacturers; Creative Labs, producers of the Sound Blaster (the Sound Blaster Live! is currently their top-of-the-line model), and Ensoniq, makers of all sorts of high-quality sound components, seem to have large and loyal groups of sound enthusiasts supporting their products. Other popular sound card manufacturers include Turtle Beach Systems, Yamaha, and Newcom, Inc. Before you make your own decision for a high-end sound card, search the Web to keep on top of the changing medium and discover which board is the hottest of the moment.

 NOTE No matter how good your sound card is, you're not going to hear the quality without a good set of speakers. Depending on what you want and need for presentation sound, there are a number of good speakers available. Basically any stereo speakers that you can plug into a sound card can be adapted for multimedia output, but some speakers—such as those specifically designed to give full-impact sound from a PC—stand out for solid sound.

Does all this sound hardware and software make you wonder what's coming next? Voice recognition is here—the latest and greatest PC models are all being sold with attached extending microphones. It won't be long until you're speaking into your portable mike from the center aisle of the presentation room, telling PowerPoint "Advance to the next slide, please." How did you prepare this presentation? Via straight dictation, with your sound card being your computer's ears and the voice recognition software deciphering and entering your words into the PowerPoint Outliner.

Today, the age of voice-directed applications is nearer than ever. Programs such as Simply Speaking from IBM enable you to command your PC by dictating. In just a few steps, you can dictate the file, export it to Word, and then pull it into PowerPoint. The process may be a little cumbersome today, but we can be sure the process will be streamlined—almost effortless—in the future.

Upgrading for Sound

Okay, so you're convinced that sound would give your presentations that extra something they need to really make your work stand out. You're sure you'll get departmental funding with a little more glitz and glamour. You know your training will go better if you can add sound to the teaching tools—charts and text—you already use.

If you are the one responsible for upgrading the system for sound, don't despair—the process is easier than ever, now that Windows includes plug-and-play technology. However, let your company's technical support person install the card unless you've been trained to know your way around a PC.

 TIP Don't pop the cover off your PC unless you know what you're doing.

Once the sound card itself is installed, the rest is up to Windows. The new plug-and-play technology will recognize supported cards (most popular cards). If Windows doesn't recognize your sound card, make sure that the card is installed properly. If it is, then use the disk included with the card to install the necessary drivers on your system.

To see what sound card Windows recognizes for your system, click Start, and then choose Settings , Control Panel , Multimedia. The Multimedia Properties dialog box for Windows 98 appears, as shown in Figure 6.2.

FIGURE 6.2

Look in the Audio tab of the Multimedia Properties dialog box to see which sound card you've got installed

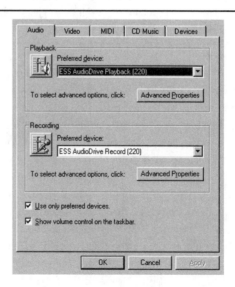

The sound card Windows has located on your system is displayed in the Preferred device box. As you can see, the device on this system is an ESS AudioDrive Playback card.

WARNING Windows' plug-and-play system should find your sound card automatically and display it in the Preferred Device box without fail. If you don't see your sound card in the Preferred Device box, click the drop-down arrow to see whether it is in the displayed list. If it's not, contact your technical support person to make sure the hardware has been installed correctly.

Other considerations in the Multimedia Properties dialog box affect the volume and quality of the recordings you play in your presentations. You can view video options, select MIDI devices, play CD music files, and set up other multimedia drivers with the various tabs in this dialog box.

Now that you know the basics of sound and the elementary considerations of sound files, software, and hardware, you're ready to see how to best use sound in your PowerPoint presentations.

Using PowerPoint's Sound Effects

One of the easiest ways to add sound to your slides is to assign a sound to the slide's transition. That is, you select a sound (called a transitional sound effect) to play when the slide advances to the next slide or when it first appears. You can either use the preset sound effects included with PowerPoint or add sound effects from another source—perhaps a multimedia collection disk or CD-ROM with sound and video files.

PowerPoint 2000 enables you to record the presenter's voice to deliver a presentation in a continuous slide show, which means you don't even need to be there to give your own presentations! Just record your voice and let it speak for itself while the presentation runs. For more about recording narrations, see the section "Record Your Own Sound," later in this chapter.

Choosing Transitional Sound Effects

To add a transitional sound effect, display the slide to which you want to add the transition and then choose Slide Show ➢ Slide Transition to open the Slide Transition dialog box. Click the drop-down arrow in the Sound box to display the available special sound effects (see Figure 6.3).

The Slide Transition dialog box gives you the option of repeating—or looping—the sound until the next sound is chosen for another slide. Or, to turn off a previously selected sound, you can click the down arrow in the Sound box and choose [Stop Previous Sound].

FIGURE 6.3

The Slide Transition dialog box provides a place where you can add transitional sound effects to your slides.

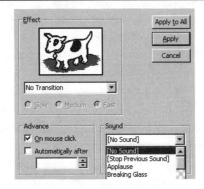

Adding Sound from Other Sources

If you have sounds on disk or CD that you're eager to try out, insert the disk in the drive and display the slide to which you'd like to add the sound. Choose Slide Show ➢ Slide Transition to open the Slide Transition dialog box.

Click the Sound box's down arrow and highlight the last item in the list, Other Sound. The Add Sound dialog box appears (see Figure 6.4). Navigate through the folders in the displayed list—if you're using a multimedia collection (perhaps using the Office CD-ROM), you'll see all kinds of folders related to different aspects of multimedia (Mpeg, Tiff, Bmpsmall, etc.). It should be obvious which folder is the one related to sound from its name (it may be named something like "Sound")—if not, look for the small sound icon next to files in the folder.

Select the file you want by clicking it and clicking OK. PowerPoint adds the name of the file to the Sound box and immediately begins playing the sound so you can decide whether that's the one you want. If you want a different sound, click the Sound box's down arrow again and choose a different file. Click OK when you've got the one you want.

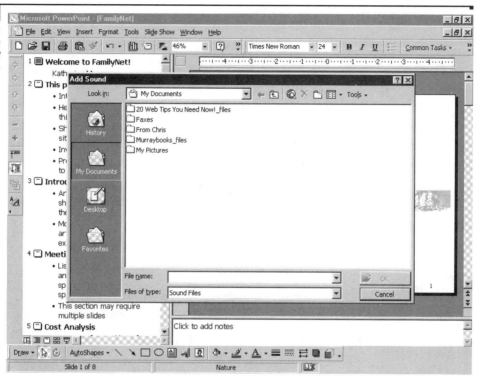

FIGURE 6.4

You can play your own sound file by choosing Other Sound and selecting the file you want to play.

TIP Sound files are like any other computer files. You can copy or delete them from your system just as you would clip art files. Just be sure to know what, if any, licensing restrictions apply to your situation.

TIP You can add sound effects from a variety of sources. Many third-party products are available in the form of sound libraries—on both CD-ROM and disk—that can give you literally thousands of sound effects for use in your presentations. Check out PowerPoint Central for additional sound clips and be sure to search on the Internet for the latest sound files and soundtracks.

PART

II

The Right Tools
for the Job

Adding Sound to Animations

In some cases, you'll want to play a sound that is connected to the appearance of a certain element on the screen. For example, you might want to play the sound of a typewriter as the title of your presentation is "typed" on the screen. Or you may attach the sound of brakes screeching to a bullet item zooming in from the side, or a bell ringing when a logo appears.

You apply sounds to objects by first clicking the object you want to assign the sounds to, then choosing Slide Show ➤ Custom Animation. When the Custom Animation dialog box appears, click the Effects tab. Then choose an effect in the Entry Animation and Sound drop-down list to activate the other drop-down lists. Next, click the drop-down arrow for the list currently displaying [No Sound]. A list of sounds available for use with the selected object appears, as shown in Figure 6.5. Click on the sound to choose it, then click OK.

FIGURE 6.5

You can assign a sound to a specific object in the Custom Animation dialog box

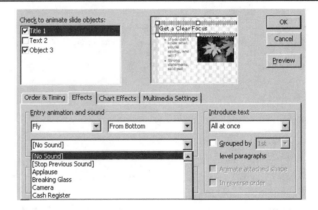

Inserting Sound Objects

Another method of adding sound to your PowerPoint presentations involves working with sound objects. A *sound object* is different from a sound effect in that when you insert an object, a sound file is placed on the current slide.

 TIP Sound files can add dramatically to the size of your presentation, so if you're running short on RAM or storage space, don't overload your system with a huge symphonic background piece when a simple 15-second intro will do.

To insert a sound file as an object on your PowerPoint slide, display the slide on which you want to begin the sound file, and then choose Insert ➤ Movies and Sounds (see Figure 6.6). A submenu of sound choices appears, from which you can choose whether to add a sound from the Clip Gallery, a file, CD, or to record a sound. To insert a prerecorded sound file, select Sound From File. The Insert Sound dialog box then appears.

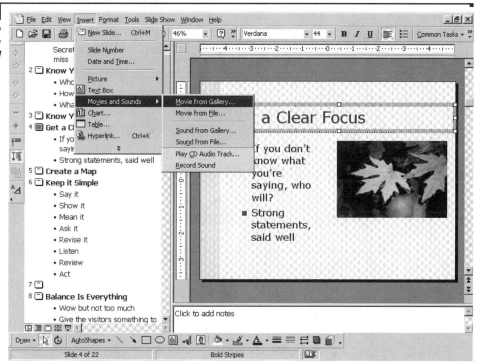

FIGURE 6.6

When you choose Movies and Sounds, a submenu of sound choices appears.

Use the Look In box to navigate to the disk and/or folder where the sound files are stored. When the files are displayed in the file area, choose the file you want to use and click OK. PowerPoint adds the file as a small sound object icon in the center of the slide.

 TIP You can drag the sound object to an inconspicuous place on the slide—no need to leave it right there in the middle of things.

Recording Your Own Sound

For some presentations, you may want to do your own recording. In fact, PowerPoint enables you to record an entire script to play along with your presentation.

The basic process of recording sound is easy. You can use either the Record Narration feature in PowerPoint or use the Windows Sound Recorder, an application included specifically for recording audio files.

Recording Narration

The first step is to plug a microphone into the sound input jack (you may find it as part of the sound card in the back of your computer or along the right or left sides of the system unit).

If you are interested in recording a script or voice-over for your presentation, you can easily do that with PowerPoint. For best results, start with a script that includes everything you plan to say. Small hesitations and stumbles in a voice-over become huge pauses and awkward phrasing and will distract your viewers.

 TIP You may want to use the Outliner to print the text in your presentation; then you can simply read that aloud as you record your narration.

To start recording your narration, choose Slide Show ➢ Record Narration. The Record Narration dialog box appears, as Figure 6.7 shows. You see how much disk space you have available to store the narration, what the quality will be, and so on. To change the options, click Change Quality. The Sound Selection dialog box appears, so that you can change the quality, file format, or other configurations (see Figure 6.8). Make any necessary changes and click OK to close the dialog box. Then click OK again to begin recording the narration.

After you complete the presentation, a message box tells you that the narrations have been saved with each slide and asks you whether you want to save the slide timings also. If you click Yes, the timing with which you advanced each slide is saved in addition to the narration you recorded. If you click No, only the narration is saved.

When you run your presentation by clicking the Slide Show icon in the lower left corner of the work area or by opening the Slide Show menu and choosing View Show, you will hear the narration you have recorded.

TIP You can change the recording and playback volumes by modifying the settings in the Multimedia panel of the Control Panel. Choose Start ➢ Settings ➢ Control Panel ➢ Multimedia and click the Audio tab. Increase the volume as needed, and click OK. Then click the Close box to return to the presentation.

FIGURE 6.7

The Record Narration dialog box

FIGURE 6.8

The Sound Selection dialog box enables you to make choices about your recording.

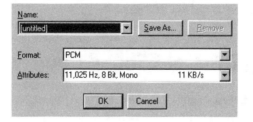

Using Sound Recorder

If you want to use the Sound Recorder to record your sound, follow the process in this section. First, start Sound Recorder by clicking the Start menu and choosing Programs ➢ Accessories ➢ Entertainment ➢ Sound Recorder. Figure 6.9 shows the Sound Recorder, with the cursor positioned on the Record button.

FIGURE 6.9

Using the Sound Recorder to record your own sounds is a simple process

Now simply click the Record button and speak into the microphone (or sing, or yowl, or whatever it is you're planning to do). When you're finished recording, click the Stop button (to the left of the Record button).

TIP You can do all sorts of things with the Sound Recorder—mix the sound with another file; insert it in another file; increase or decrease the volume and speed; add an echo; even play it backwards. For more about working with the Sound Records, see the Sybex book *Sound & Music Workshop* (1996), by Richard Grace.

After you're finished recording, be sure to use File ➢ Save As to save the file. You can then import the sound into your PowerPoint presentation, attach it to an animated object, or play it at a slide transition.

TIP You can record sounds from sources other than your own voice, such as a television show, radio interview, or some other preprocessed source. Just be sure to get the necessary permissions if you're using someone else's material.

Reviewing Different Sound Choices

We've talked about several different ways to add sound to your PowerPoint presentations. Here's a quick review of how you can incorporate sounds into your presentations:

- To play a sound object placed on a slide, click the object. You use Insert ➢ Movies and Sounds to add a sound object to a specific slide.
- If you want a sound to play automatically when slides change, use Slide Show ➢ Slide Transition to attach the sound to the slide transition.
- Use Slide Show ➢ Custom Animation to attach a sound to a specific element on your slide, such as the build text of a bullet list, a title, or an animated logo.
- To add custom voice-over notes or simple recorded sound effects, use the Windows Sound Recorder and a microphone to create your own sounds.

Some Sound Advice for Presenting

Here are a few things to keep in mind as you add sound to your presentation:

- Don't overdo it. With any cool feature comes the temptation to use it for everything. Fight the pull to assign bells and whistles to every event in your presentation. At most, you'll probably want an opening and concluding music piece with selected sound effects in between. If your presentation requires background music all the way through, don't overlay other sound effects. Remember that it's the full mix of the media—text, visuals, and sound—that makes the full statement of your presentation.

- Make sure there's a reason for the sound. Another potential pitfall in working with the creative aspects of multimedia is the craving to use something where it's really not needed. If you're doing a presentation to show the new technical specifications of a new minicomputer to a room of busy engineers, you don't need a swirling musical introduction to capture their attention. They just want to get the information and get back to work.

- Tailor the sound to the presentation. Think through the logic of the sound before you use it. If you have a special effect of a title being handwritten across the screen, for example, you wouldn't want to use the Typewriter sound effect. You wouldn't want to introduce a dry professional presentation with music stamping out a conga beat.

- Consider your presentation equipment. Before you spend a lot of time compiling, testing, and assigning sound to your presentation, think about what you'll be presenting on. If you won't have strong speakers that can project volume and quality good enough for the audience you're presenting to, don't invest your time in music production.

Chapter Summary

This chapter has introduced one of the newer media aspects of multimedia: sound. If you've never worked with sound before, you may be surprised at how easy it is to add simple sound effects and even more complicated musical scores to your presentations. A little sound adds a whole new dimension to the text and visuals on your presentation screen; so, if you've got the computer power, the time, and the desire—make those presentations sing!

CHAPTER 7

Ready, Set, Video!

I n any good presentation, all elements contribute to the final product. The text provides the information, the fonts create a certain mood, the graphics catch and hold the viewers' attention, and sound effects add liveliness that printed handouts can't offer. But video—especially good-quality, entertaining, and interesting video—does much more than any of these elements can do.

Video *moves*.

It's not just that our media-crazed culture demands sound, color, and movement in order to hold its interest. It's not just that we've become desensitized and need more and more stimulation to feel that we're getting what we came for. It's that video has something to offer that no other media has: simulated experience. Through the eyes of the video camera, you're on the French Riviera, you're the one repairing that 737, or you're in the center of that fire at 9th and Central. The movie plays and you play right along with it.

Getting Started

In a business setting, video is fast becoming an irreplaceable tool. A few years ago, in order to have video of a training course, a corporate meeting, or the installation of an assembly line, you'd have to hire a professional video company to come in and do the video for you. Then you'd have to show the video—time and time again—on your trusty VCR in order to get the video seen by all who needed it. Quite an expense—both in time and money. But these days, if you want to tape people working, presenting different products, or demonstrating procedures, you can capture the video yourself. Then import the video into a presentation that can then be circulated on disk, made accessible over a network, or set up on an open-access computer where employees can run through a self-directed demo whenever they like.

The availability of PC hardware and software to support the use of digital video has made it easier for people to use video in their presentations and other business situations. Even if you don't own a video camera yourself, you can benefit from those who have created extensive video libraries with clips you can use in your own projects.

Why Use Video Clips in Your Presentations?

A well-placed video clip in your presentation can make the difference between keeping your clients' interest and losing it. Motion, sound, color—what more do you need to get a message across? Following are a few ideas of how you might incorporate video in your PowerPoint presentation:

- Your corporate meeting begins with a video of the CEO, welcoming all attendees and announcing the corporate theme for the upcoming year.

- You put together a collection of your department's top news stories with clips from your nightly news show interspersed with still photos and text from actual articles.

- Your presentation introducing a new method of teaching includes a video showing preschool children working with your materials.

- Your presentation to promote the computerization of your company's assembly line shows a video of how it's done now and an animation (which is simply a movie made of drawings) of how it *could* be done in the future.

- Your presentation of vacation resorts includes a clip of a boat sailing on a sun-swept lake while displaying a continuing slide show of different time-share condominiums.

What You Need to Use Video

If you are planning on simply working with movie files, you need a standard multimedia computer. The more RAM, the better—32MB is passable, but 64 or even 128MB or more is better. You'll also need adequate speakers for presentation and plenty of hard disk space—video files aren't small.

If you are planning on capturing and working with the video yourself, you need a video capture board installed in your computer and a video editing package that enables you to capture the video in a digital format that can be used by your computer. And, depending on the quality, complexity, and timing of the video you want to capture, you need lots and lots of storage space! A full discussion of video capture is beyond the scope of this book, but recent editions of Mark Minasi's *The Complete PC Upgrade and Maintenance Guide* (Sybex) discuss the mechanics of video capture and purchasing issues.

 TIP What does a video capture board do? It takes the signal from your television, camcorder, or VCR—known as an analog signal—and turns it into a digital signal that the computer can understand.

Once you get the basic hardware and software in place, the Media Player applet that comes with Windows 95 enables you to choose specific clips, colorize, and edit the movie sequences you use. For more information on editing movies with the Media Player, see the section "Advanced Editing: Using Media Player" later in this chapter. For really high-end video editing, however, you'll need a program specifically designed for that purpose.

Where Do You Get Video?

Video clips for use in standard business presentations are available on a number of CD-ROMs from a variety of sources. One popular source is a company called Jasmine, which often includes clip samples on disk packaged with its multimedia collections. Many other companies, such as Kodak, offer extensive clip art and movie libraries with videos and animations ranging from funny to professional. To find these companies, check out recent computer publications such as *Multimedia Online, CD-ROM Today*, and *Multimedia World* and keep an eye on the ads.

Today's computer magazines are often packaged with a disk that includes special multimedia selections you can use in your own work. Additionally, many books on multimedia include CD-ROMs or disks with sample files you can use in your presentations.

The multimedia and computer software forums of various online services offer yet another resource for video clips, but be sure to check any files you download for potential viruses. Also, check out any licensing restrictions or shareware fees; use of the video in any product offered for sale may be restricted.

MASTERING THE OPPORTUNITIES

Checking Out Clip Gallery Live

When considering adding video to your presentations, you may not know where to look for sample video clips. Luckily, PowerPoint takes care of that problem for you by including a link to Microsoft Clip Gallery Live. This Web site gives you access to a wide range of clips—art, sound, video, and more.

To get to Clip Gallery Live, click Clips Online in the Clip Gallery toolbar. Once at the site, click the tab with the type of clip you want (in this case, Motion). You can use the Search box to enter a word related to the clip you want or click the Browse down-arrow and choose the category that best fits what you're looking for. Clip Gallery Live displays a range of choices that match your criteria in the bottom-right portion of the screen. If you see one you like, click it to preview, and then click the open checkbox if you want to download that particular file. When you're ready to leave the site, simply close your browser or move to another site.

Understanding Video Formats

Video files are available in a number of formats. The most common format is AVI, a format introduced when Video for Windows arrived on the scene. The AVI format (AVI stands for Audio Video Interleaved) interleaves audio and video data together in the same file, one after the other. Apple QuickTime for Windows is another format that mixes audio and video together.

Because video files are often so large, data compression is important. Data compression stores the data in a file that takes up less room than the uncompressed file. JPEG (Joint Photographic Experts Group) and MPEG (Motion Picture Experts Group) are two compression techniques often used with video files. JPEG removes some of the video data in order to compress the file but does it so that the change is transparent—or almost transparent—to the eye. MPEG is a higher standard of compression than JPEG, requiring an add-in board and software that is able to read and write the MPEG format. MPEG can actually "predict" what will happen next in the video and make choices about what colors or patterns should remain on the screen; it is much better quality than JPEG and now the highest standard for video. Although it requires additional hardware that used to be extremely expensive, high-end multimedia systems today are being touted as MPEG-ready.

 MASTERING TROUBLESHOOTING

What Makes Good Video Good?

Whether you've got the right video for your particular presentation depends on many different factors. The first decision you've got to make is, "What kind of movie best represents what I'm trying to say here?" If you're trying to get your potential customers dreaming about their next vacation, you would want a colorful, inspiring video that makes clients think, "Boy, I'd like to be there."

Once you decide what kind of video you'd like, you need to either videotape it yourself or find it in a video file collection. Then the issue becomes one of quality. Here are a few questions you should ask about the movie you use in your presentation:

Are the images sharp? The first criterion should be the crispness of the video image. Remember that the larger the movie object, the poorer the resolution will be. For a good-quality video, display the movie in a box about one quarter the size of the slide space. Anything larger than that size may distort the image or make it choppy. Speaking of which...

Continued ▮▶

PART

II

The Right Tool
for the Job

MASTERING TROUBLESHOOTING CONTINUED

Is the movement smooth or choppy? This may be more of a memory consideration than a video consideration, but the size of the movie file will influence how easily it is handled in your computer's RAM. If the video is jerky, try a different clip. Video with hiccups that distract your audience is worse than no video at all.

Do the colors complement the presentation's color scheme? You may spend a great deal of time finding just the right movie to fit your presentation, and then insert it onto a slide and discover that it clashes terribly with the background colors of your slides. You can fix this with PowerPoint's Recolor Picture command, available when you right-click the movie object. You can exchange one color for another (for a total of up to 64 colors), thus making sure that you get just the right mix of colors for your presentation.

Is the sound clear? Sound can make or break a movie in your presentation. If the sound is distorted, crackling, or muffled, your audience is going to be straining to make out what's being said and miss what's being shown. Before you select a movie file, make sure the sound holds up its end, too. (Note: Not all movie files include sound as part of the format. AVI, a popular format introduced with Video for Windows, incorporates both sound and video in the same file.)

Does a certain segment of the video work best in this presentation? Just because a movie segment you select is 40 seconds long doesn't mean you have to use the entire 40 seconds. You can use the Media Player to select just the segment you want.

Adding Movies to PowerPoint Slides

So you've got the movie clip you want to use and know the slide on which you want to use it. To put the movie in the presentation, you'll start by displaying the slide in which you want the movie to begin playing.

Now you have a choice to make: do you want to display the movie as a poster or an icon? A movie poster displays the first frame of the movie on the slide. A movie icon shows up as an icon that you click to play.

PowerPoint enhances AVI movie capability. Now you can play AVI movies—that's sound and video together—and get better, smoother playback and truer colors as well.

Making Movie Posters

The easiest way to add a movie to your PowerPoint presentation is to choose Insert ➤ Movies and Sounds. A pop-up menu appears, as Figure 7.1 shows, enabling you to choose whether you want to select a movie from the Clip Gallery or from a file. When you click Movie from File, the Insert Movie dialog box appears, as shown in Figure 7.2; choose the movie file you want and click OK.

After a moment, the file appears in a small (approximately 2.5 × 2 inches) window on the screen. There's the movie—now you can move, resize, edit, open, and even recolor it.

FIGURE 7.1

Preparing to insert a movie file

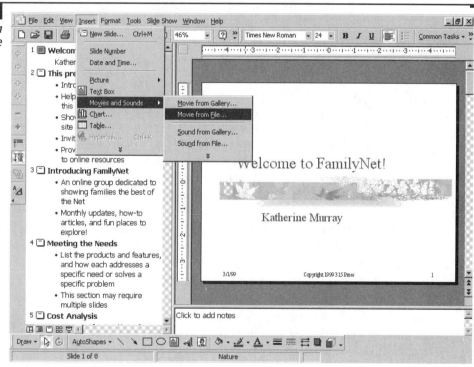

FIGURE 7.2

Choosing a movie file
to use in your
presentation

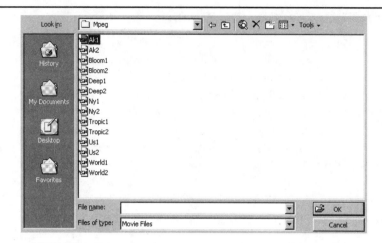

Adding a Movie Icon

Instead of including a movie clip with the first frame of the movie showing, you may want to include the movie as an icon so you have the option of activating it manually during your presentation. You might do this, for example, with a video clip that shows a segment of a training program. Suppose that you know you will give your presentation several times—once to managers, once to line workers, and once to shareholders. You might want to show the training video to the line workers and the managers, but not the shareholders. In this case, using an icon lets you control whether the movie plays, saving you presentation time by allowing you to customize the presentation to your audience's needs.

Including a movie as an icon uses a different process than making it a poster. Again, display the slide on which you want to place the movie object, but choose Insert ➤ Object. The Insert Object dialog opens, so you can find the movie file for which you want to create the icon. Click Create from File (see Figure 7.3). Next, click Browse to display the Browse dialog box in which you can search for the movie file you want, or type the path. When you locate the file in the file list area, click the file you want and then check the Link checkbox if you want to maintain the link to the movie file as opposed to adding the file itself to your PowerPoint file.

FIGURE 7.3

You can use Insert ➢ Object to select the movie file you want to include as an icon.

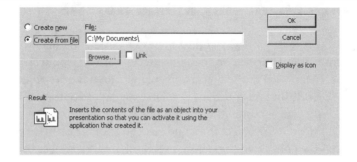

 NOTE When you add a movie to a slide, the movie is linked rather than embedded. A linked file maintains its link to the original file, so if the movie in the original file is edited, the changes are reflected in the PowerPoint file. If the file was embedded, the movie would actually be stored in with the PowerPoint file. Because of the size of most video files, embedding is impractical and taxing on your computer's resources.

To finish, click the Display As Icon check box. An icon appears beneath the check box, showing a default icon that will be used on your presentation slide. To select a different icon, click the Change Icon button to see additional choices and click the one you want. Figure 7.4 shows both the default movie icon and your choices in the Change Icon dialog box. To change the caption displayed beneath the icon, type a new caption in the Caption box.

FIGURE 7.4

Customizing the icon appearance of a movie object

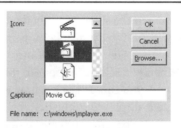

After you click OK in the Insert Object dialog box, PowerPoint redisplays the current slide and shows the movie icon you selected in the Insert Object dialog box. You can now drag the icon to a convenient point on the screen.

Resizing and Moving Movie Objects

If you've decided to add the movie as a poster, you may want to change the size of the movie as it appears on the slide. Resize it as you would any PowerPoint object: drag a corner or side of the object and enlarge or reduce the object as necessary. When the object is the size you want it, release the mouse button. If you change the proportions of the movie poster, the video frame is reproportioned to use the allotted space.

Moving the object from one place to another is also easy now—just position the mouse pointer on the object, press and hold the mouse button, and drag the movie to the new location. When the movie poster is positioned where you want it, let go of the mouse button.

Playing Movies

Once you find the clip you want and get it positioned on your slide, you'll be anxious to check it out in your presentation. This section shows you how to test the movie clip you've added and make choices about when you want the movie to play.

Testing the Movie Clip

If you're like most people, you're anxious to see how that movie looks the moment you position it on the slide. You don't want to wait until the presentation to find out that the clip really doesn't fit your topic.

You can play the movie without running the presentation by positioning the mouse pointer on the movie object and double-clicking.

Choosing When You Want the Movie to Play

The movie is now in the slide; the only remaining task is to define when it plays during the presentation. You can display a menu of movie options by right-clicking on the movie object (see Figure 7.5). To control when the movie plays, select Custom Animation. When you select this option, the Custom Animation dialog box appears. In this dialog box, you can determine how you want the movie object to "act" when the current slide is displayed in the presentation. Do you want the movie to play automatically or sit dormant until clicked?

FIGURE 7.5

Right-click the movie object to see movie options.

 NOTE When you right-click a movie object, the names and number of options in the menu displayed will depend on the type of movie file it is.

Figure 7.6 shows the Custom Animation dialog box. The Effects tab is displayed by default. First select an effect for the object (Appear is fine) so the other options are made available. Next, click the Order & Timing tab to set the play options. When that tab is displayed, click the object name in the Check to Animate Slide Objects box in the upper-left corner of the Custom Animation dialog box. Now all the other choices are enabled. If you want the movie to play automatically, click that option in the Start animation box and enter the number of seconds you want to delay the start of the video clip (see Figure 7.7).

FIGURE 7.6

The Custom Animation dialog box

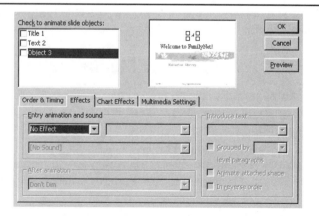

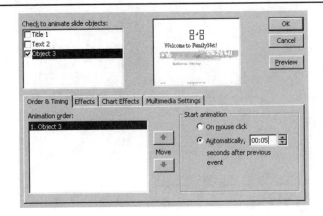

Editing Movies

The commands for editing your selected movie file are also tucked away in the pop-up menu that appears when you right-click the movie object.

Simple Editing

The first three commands—Cut, Copy, and Paste—are standard editing commands. You can cut and paste a movie from one slide or presentation to another; you can even cut and paste a movie from your PowerPoint presentation into your Word document (or vice versa).

Advanced Editing: Using Media Player

When you position the pointer on the movie object and right-click the mouse, the pop-up menu appears. Here you will see different things, depending on how you added the movie object.

If you added the object by choosing Insert ➤ Movies and Sounds, choose Edit Movie Object from the displayed menu; you will see a small pop-up box that allows you to change whether the movie repeats (called *looping*) and whether you want the movie to rewind when it finishes.

If you added the object using Insert ➤ Object ➤ Create from File, you will be presented with the option Media Clip Object ➤ Edit. When you select the Edit option, the Media Player appears, along with tools for editing the movie clip.

The Media Player enables you to do the following things:

- Edit video
- Select clips of video you want to use in your presentation
- Move through a video clip forward and backward
- Control the volume for AVI clips
- Determine whether you want a border around the clip
- Choose whether you want the control bar displayed at the bottom of the clip
- Make copies of video clips you select

 TIP Time is just one of the ways you can display the different aspects of your video. You can also choose to display the movie by frames or by track (for sound). The only difference is the method of selection—some people find it easier to cut a piece from 370 to 385 than from 00:00:24 to 00:00:34. To change the sequence scale, click the Scale menu and choose the sequence style you want to see.

Media Player includes different menus than the ones you're accustomed to in Power-Point. Table 7.1 gives you a quick rundown of Media Player features; Table 7.2 introduces you to the tools in the Media Player toolbar.

TABLE 7.1: MEDIA PLAYER MENUS

Menu	Contains Commands For
File	Opening, saving, packing, and sending movie clips
Edit	Copying movies, setting movie options (such as displaying the control bar, setting Auto Rewind and Auto Repeat, and options for the display and playing of the object in the current presentation)
Device	Adding a new video clip, reviewing file properties, or controlling volume
Scale	Choosing the measurement by which the file is sequenced: time, frames, or tracks
Help	Accessing Media Player help

PART

II

The Right Tool
for the Job

TABLE 7.2: TOOLS IN THE MEDIA PLAYER TOOLBAR

Tool	Description
Play	Begins playing the movie from the selected mark
Stop	Stops the movie being played
Eject	Closes Media Player and abandons changes
Previous Mark	Rewinds the movie to the preceding marked place
Rewind	Rewinds the movie to the beginning of the clip
Fast Forward	Fast forwards the movie to the marked spot
Next Mark	Forwards the movie ahead to the next marked place
Start Selection	Marks the beginning of a selected sequence of the movie
End Selection	Marks the end of a selected movie sequence
Scroll Backward	Moves backward through the movie a frame at a time
Scroll Forward	Moves forward through the movie a frame at a time

Setting Video Options

Some things that look impressive on-screen are actually very easy to do. For example, you can add a great deal to a continually running presentation with an Auto Repeat feature, which will run your video over and over again until you tell it to stop. Or, if the presentation is a user-controlled demo, you could turn on the Auto Rewind option so the user can repeat the video. Both of these features, and others, are set in the Options dialog box (see Figure 7.8), accessible by choosing Edit ➤ Options. To turn on Auto Rewind and/or Auto Repeat, simply click the corresponding check boxes.

Auto Rewind and Auto Repeat aren't your only options, however. To remove (temporarily or permanently) the control bar that appears beneath the movie, click Control Bar On Playback. (Removing the check mark hides the control bar; adding the check mark displays it.)

You can also enter a new caption to be displayed beneath the movie until the movie begins. For example, you could type an instruction ("Click here to start!"), your company name, or the name and title of a person interviewed in the movie sequence.

FIGURE 7.8

*You can control the
way the movie plays
and the controls that
are available in the
Options dialog box.*

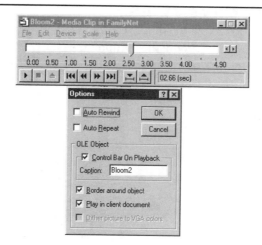

Getting the Clip You Want

Whether you are using video created just for your presentation or a movie from a collection of video clippings, you will probably need to trim the clip to include only the images you want in your presentation. Many popular multimedia CD-ROMs include a number of video files, and some of those are a compilation of short movies from which you can cut the pieces of video you want.

Entering Timing Coordinates

It's easy to clip just the part you want out of a larger movie by displaying the movie as a poster on the slide of your choice, then right-clicking the mouse on the object. When the Media Player appears, choose Edit ➤ Selection to open the Selection dialog box shown in Figure 7.9. Now you can type the timing coordinates of the segment you want (if you know them) by typing the timing value in the appropriate box. If you don't know the exact coordinates of the video clip you want, you can easily select the clip yourself using the process described in the next section.

FIGURE 7.9

The Set Selection dialog box enables you to choose the section of video you want for your presentation.

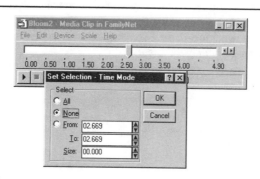

Making Your Video Selection

If you don't know the timing coordinates, you can simply drag the markers on the sequence bar to choose the portion of the movie you want.

Start by clicking the Start Selection marker (at the far left of the sequence bar) and dragging it to the beginning of the section you want. As you drag the marker, the video changes to show the current movie segment (see Figure 7.10), so you can see where you are.

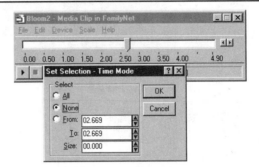

Next, specify where you want the movie to end by clicking Play. As the movie clip continues, anticipate where you want to stop the video. (The film runs at a rate of about 30 frames per second.) When the movie gets to that point, click the End Selection button. Notice that a colored bar shows the segment in the sequence bar you have selected.

Does your Set Selection dialog box show all zeros? This is because you haven't yet chosen a selected sequence. Once you choose a selection, it is reflected in the dialog box (as well as in the sequence bar) until you choose a different sequence or insert a different clip.

TIP If you want to choose a different movie selection, display the Set Selection dialog box and zero out all the timing values. If you want to edit the settings, use the up arrow and down arrow in the From and To boxes to modify the beginning and end points of the segment (or drag the slider).

Using Volume Control

Especially in a multimedia presentation, setting the volume to a good healthy balance that neither deafens your audience nor makes them strain is an important part of conveying your message. Volume control is a global Windows setting that you may or may not have already discovered for yourself. Choose Device ➤ Volume Control to display the Volume Control dialog box (see Figure 7.11).

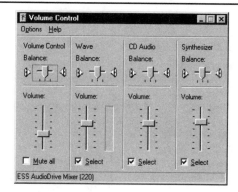

You can set the volume control by using the slide controls in each of four areas: Volume Control, Wave (this affects sound and movie files you use in your presentations), CD Audio, and Synthesizer files. (The latter three all control additional sound output devices; Volume Control controls the basic sound system of the PC.) When you're finished changing the volume settings, click the Close button in the upper-right corner of the window. The number of controls you'll see depends on the sound mixer you have installed on your machine.

You can also display the Volume Control dialog box from any point in Windows 95, assuming the volume control is present, by double-clicking the speaker icon in the bottom-right corner of the taskbar.

TIP When you've finished editing your video clip in the Media Player and are ready to return to PowerPoint, simply click outside the movie area. The PowerPoint work area is redisplayed and the movie object is shown highlighted, with handles at the corners and along the sides of the object.

PART

II

The Right Tool
for the Job

Cropping the Movie Object

In some cases, you may want to crop your video to display only the portion you need. Suppose, for example, you want only the top portion of the revolving world showing behind the text on a series of slides. You can crop the video of the world spinning to get only the portion you want.

To crop the movie, right-click on the movie object to open the pop-up menu. Click Show Picture Toolbar, and the tool palette appears (see Figure 7.12). Click the Crop tool. You can now crop the movie object displayed as a poster by clicking in its corner (or along its side), then dragging the corner or side to its new position. When the object has the view you want, release the mouse button. Click outside the object to finish and return the pointer to its normal shape.

FIGURE 7.12

You can crop a movie to hide the portions that you don't want your audience to see.

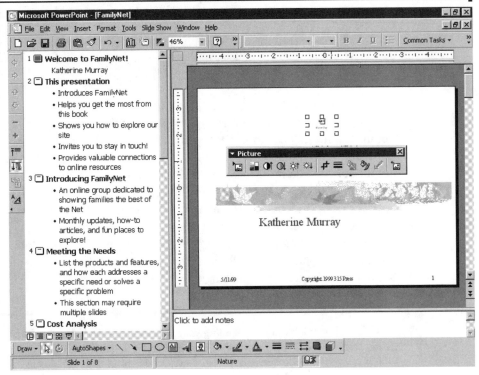

Recoloring Images

Sometimes some of the background color or primary colors of the video may not mesh the way you'd like with the color scheme you've selected for your PowerPoint presentation. The Recolor Picture tool in the Picture toolbar lets you change the colors in the video to either make the color scheme more consistent or create stunning color special effects.

Start by displaying the Picture toolbar (right-click the movie object and choose Show Picture Toolbar). When the toolbar appears, click the Recolor Picture tool. The Recolor Picture dialog box then appears.

To change a color in the picture, check the check box beside the color you want to change in the Original column. Next, click the down arrow of the color in the New column and select the new color from the palette that appears. To choose from the larger scheme of colors, click Other Color.

For best results, preview your changes before you click OK and have them recolored in the movie. Select the poster and click on Recolor Picture. You'll see a message box that says, "The object is a bitmap." To recolor it, you must use an image editor such as Microsoft Photo Editor.

 TIP If you return to the slide and realize that you really don't like the color change, choose Edit ➤ Undo Recolor Picture or press Ctrl+Z to restore the video to its original color scheme.

Chapter Summary

This chapter explored the basics of adding movies to your PowerPoint slides, using either movie files from other sources or, if you have the right hardware and software, video input from your TV, VCR, or camcorder. With a mix of video, sound, graphics, charts, and text, your presentation is nearly complete.

The next chapter shows you how to finish up the fine points for presenting, including how to set slide transitions and add special effects, like animation, to your presentation.

CHAPTER **8**

Finishing the Slide Show

Up to this point in the book, you've concentrated on compiling all the different elements of your presentation. You wrote and edited the text, created and modified the charts, designed and/or imported graphics, added sound, and inserted movie objects. What's left to do besides give the presentation?

A few subtle techniques can make a big difference in the way your presentation comes across. These techniques can make a big difference in the way your slides make the transition from one to another and how quickly or slowly you "turn the page" during the slide show are the focus of this chapter. You'll also learn about the new features PowerPoint adds to strengthen your presenting power—things like on-screen drawing, Meeting Minder notes, and presentation conferencing.

 TIP If you're not thrilled about standing up in front of a group and giving that presentation, practicing it a few times can help you learn what to expect while you're presenting. You'll be less nervous at show time if you've rehearsed the presentation enough to know it well.

What Is a Slide Show?

In its simplest state, a slide show is an on-screen presentation of slides. When you click the Slide Show button or choose View ➤ Slide Show (and then click the Show button), PowerPoint displays the slides, one at a time, in full-screen view. The selected slide is displayed complete with all text, art, graphs, and any other items you added.

You can display a slide show at any time during the creation process. When you want to see how a single slide will look, how a particular piece of video will appear, or how a sound effect will sound, you can display the slide show in its unfinished form.

 TIP Click the Slide Show button, and check out how your developing presentation is looking at various stages throughout the creation process. Seeing the slide in Slide Show view gives you a much better idea of how the screen will look, because it gets rid of the clutter of the menu bar and toolbars.

Adding the Finishing Touches

By this stage in the presentation creation process, your slides should be finished at a point where you're happy with them. The text is where you want it, the charts appear the way they will in the presentation, and you've conscientiously used the Spelling Checker and Style Checker to make sure that the basic content and layout of your presentation look as professional as possible.

 TIP If you haven't used the Spelling Checker—or if it's been a while since you did—take a minute and do so before continuing. You'll find the command in the Tools menu, or you can press F7 to start the utility.

While focusing on building slides, you are also working from an up-close perspective, asking yourself questions such as "What would look good on this side of the slide?" or "Is there too much text in a bullet list?" Your attention is given to each individual slide to make sure it meets its goal.

Once you get all the elements in place, your vision becomes more global: you begin thinking of the presentation as a whole. "How much time will this presentation take?" or "How many different transitions should I use in a 25-slide presentation?" or "How do I know how much time to leave for each slide in order to get them all in?" become the questions you're more concerned with now.

The answers to each of these questions help you add the finishing touches to your presentation. In the next section, you will learn how to work with features that help your presentation really shine.

PowerPoint "Polishing" Tools

PowerPoint includes a number of features that make the finishing step one of the easiest:

- Dozens of transitional effects, such as wipes, fades, and dissolves, to keep your audience's attention.
- A hidden slides feature that lets you include backup slides for more information but display them only when needed.
- A rehearsal feature that lets you rehearse the presentation with a recording timer so you can set just the right amount of time for individual slides.
- A Slide Meter that enables you to compare your actual presentation timing to your rehearsal timing, so you can gauge how accurate your projections were and decide whether you need to make modifications.

- An on-screen draw feature that lets you write notes, circle important items, or underline important concepts, using a variety of colors and pen styles.
- The Meeting Minder feature that lets you take notes during the meeting or presentation. You can assign priorities to the notes and even export them to use in other applications.
- Presentation conferencing that enables you to give the presentation over your network, so others can log in on the process and participate online.

Setting Slide Transitions

A slide transition is the effect PowerPoint uses to remove the current slide and bring in a new one. By default, PowerPoint doesn't assign any special transitional effect; until you specify the transition you want, one slide is simply replaced uneventfully with the next. But PowerPoint can supply dozens of interesting transitional effects, such as fades, wipes, blinds, and checkerboards.

Choosing the Transition

To choose a transitional effect for your slide, first select the slide to which you want to apply the transition when the slide appears. If you are in Normal view, the transitional effect will be applied to the current slide. If you are displaying Slide Sorter view, you need to click the slide to which you want to add the transition. You can display the Slide Transition dialog box necessary to add transitions in three different ways:

- You can choose Slide Show ➤ Slide Transition.
- You can click the right mouse button on the slide for which you want to set the transition in Slide Sorter view, and choose Slide Transition from the pop-up menu that appears.
- You can click the Slide Transition button on the far left side of the special effects bar.

Figure 8.1 shows Slide Sorter View. If you know the name of the transition effect you want to apply to a slide, you can choose it from the Slide Transition drop-down list.

FIGURE 8.1

You can select the transition you want by choosing it from the Slide Transition drop-down list.

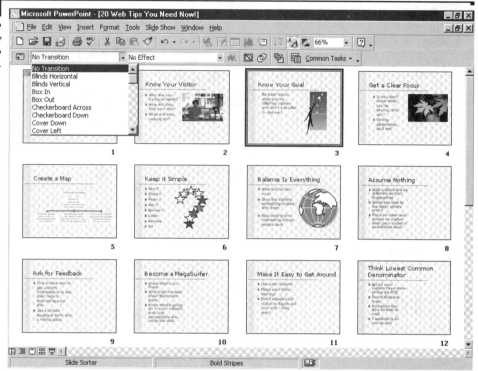

PART

II

The Right Tool for the Job

 TIP Although PowerPoint lets you work in either Normal view or Slide Sorter view when you're adding transitions to your slides, it's often easiest to work in Slide Sorter view when you're putting together the final elements of your presentation and preparing a slide show. All the tools for the slide show are right there on the Slide Sorter tools row, and you can immediately see the effects you create.

The Slide Transition dialog box lets you try out all the different transitional effects on the dog picture before you add them to your slides (see Figure 8.2).

FIGURE 8.2

*The Slide Transition
dialog box*

When you first display the Slide Transition dialog box, the setting No Transition is displayed in the Effect box. To show the list of potential transitions, click the drop-down arrow (see Figure 8.3).

FIGURE 8.3

*Displaying transition
choices*

What you see in the Effects list isn't all there is: click the drop-down arrow on the scrollbar to see the entire list. The names may not tell you much, however—it's hard to tell exactly what the effect does until you see it in action. By watching the little dog in the preview picture as you try each effect, the picture will change to a key picture. When you try another effect, the dog appears again. This variance makes it easy for you to see exactly what the effect does. If you don't want to work your way through the list to see what each effect does, look at Table 8.1.

TABLE 8.1: SLIDE SHOW TRANSITIONAL EFFECTS

Effect	Description
No Transition	No transitional effect has been applied to this slide.
Blinds Horizontal	Horizontal strips close, revealing the next slide.
Blinds Vertical	Vertical strips close, revealing the next slide.
Box Out	Next slide starts as a small box in center of the former slide and spreads outward.
Box In	New slide spreads inward from the outer edges.
Checkerboard Across	A checkerboard pattern fills in the new slide from left to right.
Checkerboard Down	A checkerboard pattern fills in the new slide from top to bottom.
Cover Left	The new slide slides in from the right.
Cover Up	The new slide slides up from the bottom.
Cover Right	The new slide slides in from the left.
Cover Down	The new slide slides down from the top.
Cover Left-Up	The new slide slides up from the bottom right corner.
Cover Right-Up	The new slide slides up from the bottom left corner.
Cover Left-Down	The new slide slides down from the top right corner.
Cover Right-Down	The new slide slides down from the top left corner.
Cut	A quick exchange inward reveals the new slide.
Cut Through Black	A quick exchange reveals the new slide after a momentary blackout.
Dissolve	The old slide dissolves into the display of the new slide.
Fade Through Black	The old slide fades to black and the new slide appears gradually.
Random Bars Horizontal	Random horizontal bars reveal the new slide.
Random Bars Vertical	Random vertical bars reveal the new slide.
Split Horizontal Out	The new slide begins as a horizontal line in the center of the screen and spreads outward.
Split Horizontal In	The new slide begins along the top and bottom of the screen and spreads inward.
Split Vertical Out	The new slide starts as a vertical line in the center of the slide and spreads outward.
Split Vertical In	The new slide begins at the left and right edges of the screen and spreads inward.
Strips Down-Left	The new slide builds in diagonal strips from the upper right corner to the bottom left corner.
Strips Down-Right	The new slide builds in diagonal strips from the upper left corner to the bottom right corner.
Strips Up-Left	The new slide builds in diagonal strips from the bottom right corner to the upper left corner.

Continued ▶

PART

II

The Right Tool
for the Job

TABLE 8.1: SLIDE SHOW TRANSITIONAL EFFECTS (CONTINUED)	
Effect	**Description**
Strips Up-Right	The new slide builds in diagonal strips from the bottom left corner to the upper right corner.
Uncover Left	The old slide is removed from the left, revealing the new slide.
Uncover Up	The old slide is removed from the top, revealing the new slide.
Uncover Right	The old slide is removed from the right, revealing the new slide.
Uncover Down	The old slide is removed from the bottom, revealing the new slide.
Uncover Left-Up	The old slide is removed from the upper left corner, revealing the new slide.
Uncover Right-Up	The old slide is removed from the upper right corner, revealing the new slide.
Uncover Left-Down	The old slide is removed from the bottom left corner, revealing the new slide.
Uncover Right-Down	The old slide is removed from the bottom right corner, revealing the new slide.
Wipe Left	The old slide is wiped off to the left, revealing the new slide.
Wipe Up	The old slide is wiped off the top, revealing the new slide.
Wipe Right	The old slide is wiped off to the right, revealing the new slide.
Wipe Down	The old slide is wiped off the bottom, revealing the new slide.
Random Transition	PowerPoint chooses any transitional effect.

After you've decided on the transition you want and are ready to exit the Slide Transition dialog box, leave the one you want highlighted, and click OK. But if you want to set other options—such as manual or automatic advance or adding sound effects—don't click OK to close the Slide Transition dialog box just yet.

Once you've chosen the effect you want from the Slide Transition dialog box, the slide in Slide Sorter view shows a small icon in the bottom left corner, indicating that you have added a transitional effect (see Figure 8.4).

 TIP When you click OK to close the Slide Transition dialog box, PowerPoint displays the slide and its transition in place in Slide Sorter view without going into the slide show.

FIGURE 8.4

After you choose a transitional effect, PowerPoint adds an icon to show that an effect has been applied to the slide.

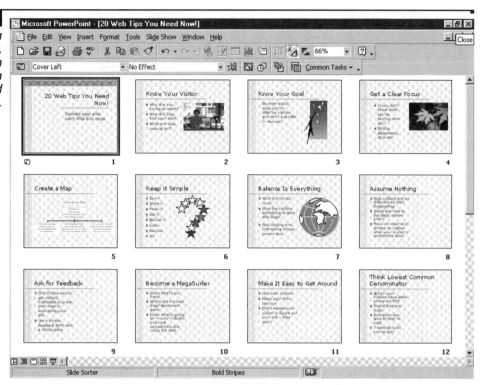

Choosing Transition Speed

Some transitional effects work better at different speeds than others. All effects are set to a fast speed at first, but you can change the speed in the Slide Transition dialog box. Some effects, such as the Cut Through Black transition, are available in only one speed.

For example, the Uncover Up effect moves very quickly to pull the old slide off the screen. You might want to slow it down for your presentation. Start in the Slide Transition dialog box. In the Speed area, choose whether you want Slow, Medium, or Fast. Again, the preview window shows you the effect of the change.

TIP Don't be afraid to mix and match the speeds of transitional effects. Some naturally work faster than others. The speed of the checkerboard effect, for example, might be plenty slow enough for you, but the Uncover or Wipe effects might work too quickly.

PART

II

The Right Tool
for the Job

Choosing Manual or Automatic Slide Advance

Certain presentations need a fair amount of flexibility built in, with the opportunity to stop and discuss important points or areas that require more elaboration. For this type of presentation, you would use manual slide advance, so you control when each slide is replaced with the next. This way, you can make sure your audience has enough time to register the information before you move on to the next topic.

Other presentations are geared more toward communicating general information, often giving an overview of a company's progress, an introduction to a new product line, or the "look and feel" of a new organization. For these presentations you may choose to use an automatic slide advance, which has a timer and advances the slides automatically after a specified period of time has elapsed.

Both situations are needed at different times, and PowerPoint includes a number of features to support both types of presentations.

Manual Advance

By default, PowerPoint's slides are set to manual advance. You see this in the Slide Transition dialog box, where On Mouse Click is selected in the Advance area. When you display the presentation in a slide show, you must click the left mouse button to move to the next slide.

During the presentation, an Options button appears in the lower left corner of the display. You can click this button (or you can click the right mouse button anywhere on the slide) to display a pop-up menu of choices. Using these options, you can move to the next (or previous) slide in the presentation or go to a specific slide. If you want to end the presentation, you can click End Show (see Figure 8.5).

 NOTE For more about navigating through the various slides in your slide show, see "Moving through a Slide Show," later in this chapter.

PART

II

The Right Tool
for the Job

FIGURE 8.5

If you have chosen Manual slide advance, you can use options in the pop-up menu to navigate through the show.

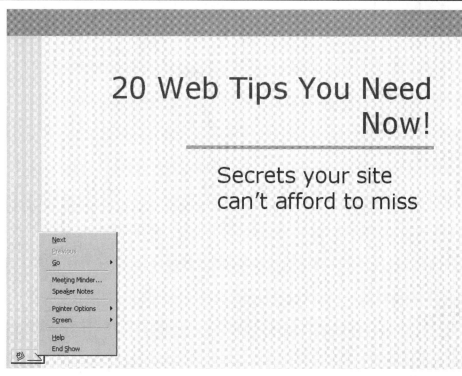

Automatic Advance

You can have PowerPoint automatically advance the slides in your presentation by choosing Automatic advance in the Slide Transition dialog box. First, click the slide for which you want to enter the automatic advance settings; then, in the Advance options, click Automatically After, and enter the number of seconds you want to wait before the slide advances in the Seconds box (see Figure 8.6). The default is 0 (zero).

NOTE   When you work with automatic slide display, PowerPoint advances the slides for you. In return for this convenient feature, you also lose some control, so it's important that you get the timing just the way you want it before you present. You can practice and fine-tune the timing of your slide display by using PowerPoint's rehearsal feature. For more information, see "Rehearsing Slide Display Timings," later in this chapter.

FIGURE 8.6

Entering automatic settings

After you click Apply, PowerPoint assigns the amount of time you entered to the selected slide. (You must set the timing for each slide individually unless you click Apply to All in the Slide Transitions dialog box, which assigns the same time to each slide in your presentation.) The time value is shown below the slide in Slide Sorter view (see Figure 8.7).

FIGURE 8.7

In Slide Sorter view, the timing for automatic advance is shown beneath the slide.

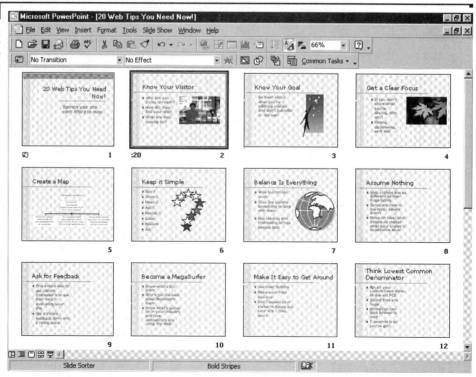

TIP You can change the time allotted for the display of any slide by displaying the Slide Transition dialog box and changing the Automatic Advance value. This modifies the time advance settings for the selected slide, overriding any other settings (such as the ones you set in Rehearsal mode).

Adding Sound Effects

In Chapter 6, "Adding Sound," you learned the ins and outs of adding sound effects and sound files to your PowerPoint presentations, so we'll just touch on the process here briefly. Remember that even though PowerPoint includes a few sound effects you may want to use in your presentations, many third-party libraries of sound effects are available that you can add to your slide transitions.

In the Slide Transition dialog box, the Sound area controls whether a sound is added to the transition of your slide. By default, No Sound is selected.

 TIP If you want a sound to play automatically when the selected slide appears, add the sound as a sound effect in the Slide Transition dialog box.

To see what sounds are available, click the Sound drop-down list (see Figure 8.8).

FIGURE 8.8

Scrolling through available sound effects

Scroll through the list until you find the sound you want. If you want to add a sound from disk or CD-ROM, scroll down to Other Sound. When you select that option, the Add Sound dialog box appears, as shown in Figure 8.9. Navigate to the disk and/or folder you need, click the sound file you want to use, and then click OK. PowerPoint adds the filename to the list in the Sound area.

After you've selected the sound you want in the Sound list, you need to decide whether you want the sound to play only once or repeat. PowerPoint calls this looping.

TIP If you've used a looping sound and want to turn it off at the beginning of the next slide, select the slide on which you want the sound turned off, display the Slide Transition dialog box, and in the Sound area, choose either another sound or Stop Previous Sound.

Creating Hidden Slides

Why create a slide if you just plan to hide it? In some cases, you may want to create backup slides that offer more information about a specific topic. For example, suppose that it's your job as personnel manager to explain a new benefits program your company is offering. You've got all kinds of data on various programs and benefits.

You're a little concerned that the profit-sharing plan may be confusing to people who are seeing it for the first time. For this reason, you create additional slides showing graphs and bullet lists that can help explain the basic concepts. However, the time you have for giving your presentation is limited, so you only want to show as much information as is necessary. If everyone in the audience already understands the profit-sharing plan, you won't display your backup slides. But if they need a little more of an explanation, you'll have that explanation already prepared and right at your fingertips. *That's* why you can hide slides in PowerPoint.

Hiding a Slide

To hide a slide, follow these steps. In Slide Sorter view, click on the slide you want to hide. Now, click the Hide Slide button in the tools row, or open the Slide Show menu, and choose Hide Slide. A small box appears around the slide number (in this case, slide 5), indicating that it is hidden (see Figure 8.10).

FIGURE 8.10

The page number is enclosed in a box, indicating that the slide is hidden.

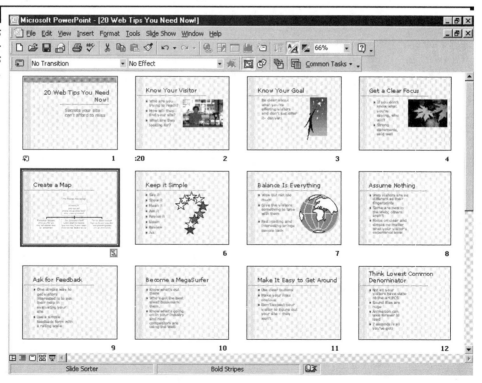

TIP You can unhide a slide as easily as you can hide one: just click the slide, and click the Hide Slide button (or choose Hide Slide again in the Slide Show menu).

Displaying a Hidden Slide

But how do you get to the slide when you need it? PowerPoint knows automatically when you come to a hidden slide. Your presentation will skip right over the slide as though it were never there.

If you want to display a hidden slide (or slides) as you are giving the presentation, just press *H*. PowerPoint moves directly to the hidden slide.

If you prefer to see what you're doing, you can display the hidden slide by clicking the control button in the lower left corner of the screen. When the pop-up menu appears, as shown in Figure 8.11, point to Go, By Title, and choose the title of the hidden slide.

FIGURE 8.11

Use the control button to display hidden slides.

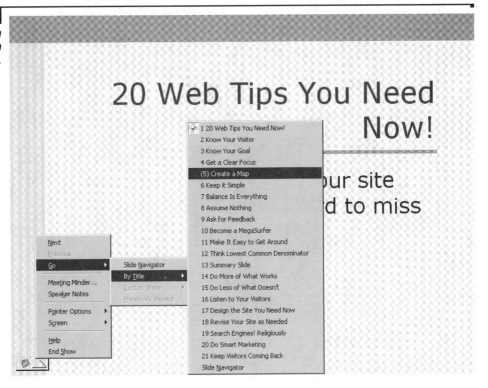

TIP If the control button does not appear while you are giving your presentation, move the mouse pointer to the lower left corner of the screen. The button will appear.

Rehearsing Slide Display Timing

When you want to rehearse the timing of your presentation, simply click the Rehearse Timings button in the Slide Sorter tools row. PowerPoint displays the slide show, beginning with whatever slide you had selected, and starts a timer in the upper left corner (see Figure 8.12).

PART

II

The Right Tool
for the Job

FIGURE 8.12

The rehearsal timer

20 Web Tips You Need
Now!

Secrets your site
can't afford to miss

The Rehearsal timer helps you get your spoken presentation synchronized with your slide show. The timing value on the left shows the amount of time expended so far in the presentation; the box on the right shows the amount of time assigned to the current slide. Table 8.2 explains the different buttons in the Rehearsal timer.

TABLE 8.2: REHEARSAL TIMING BUTTONS

Button	Name	Description
➡	Next	Advances to the next slide, and begins timing.
⏸	Pause	Pauses timing.
0:00:03	Slide Time	Shows the timing for the current slide.
↩	Repeat	Restarts the timing for the current slide.

While you record the time you spend on each slide, you can go through your notes, pretend to answer questions, or just sit and wait out the amount of time you feel is appropriate. When you are ready to move on to the next slide, click the Next button. If you want to stop recording, click Pause. To retime the current slide, click Repeat.

WARNING The clock in the Rehearsal timer may appear to stop while PowerPoint adds special text effects. PowerPoint is still timing the slide, however; after the special effects have been added, you'll notice that the Rehearsal timer shows that it has added the time.

When you're finished recording the time, whether you've completed the entire slide show or just want to stop rehearsing, PowerPoint tells you the total time your presentation took and asks whether you'd like to record the time settings (see Figure 8.13).

If you want to save the timings, click Yes. The new settings are displayed beneath the slides in Slide Sorter view. To discard the timing settings, click No.

TIP Another feature, called the Slide Meter, lets you compare the slide timings you set up during rehearsal with the actual timings you use in manual advance in your presentation. Right-click the mouse when in Slide Show View and you'll see a representation of how your planned and actual timings compare.

FIGURE 8.13

Elapsed time of the presentation

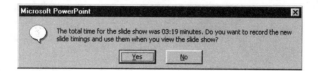

Starting a Screen Show

You may not want to wait until you've finished the entire presentation to display a slide show. Displaying a show as you're creating slides can help you see what you've done and judge the effectiveness of a certain element, font, or color.

You can start a screen show several ways:

- Click the Slide Show button in the lower left corner of the screen.
- Choose View ➢ Slide Show.
- In Slide Show view, you can choose Slide Show ➢ View Show (or press F5).

 TIP Even if you don't plan to display your presentation on a computer monitor and will only print it out for a meeting, moving through the slides in sequence can help you make sure you've made the most effective statement possible.

Working with the Set Up Show Dialog Box

You can set a number of other options to further customize the way your slide show displays. Open the Slide Show menu, and click Set Up Show to display the dialog box in Figure 8.14.

PART

II

The Right Tool for the Job

FIGURE 8.14

*The Set Up Show
dialog box*

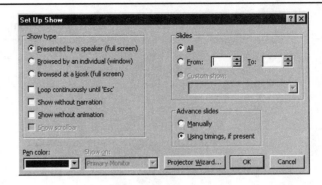

In the Set Up Show dialog box, you can select the type of show you want to give. PowerPoint gives you a number of options:

- You can have the show display full screen.
- You can display the show in a window so an individual can browse the slides at will.
- You can set up the show to be browsed at a kiosk in full-screen style.

The next set of options enables you to choose whether the show will loop continuously until you press Esc. *Looping* means the presentation will start over as soon as it completes. You can also opt to present the show without narrations and/or without animations.

The Set Up Show dialog box also lets you control which slides are displayed and how they advance. To choose only a few slides for display, enter the beginning and ending slide numbers of the sequence in the From and To boxes. Finally, in this dialog box you can select Use Slide Timings to instruct PowerPoint to control the slide display for you, or you can choose a Pen Color for your notes and diagrams that you add during the presentation.

 TIP If you plan to use a projector to give your presentation, click the Projector Wizard button in the bottom of the Set Up Show dialog box. PowerPoint walks you through the process of preparing your data projector for display.

Moving through a Slide Show

If you jumped right in and started the slide show by clicking the Slide Show button, you are ready to navigate your way through the slides. The following commands make it easy:

- To move to the next slide, click the left mouse button, press the N key, or press Enter or Page Down.

- To move to the previous slide, press Page Up or the P key.

- To cancel the slide show and return to the presentation work area, press Esc.

- If you prefer working with a menu, click the right mouse button anywhere on the slide. A pop-up menu appears. You can then choose the command you want, depending on the direction you want to go (see Figure 8.15). You can also click the button in the lower left corner of the display to show this same menu.

FIGURE 8.15

*Displaying the Slide
Show menu*

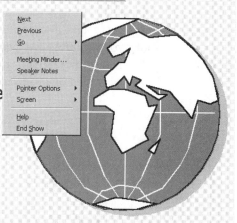

Using the Slide Navigator

If you want to jump directly to a specific slide—perhaps a slide that you've already displayed—you need the Slide Navigator. Display the Slide Show pop-up menu by clicking the right mouse button anywhere on the slide when you're giving a slide show. Click Go, and from the pop-up submenu, choose Slide Navigator. The Slide Navigator dialog box appears, as shown in Figure 8.16.

The Slide Navigator lists the different slides in your presentations by title. The current slide is highlighted, and any slides you've hidden are displayed with the slide number in parentheses. At the bottom of the dialog box, the Last Slide Viewed area shows you the last slide you displayed.

To change to the slide you want, simply click it, and then click the Go To button. The Slide Navigator closes, and you are returned to the presentation.

MASTERING TROUBLESHOOTING

Tips for Presenters

The more you create and give your own presentations, the more you'll discover the individual challenges and pitfalls your particular industry or business presents. As you're starting out, remember that each situation will have its own unique issues, so it's a good idea to keep a notebook of the tips you discover along the way.

Continued ▌▶

MASTERING TROUBLESHOOTING CONTINUED

Practice, practice, practice. Especially if you are a first-time presenter or will be presenting in an area or forum new to you, make sure you know your topic—and your presentation—inside and out. Many people prefer to practice in front of a mirror, so they can check out their expressions and gestures. Some people are more comfortable practicing in front of small groups of friends or coworkers. Others videotape the presentation so they can review the result more objectively later. Whatever mode of practice you're most comfortable with, remember to put yourself in the audience and watch yourself from a distance. How are you coming across? Are you enunciating clearly? Do your slides—and slide timings—give your audience a clear picture of what you're trying to say? What can you do to improve your message?

Invite feedback before the event. Few of us like to have our work scrutinized. We don't want to see a red line through a headline we particularly liked or watch someone shake their head while we're giving a presentation. It's not fun to listen to a group of people tell you what's wrong with your work when so few people will take the time to tell you what's right. But toughening your skin and inviting input can dramatically improve the quality and effectiveness of your presentation.

Everyone processes information and reacts to it a little differently. Getting input from a variety of people about what works for them and what doesn't will serve to make your presentation more appealing to a wider variety of people. To some degree, you can control the input you get by asking targeted questions, such as, "If you could do one thing to improve the text (or charts or graphics) of this presentation, what would you change?" This makes your reviewer think about a solution rather than just making a broad judgment like "It stinks!"

Speak simply. Remember that your audience may represent a wide range of education and intelligence levels. Don't shoot for the Mensa crowd, using four-syllable words and obscure analogies. Simple and straightforward is best, especially if you're talking to a high-end audience. Even people who do heavy brainwork for a living appreciate communication that's easy to understand and implement.

Show, don't tell. This is a basic philosophy, but it is probably one of the primary motivations you have in giving the presentation at all. Your presentation—and multimedia in general—gives you the option of creating for your viewer an experience that is much different from a book, a lecture, or a videotape. You've got all the elements—text, sound, video, art—and you can use them interactively to create a totally unique experience. After you finish the first draft of your presentation, display it in a slide show and ask yourself what carries the bulk of your message. If most of your message is in the text,

Continued ▮▶

PART

II

The Right Tool
for the Job

MASTERING TROUBLESHOOTING CONTINUED

you've missed the boat. Text—the on-screen text in bullets, paragraphs, notes, and titles—and the script you recite (or wing, depending on your style) should be **supporting** what the audience is viewing. With the brain, sight goes right in, but hearing has to be decoded and processed. Don't make your audience read your message. Use your multimedia resources to show it.

Start with the end in mind. Presentations can be given for all kinds of reasons. Whatever your reasons are—whether you are there to inform, entertain, enlighten, motivate, inspire, or educate—keep your goal in mind throughout the presentation. Your voice, your expression, and your body movements should all be in alignment with your goal. Everything about you communicates something to your audience, so stay focused to make sure that you're sending the right message.

Presentation Special Features

Several of PowerPoint's newest features add to your ability to present. In previous versions of PowerPoint, you had an on-screen drawing feature that let you write notes or circle and underline things to visually emphasize points on the slide during your presentation. The on-screen drawing feature has been enhanced in PowerPoint so that you can choose colors in a variety of places, making it easier for you to get just the right color contrast for your on-screen notes.

 TIP In some cases, you may want to remove the drawing pointer altogether. Press Ctrl+H to hide the pointer while it is inactive on this slide, or press Ctrl+A to hide the pointer for the rest of the presentation. If you hide the pointer and then want to redisplay it later, press Ctrl+A to return the pointer to the display.

PowerPoint includes other features, as well, including the new Meeting Minder—a note-taking utility that allows you to take notes while you present, assign them priorities, and even export them to Microsoft Word so that you can use them again without retyping them.

TIP For more information on working with Meeting Minder notes, see "Creating On-the-Spot Notes with Meeting Minder," later in this chapter.

Finally, a presentation conferencing feature makes it possible for you to give your presentation over a network, so you can get feedback from a number of sources while you're still in the development stages of your presentation. Or if you've completed the presentation and need to present to seven top executives scattered across the world, you can use PowerPoint's broadcasting features to actually link everyone up and present in real time through the wonders of telecommunication.

Drawing on Screen

One of the most interesting things about PowerPoint's display possibilities is the addition of an on-screen marker you can use to annotate your slides during a presentation. Suppose that you are explaining the pecking order of a new division in your corporation and have an organizational chart displayed on screen. If someone in the audience doesn't understand how a project moves from one department to another, you can use the on-screen drawing feature to help highlight points while you talk.

To start drawing on screen, press Ctrl+P, and start moving the mouse on screen. Or if you prefer, you can click the right mouse button to display the slide show pop-up menu and click Point Options ➢ Pen.

You can choose the Pen Color at several different points. In the Set Up Show dialog box (display the dialog box by choosing Slide Show ➢ Set Up Show), click the Pen Color drop-down arrow, and choose the color you want. If you're already running the presentation, display the pop-up menu, choose Pointer Options, and select Pen Color, as shown in Figure 8.17.

 TIP Go ahead and scribble on your slides—those on-screen markings aren't recorded. The next time you give the presentation, they will be as good as new.

FIGURE 8.17

Choosing a new pen color in the middle of a presentation

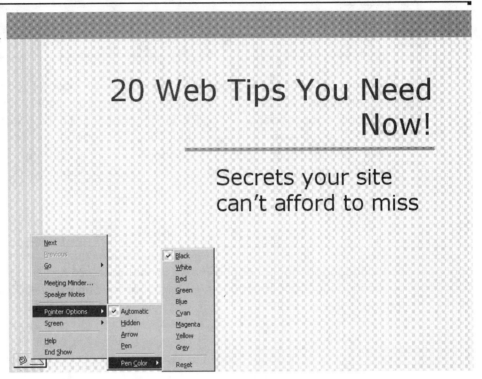

Creating On-the-Spot Notes with Meeting Minder

In some situations, you may be giving your presentation as part of a small brainstorming session. Your coworkers may be evaluating the presentation itself, giving you pointers or suggesting additional information to include or points you could clarify. Or you may be gathering information for the next stages of a project, taking notes, and deciding on the next logical step in your reach for a particular goal.

Whatever the scenario, PowerPoint now includes a feature called Meeting Minder that makes it easy for you to take notes during the presentation. Once you record the notes, they stay with the presentation (although, by default, they're not visible on your slides). You can, however, export the notes to a Word document, or you can move them to the Notes Pages of your presentation and print them with your slides.

To take notes during a presentation, click the right mouse button, and choose Meeting Minder from the pop-up menu that appears. If you're not currently in a presentation, choose Tools ➤ Meeting Minder and the Meeting Minder dialog box will appear, as shown in Figure 8.18. Enter the notes as necessary in the Meeting Minutes page. When you're finished, click OK to return to the presentation.

FIGURE 8.18

Displaying the Meeting Minder dialog box

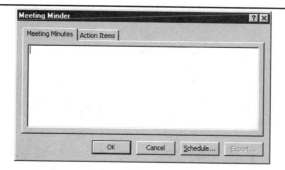

 NOTE If you have already entered notes in the Meeting Minder, the notes attached to your current presentation will appear. Otherwise, the Meeting Minder dialog box will be blank.

 TIP We've all been there—sometimes meetings turn into exercises in futility, where everyone voices his or her opinion about a topic and nothing really gets done or decided. The Meeting Minder includes a tab for Action Items, where you can record and prioritize the most important issues discussed and the things you most need to take action on.

Adding Meeting Minutes

Especially when you are working in a group, you'll find it helpful to keep track of your project and the tasks it requires. The Meeting Minutes tab of the Meeting Minder can help you keep your thoughts tied to the items you need to act on in order to get the presentation done. Figure 8.19 shows sample notes added to the Meeting Minutes tab.

PART

II

The Right Tool
for the Job

FIGURE 8.19

*Taking notes in
Meeting Minutes*

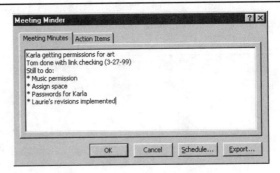

Exporting Meeting Minder Notes to Word

Sometimes the information you come up with in a meeting can be really beneficial. Perhaps someone came up with a new slogan, a new topic to introduce, or a new way of handling or solving a particular challenge. If you've captured the notes in the Meeting Minder, you can easily export the notes to Word, so you can circulate the ideas in memos to the necessary people to get things done.

When you want to export Meeting Minder notes, open the Meeting Minder, and display the page of notes you want to export. Then click the Export button in the lower right corner of the dialog box. A pop-up box appears, as shown in Figure 8.20.

The first option—Send Meeting Minutes and Action Items to Microsoft Word—is selected by default. When you click the Export Now button, Microsoft Word starts, and a new document is opened, with your note text inserted. Remember to save the file by choosing File ➤ Save before you exit Word.

FIGURE 8.20

*Exporting Meeting
Minder notes to
Microsoft Word*

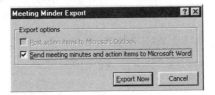

 TIP When you export the notes from Meeting Minder, the notes from *all* of your presentation slides are exported into the Word file. If you only want to keep some of the notes, you can select and delete any unwanted text with normal text-editing operations.

Presentation Comments and Review

PowerPoint allows you to add your very own custom "sticky notes" to presentations, reminding yourself of work to be done, changes to be made, or suggestions to be implemented. Later, you can use Microsoft Outlook to e-mail the note to another person on your work team, if you choose.

To add comments to your presentation, make sure you're in Normal View, then open the Insert menu, and choose Comment. A small yellow note appears in the upper left corner of the presentation page, with the name of the registered user already entered. A short Review toolbar also appears, with seven tools you can use as you add and use notes: Insert Comment, Show/Hide Comments, Previous Comment, Next Comment, Delete Comment, Create Microsoft Outlook Task, and Send To Mail Recipient (as Attachment) (see Figure 8.21). To add the note, simply type your comment. When you're finished, click outside the note area.

PART

II

The Right Tool
for the Job

FIGURE 8.21

Adding a sticky note to a presentation page

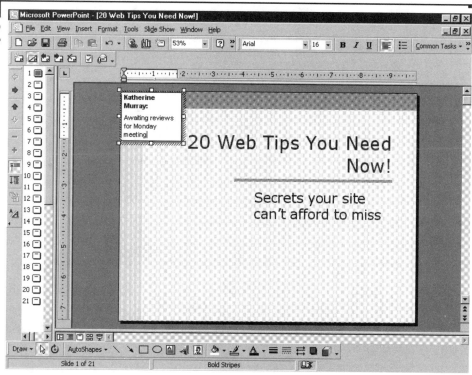

Presentation Collaborating

PowerPoint makes it simple for you to work with others as you build your presentation whether you work with a team on site or with a team spread out in offices on separate continents. By using the Online Collaboration feature, you rely on Microsoft NetMeeting to set up online conferencing as you view, review, and remark on the presentation under construction. To start the online collaboration process, open the Tools menu, and choose Online Collaboration. A pop-up menu appears, giving you the choice of Meet Now, Schedule Meeting, or Web Discussions.

When you choose Meet Now, PowerPoint calls on Microsoft NetMeeting, and the NetMeeting information screen appears if you've never used NetMeeting before (see Figure 8.22). Fill in your information (make sure you're online first), and click OK. NetMeeting locates the server you selected. (The others participating in your conference need to go to the same server as well.) Scroll through the list, and click the names of your collaborators; then click Call to initiate contact.

FIGURE 8.22

PowerPoint jump-starts NetMeeting to take care of the online collaboration work.

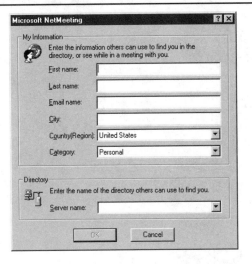

When you choose Web Discussions from the Online Collaboration submenu, you are presented with a Wizard that helps you set up discussion servers (see Figure 8.23). Enter the information from your system administrator or ISP; then click OK to continue.

PART

II

FIGURE 8.23

You can also participate in Web discussion groups related to your presentation topic or any topic of your choosing. But first you need to enter the server information provided by your system administrator or ISP.

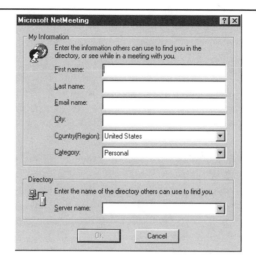

Chapter Summary

This chapter has introduced you to the ins and outs of presenting your PowerPoint Slide Show. PowerPoint makes displaying your slides easy, and if you are working in Slide Sorter view, all the tools you need are there on the screen within easy reach. New presentation features, such as the Meeting Minder and Presentation Conferencing, make it easy for you to enhance the concept, content, and charisma of your presentation by collecting feedback from a variety of sources.

The next chapter explains how you can customize the color selections in your presentation to produce just the right mix of color for the effect you want.

The Right Tool
for the Job

PART III

Quintessential PowerPoint

LEARN TO:

- *Work with color in your presentations*

- *Print slides and handouts*

- *Turn your presentation into a Web site*

- *Manage multimedia files*

- *Rehearse, present, and evaluate information*

CHAPTER <u>9</u>

Coloring Your Presentation

L ife is colorful—there's no denying that. If you want to bring life into your presentations, color is one of the most effective and enlivening tools you have, whether it's in the form of photographs, video, or background illustrations.

If you use color well, you can dazzle your audience. If you aren't particularly adept at mixing and matching colors, you could drive your viewers batty (or worse, give them headaches). Recognizing that we're not all equipped with a natural instinct for putting colors together, PowerPoint includes sets of colors known as *color schemes* with each template or presentation design. However, even though the colors for the background, text, graphics, and clip art are already set, you can change any or all of the colors on your own. You can also easily change your color presentation to a black-and-white presentation to see what your slides will look like when printed on a single-color printer.

This chapter explains how you can do a variety of things with color, including choosing a new color in a color scheme, creating your own colors, and using special illustrations for background color in your presentation.

How Do You Use Color?

Using color to your best advantage is one of the surest ways you have of grabbing and holding your audience's attention. Even though PowerPoint sets up the colors for you automatically, here are a few examples of situations in which you might want to change the colors PowerPoint assigns:

- You want to change selected words in a bulleted list to highlight them, as Figure 9.1 shows. (For example, you might change the key words from black to red so they stand out against the background.)

- You need to change the background of the slide to better complement the main colors in a color photograph you're using on the current slide.

- You want to choose a different color for the headline text to distinguish it from the main text.

- You'd like to create a custom-drawn logo that you want to fill with a color not included in the original color scheme.

 TIP Changing colors isn't just about color—you can also change the pattern, texture, and shading of the colors you use to create a myriad of effects.

FIGURE 9.1

You can change the color of selected words to highlight them.

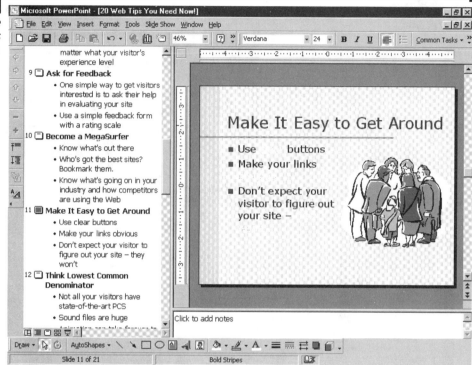

A Shortcut to Color Choices: Templates

If you haven't yet taken advantage of the templates that come with PowerPoint, look them over now. The templates—also known as *presentation designs*—have all the colors preset for you. You can display the variety of templates and presentation designs available by choosing File ➢ New and clicking the Design Templates tab. To see the basic colors of the different designs, click the design file once to display it in the Preview window (see Figure 9.2). When you've got the one you want, click OK.

Templates also can help you find which colors go together—you can learn from the combinations put together by the developers of the software. If you find a set of colors you like, your color problems are over: PowerPoint has done it for you. Turn to Chapter 2 for more information on choosing and using templates.

PART

III

Quintessential
PowerPoint

You can scroll through the presentation designs to choose the color scheme you like.

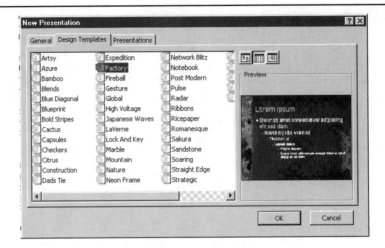

 TIP PowerPoint includes a "consistent color" feature that helps you keep the same colors in your various Office programs. When you copy a shape from Word to PowerPoint, for example, you can be sure the green rectangle you created in Word is the same green in PowerPoint.

Making a Fast Color Change

When you know you want to change a color and are ready to change it, two options allow you to make your color choices quickly: one is to change the color of text, and the other is to change the color of the inside or outside of a text box, graphic object, or chart.

Changing Text Color

The most common color change involves changing the color of text. To change text color, highlight the text you want to change, and choose Format ➤ Font to open the Font dialog box. Click the Color drop-down arrow to see the color choices for changing the text (see Figure 9.3). If you aren't happy with the choices you have, display more colors by clicking More Colors.

TIP If you want to highlight a word, you don't need to select it. Just position the cursor in the word before you choose Format ➤ Font. PowerPoint will change the color of the word at the cursor position.

After you've selected the color you want, click OK. PowerPoint applies the new color to the selected text.

FIGURE 9.3

Changing text color with Format ➤ Font

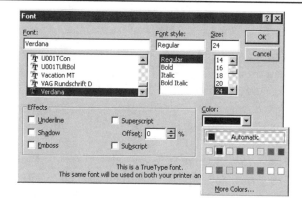

Changing Object Color: Inside

To change the color of an object, first click it to select it, and then click the Fill Color tool in the Drawing toolbar.

The Fill Color tool displays a pop-up color menu with a variety of choices, as shown in Figure 9.4. You can select from the displayed colors (representing only a small part of the entire selection available). To change the shade, pattern, texture, or background color, click Fill Effects. If you want color choices other than those shown in the displayed palette, click More Fill Colors. When you make your selection, the inside of the object selected changes to the new color.

 TIP You can also use the Format menu to change the color of an object. Select the object, and then choose Format ➤ Colors and Lines to change the internal and external colors of the object. To change the entire color scheme of the presentation, choose Format ➤ Slide Color Scheme.

PART

III

Quintessential
PowerPoint

FIGURE 9.4

Displaying the menu
for Fill Color

Changing Object Color: Outside

The Line Color tool changes the lines in the object. If you've selected a graphic, chart element, or text box, the line that surrounds the object changes, not the contents. This means that if you click a piece of clip art and expect to see all the lines in the drawing change when you choose red in the Line Color palette, you're going to be disappointed. Only the border of the object will change.

TIP   What does No Fill mean? In the Fill Color pop-up menu, No Fill means that the selected object takes on the color of the background—or is transparent. In other words, when you've selected a text box in which the text appears to be placed right on the background of the slide (as opposed to appearing in a colored box layered on top of the background), No Fill has been selected as the Fill Color. To do away with the line surrounding the object, choose No Line in the Line Color pop-up menu.

Again, you can choose the color or other option you want from the displayed pop-up menu; PowerPoint changes the selected object to reflect the modifications you made.

What If You Want More Colors?

Whenever you have displayed the Font dialog box to change text color, the Fill Color pop-up menu to change the internal color of an object, or the Line Color pop-up menu to change the lines surrounding an object, you have the option of selecting More Colors.

Clicking More Colors displays a "honeycomb" of available colors from which you can choose (see Figure 9.5). The Colors dialog box contains a wide array of color choices. The current color is highlighted in the palette and appears in a preview box in the lower right corner of the dialog box.

FIGURE 9.5

Choosing a color from the Colors dialog box

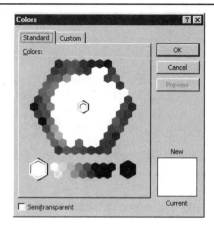

The Standard tab of the Colors dialog box broadens your color horizons, but there are still more colors to see. You can define your own color by choosing the Custom tab. This lands you squarely in the world of custom color definition.

Creating Custom Colors

It's not likely that you'll search through all of PowerPoint's color schemes without finding the one you want. If you're particular about the color you need (or if you're trying to replicate something that needs to be a certain color, such as a company logo or an important piece of art), you do have the option of mixing a custom color.

When you choose the Custom tab of the Colors dialog box, you're presented with a mixing board on which you can create a new color, as shown in Figure 9.6.

The crosshair shows the current color as well as the levels of red, green, and blue it contains and its hue, saturation, and luminance settings. You can create a custom color in either of two ways:

- Click the color scale at any point where it displays the color you want.
- Manually adjust the Red, Green, and Blue settings by entering new numeric settings.

To choose a new color by clicking the color scale, position the pointer on the color you want, and click the mouse pointer. The New area of the box in the bottom corner of the dialog box changes to reflect your choice, while the Current area continues showing the current color.

PART

III

Quintessential
PowerPoint

FIGURE 9.6

*Defining a
custom color*

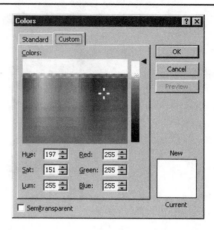

If you want to adjust the settings by altering the amount of red, green, and blue in the mixed color, click the spin buttons beside the color you want to change, or type in a new value. As you make the change, the crosshair moves to show the color you are selecting, and the New area of the box reflects your choice in comparison with the color you have chosen to replace (the Current color).

NOTE   Although you'll probably find it much easier to use the crosshair cursor to change color mixes, typing in values lets you duplicate a specific color, such as "dialog box gray" (192 192 192).

When you've got the color you want, click OK to add it to the selection of colors at the bottom of the Fill Color pop-up menu.

Changing Entire Color Schemes

The color scheme of your presentation defines the color of different elements in your presentation:

- Slide background
- Title text
- Smaller text and lines

- Fill colors
- Three different accent colors for chart elements

 TIP One of the greatest things about using a color scheme is that you can easily search and replace one color with another. If you want to replace all blue-green with olive, for example, you can do that with a few quick clicks of the mouse.

Viewing and Changing the Current Color Scheme

A presentation that you've begun already has its own color scheme. How do you find out which one it's using?

Open your presentation, and choose Format ➤ Slide Color Scheme. The Color Scheme dialog box appears, as shown in Figure 9.7. The Color Schemes area shows you what color schemes are currently available—the one currently in use has a border around it, indicating that it is selected. Take a few minutes and consider the variety of colors used. Do they give you enough contrast? Do you like the colors shown for chart elements? For text? Is the background color the color you want? If not, you can change a color or create your own mix.

 TIP Want to see which color is assigned to which element? Click the Custom tab. The Scheme Colors area shows you which color is used for title text, for text and lines, for the background, and so on.

By default, you have several different color schemes—color and black-and-white— you can use right away. You can create up to a total of sixteen schemes for each presentation. For more information on creating your own color scheme, see "Creating a Custom Color Scheme," later in this chapter.

To choose a different color scheme for your presentation, click the one you want, and click either Apply to apply the new colors to the currently displayed slide only or Apply to All to apply the color to all slides in the presentation. PowerPoint makes the change and returns you to the presentation.

FIGURE 9.7

The Standard tab of the Color Scheme dialog box

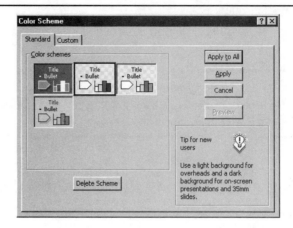

Creating a Custom Color Scheme

If you want to create a custom color scheme, click the Custom tab in the Color Scheme dialog box. You'll see the basic set of colors you can choose from to create the new color scheme (see Figure 9.8).

To choose a new color for an element, select the element you want to change (for example, Title Text) and then click the Change Color button. The Title Text Color dialog box appears—it's the same dialog box you saw when you selected the Custom tab of the Colors dialog box. Choose the new color for the title text by clicking the color in the honeycomb, or create a new color on the Custom tab, as explained in the Creating Custom Colors discussion earlier. Click OK to return to the Color Scheme dialog box.

When you're finished making changes to the color scheme, you can save it by clicking the Add as Standard Scheme button. This saves the color choices you have made and displays the new color scheme in the Standard tab of the Color Scheme dialog box.

To make the color changes in the presentation, click Apply to All to change the title text color for the entire presentation, or click Apply to change the color for the currently displayed slide only.

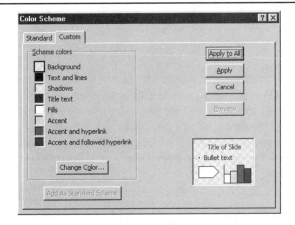

FIGURE 9.8

Choosing colors for a custom color scheme

Using Apply to All to Globally Replace a Color

There may be times when you are mostly happy with a color scheme but want to replace a certain color. Apply to All, available in the Color Scheme dialog box, will seek out every occurrence of a color, even an accent color used for a text item, and replace it with the new color you have chosen.

For example, suppose that you like using a particular shade of pink against a sky blue background. However, after getting raised eyebrows from your coworkers ("Do you think Henderson is going to go for *hot pink*?") and a little doubt of your own, you change your mind about the color. Maybe you'd better use something a little more traditional.

To change that color throughout your presentation, display the Custom tab of the Color Scheme dialog box, click the color, and choose the Change Color button. Then choose the new color you want to replace the hot pink with, and click Apply to All. PowerPoint then finds the hot pink in the presentation and replaces it with the color you selected.

NOTE If you have assigned a color to more than one element, you must change the color for each type of element individually.

As you work with color schemes, you'll realize how drastic a change you can make with a few clicks of the mouse. You can take a finished presentation and completely change its look with a simple change of background or text color. This is helpful if you travel to different locations to present in places where the lighting is not within your control. You can quickly change from lighter to darker backgrounds to suit the lighting conditions.

 TIP You can use accent colors to apply color to any special elements on your slides—items you draw yourself, pen color, object borders, even the background for clip art or charts—without using a color that's already being used for something else. This gives your presentation a consistent look and feel and helps you fine-tune your color choices.

Working in Black-and-White

To convert any color presentation to black-and-white, you need only to click the Grayscale Preview button in Standard toolbar, or you can choose View ➢ Black and White.

Why would you use black-and-white? For starters, you can produce a presentation with simpler hardware requirements: you can print out the slides, copy them to transparencies, and give the presentation with just an overhead projector; you may want to double-check the appearance of the handouts for your presentation; or perhaps your ultimate goal is not to actually give a presentation at all but to explain your message with handouts. Even if none of these scenarios apply to you, having a good balance of dark and light colors gives your slides and printouts a more polished, professional look.

When you click the Grayscale Preview button (in the Tools palette available to the right of Font box), the presentation screen changes to black-and-white. A small Color View window appears in the upper right corner of the presentation that shows the presentation's original color scheme (see Figure 9.9).

FIGURE 9.9

When you view the presentation in black-and-white, a Color View window shows you the slide as it appears in color.

TIP When you're working with the Color Scheme dialog box, you can choose a black-and-white color scheme from the Standard tab. Click the color scheme, and then click OK.

Setting Black-and-White Options

You still have many tone options, even in a black-and-white presentation. Many shades of gray are available in the Fill Color and Line Color pop-up menus. You also have the option of choosing black text on a white background or white text on a darker background.

To see the options you have for black-and-white, click the object you want to work with in the black-and-white slide. (If you haven't activated B&W View, do so now.) Now, right-click the object to open its pop-up menu. Choose Black and White. Another menu appears, as shown in Figure 9.10.

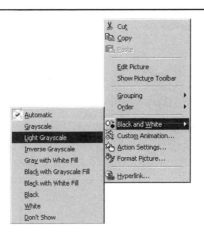

This menu appears whether you have selected a text object, graphic, or chart. As explained in Table 9.1, the different options enable you to control just the right mix of grays, blacks, and white.

PART

III

Quintessential
PowerPoint

TABLE 9.1: BLACK-AND-WHITE OPTIONS	
Option	**Description**
Automatic	Automatically sets the black-and-white scale as the slide is converted from color to black-and-white.
Grayscale	Displays the selected object in shades of dark gray.
Light Grayscale	Displays the object in shades of light gray.
Inverse Grayscale	Displays the object with its colors inverted, so light gray becomes dark gray and dark gray becomes light gray.
Gray with White Fill	Outlines the selected object with gray and fills it with white.
Black with Grayscale Fill	Displays lines in black and shows other object elements in gray.
Black with White Fill	Outlines the object in black and fills the internal area with white.
Black	Draws and fills the entire object with black.
White	Draws and fills the entire object with white.
Don't Show	Hides the selected object.

Do I Need a Black-and-White Color Scheme or Just a Black-and-White View?

Whether you need a change in color scheme or just a grayscale view of the color scheme depends on your final product. If it's your goal to produce a black-and-white presentation, either for print or for screen display, your best bet is to use a black-and-white color scheme. This enables you to easily control the different grays, blacks, and whites used for the different elements in your presentation. If you prefer, you can use the Custom tab to create your own black-and-white palette.

If you're more interested in checking out how the presentation will look in print than you are in creating the most effective on-screen look, use the B&W View button. When you're working in color, it's easy to distinguish between shades. When everything is converted to shades of gray, subtle differences may be harder to see. You can control the grayscales to make the contrast greater by experimenting with the black-and-white options in the pop-up menu.

Recoloring Clip Art

Those of us who were at the candy machine when art talent was passed out are really grateful for clip art. It makes our presentations sparkle, adds humor, and generally provides interesting and informational effects we'd have a tough time creating on our own.

But sometimes the art doesn't come in just the way you want it. You really wish that trumpet were green instead of yellow, or you want the tree to be orange instead of green.

PowerPoint's Picture toolbar makes it easy to recolor clip art. Click the object; then, if the Picture toolbar does not display, right-click the object to open its pop-up menu. Now choose Show Picture toolbar. To change the colors, choose this toolbar's Recolor Picture tool, as shown in Figure 9.11. This displays the Recolor Picture dialog box. You can either select multiple items to recolor or simply exchange all of one color (for instance, white, like the white keyboard and drum) with another color to change them all at once. You don't have to ungroup the object unless you want to apply recoloring to only specific items in the group. If you don't ungroup, the color change will be applied to all items in the group with the same original color.

FIGURE 9.11

Choosing the Recolor Picture tool

The Recolor Picture dialog box appears, as shown in Figure 9.12.

FIGURE 9.12

You can recolor the fill or line color of the selected object.

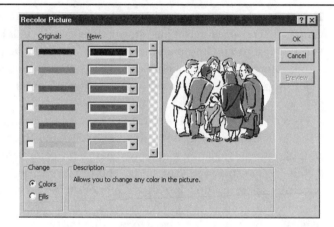

Indicate whether you want to change the Colors or Fills of the object in the lower left corner of the dialog box. Fills affects only the internal color fills—lines are not affected by the change. If you choose Colors, you can change any color in the picture.

Next, click the check box of the color you want to change. In the Original column, you see the color of the object as it was before you changed it. In the New column, choose the new color you want to use.

To change the trumpet from yellow to green, for example, you'd select Colors as the Change option; then scroll down to the yellow color, click its arrow, and select green from the pop-up color palette that appears. The preview window shows the change. When you're happy with the recoloring of the object, click OK.

 TIP You can use Recolor Picture to change colors in any line-art object, such as Clip Gallery clip art and Windows metafiles. You cannot, however, recolor bitmaps, such as photographs and video.

Working with Slide Backgrounds

Like a color scheme, the choice of a slide background sets off your presentation. Substantial offerings are available in PowerPoint.

Start with the presentation you want to change, and choose Format ➤ Background. The Background dialog box appears, as shown in Figure 9.13.

The Background dialog box

To choose a different color for the background, click the drop-down arrow in the selection box, just beneath the Background Fill display. As you see in Figure 9.14, a pop-up menu appears, similar to the one you see when you click the Fill Color or Line Color tools in the Drawing toolbar.

Choosing a new color for the presentation background

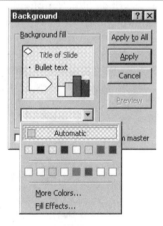

Using the color scheme colors displayed in the pop-up menu, you can create a unique effect with little effort. The color options speak for themselves: your background will be set to the color you choose.

Another option in the pop-up menu, More Colors, displays the honeycomb palette that we've discussed before, in which you can choose just the color you want. Make your choice, and click OK to return to the Background dialog box.

The Fill Effects option displays a dialog box with four tabs—Gradient, Texture, Pattern, and Picture—which are fun to work with and can produce really dramatic effects. But be warned: this is your *background*. You don't want to distract your audience from your central message.

 TIP If you want to blank out the background—removing any graphic elements, logos, or other artwork you may have positioned there—click the Omit Background Graphics from the Master check box at the bottom of the Background dialog box.

Shaded Backgrounds

When you choose the Gradient tab in the Fill Effects dialog box, you can choose how you want the background shaded (see Figure 9.15). The color of your choice is blended with black, white, or another color of your choice along a continuous gradient, producing the effect of day fading to night across the screen (or a variation on that idea). You can either pick your colors or choose from a menu of preset combinations. When you've got a color combination you like, choose the orientation of the gradation (for example, horizontal, vertical, or diagonal), and click OK.

FIGURE 9.15

Creating a shaded slide background

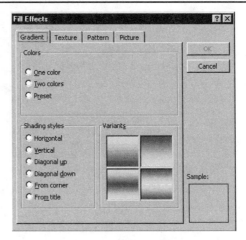

Textured Backgrounds

Textures can produce a really cool effect—try them at least once. You can choose from a wide variety of textures that look like wood, stone, cloth, or even water drops.

To see the textures, click the Texture tab in the Fill Effects dialog box, as shown in Figure 9.16. You can scroll down to see many more choices.

FIGURE 9.16

The Texture tab shows you what PowerPoint textures look like.

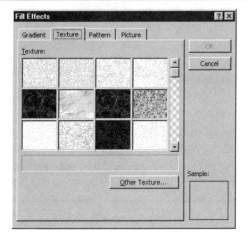

 TIP You can also add textured backgrounds not included in PowerPoint to your presentations. Click the Other Texture button to display the Select Texture dialog box, and navigate to the drive and folder that stores the background file you want to use. Click the file you want, and click OK to add the file. The file is then added to the Texture tab in the Fill Effects dialog box and is available for future presentations.

After you've selected the texture you want, click OK. PowerPoint then applies the new texture to the sample shown in the Background dialog box so you can decide whether you want to apply it to your presentation.

Patterned Backgrounds

When you choose the Pattern tab, you create a pattern by combining two colors of your choice according to any one of 48 different pattern options, as shown in Figure 9.17.

PART

III

Quintessential
PowerPoint

FIGURE 9.17

The Pattern tab enables you to add a pattern to your presentation background.

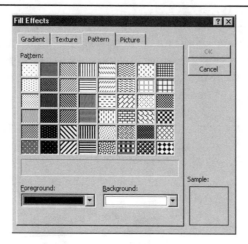

You can choose the colors you want as the Foreground and Background choices. Try reversing them or choosing other colors to experiment with the effects.

TIP Make your selection, and click Preview to assess the change before you actually make it. The background changes. (You can see it even though the Pattern Fill dialog box is still open on the screen.) If you like the look, click OK. If you don't, change it and Preview again.

When you've made your choices, click OK to return to the Custom Background dialog box.

Picture Backgrounds

The final tab in the Fill Effects dialog box lets you use a picture from another source as your background. Click Select Picture, as shown in Figure 9.18, to go to the Select Picture dialog box, similar to the Open dialog box. Choose the drive, folder, and file type you want. All Pictures includes most graphic file types, or you can choose the specific type you want (.jpg, .tif, .gif, etc.) or All Files.

FIGURE 9.18

With the Picture tab you can import backgrounds from outside PowerPoint.

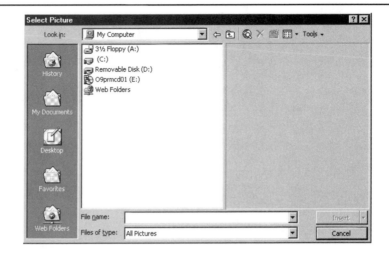

Chapter Summary

PowerPoint makes it easy for you to leave the color choices to the professionals. But when you want to make other color decisions or further customize your presentation by adding a shaded, textured, or otherwise customized background, you can easily make changes to PowerPoint's color schemes. The Color Scheme dialog box gives you the power to easily make subtle updates or sweeping changes to a large group of slides.

This chapter has explored the various ways in which you can modify and enhance your use of color in your presentations. The next chapter will help you prepare the handouts you'll print to accompany your presentations.

PART

III

Quintessential
PowerPoint

CHAPTER 10

Printing Slides and Handouts

Even though your audience may be dazzled by on-screen effects and riveted by interesting video and colorful designs, there's something convincing about having printed pages in hand.

Think about it. When you're considering buying a new car, you might dial up an online service and look at a few pictures of new cars. You might even send away for a CD-ROM demo disk from a car manufacturer that shows your favorite models in any color you imagine, with any number of options you envision. You might even receive a custom presentation originally produced in PowerPoint. But until you've got some sales literature in your hands—something you can take to your desk and look through at your own pace (perhaps again and again), you're probably not going to feel comfortable writing that check.

When you're creating a presentation, the printouts you create along with the presentation can be almost as important as the presentation itself. The handouts you create do the presenting for you when you're not around to do it yourself.

Today's affordable color printing technology makes it easier than ever to produce slides and/or handouts in full color, close to what appears on the screen. This chapter introduces you to the benefits of printing and describes procedures for printing slides and handouts to accompany your PowerPoint presentations.

Why Print Your Presentations?

You may wonder why you need to take the time to print handouts. Won't the audience see what you're doing? Why would they want the same thing in their laps? Here are a few ways you can benefit from creating handouts to accompany your presentation:

- In some cases, the presentation you give may *be* the printed presentation. If you don't have the means to display the presentation for a group on the screen, you can still print and copy the slides onto transparencies. Or you could create a set of slides, printed and either bound or stapled, to hand out. The actual presentation, in this case, is really made with the printed pages. (If you can make color printouts, so much the better.)

- Your printed presentation can travel farther than you can. Suppose you are giving a presentation on a new product line to the top fifteen sales managers in your company. They are flying in from all over the country, representing a sales force of over 100 representatives nationwide. Each of these managers will attend your presentation and then go back to their regions, prepared to brief their salespeople. With printouts, the managers can show the slides to the salespeople, answer questions, and stay much closer to your original message because they've got it right there with them and aren't relying on memory to get it right.

- Printouts are easy advertising. If you're competing for attention with a number of other vendors, you can use your printouts not only to remind people of your message but to get your contact information into their hands. Make sure the logo is on all the slides, and put the company name and numbers in the header or footer. A little corporate ID can go a long way.

- If you are working on a group project and need feedback from coworkers before you continue, you can print handouts of the presentation and invite written comments from the people on your team. You can then mull over the changes you want to make based on the comments made on the printouts and easily implement any necessary revisions.

TIP If you are working on a group project and are hooked up to a network, you can use PowerPoint's presentation conferencing feature to give the presentation to several people on your team at the same time. Team members can use the pen feature to write comments on the slides so you get immediate written feedback without printing. To find out more about presentation conferencing, see Chapter 8, "Finishing the Slide Show."

Getting Started

PowerPoint gives you a number of choices for your printouts: color or black-and-white, single slides or several slides per page. You can also add frames around the slides or scale the slide to fill the entire page. You'll make all these choices in the Print dialog box.

PART

III

TIP The type of printer you have will, to some degree, affect the kind of printout you can make. If you have a single-color printer, for example, the chances that you're going to get a full-color printout are pretty remote! Check out the type of hardware you have available before you invest a lot of time in planning your printouts.

Printing Decisions You Need to Make

Before you start the printing process, consider the answers to the following questions (because sooner or later, PowerPoint will want to know what to do about each of these issues):

- Will you be producing the presentation both on screen and on paper?
- How large do you want the slides to be?
- Do you want the slides to be printed in Portrait or Landscape orientation? How about your notes, handouts, and outlines?

 NOTE *Orientation* is a typographical term used to describe the way the item is printed on the page. *Portrait* refers to the standard, 8½ x 11-inch format; *Landscape* refers to the lengthwise, 11 x 8½-inch format. If you're printing a single slide on a page and want it to fill the available space, choose Landscape orientation.

- How many copies do you want?
- Will you print to a file or to the printer?
- Do you want to print only the current slide, the complete presentation, or a selected range of slides?

PowerPoint uses the options you choose in the Page Setup and the Print dialog boxes to get the answers it needs to these questions. The next section explains how to check the setup of the slides for your presentation.

A Few Printing Ideas

- When you need to conserve space in your printouts, print slides three to a page. Make sure you use the header and footer to convey any important contact information about your business or project, and number your pages so your readers won't get lost.
- Print sets of full-page slides, and put them in folders or envelopes for your sales managers to deliver to their salespeople. Back in their regions, they can use the printouts to create transparencies for their own training sessions.

 TIP Use PowerPoint's Pack and Go Wizard to send copies of your actual on-screen presentation back with the sales managers. For more information about Pack and Go, see Chapter 11.

- Print slides with notes pages to help others give the presentation at a later time, independent of you.

- If color printing is at a premium in your office, print the first—or cover—slide in color, and then print the rest in black-and-white. (If color is available for all slides, of course, your output will look much better.)

- Unless you're dealing with guarded information, print hidden slides, too, when you print the presentation. That way, audience members who need the additional information can look through it on their own time.

Checking Page Setup for Slides

One of PowerPoint's biggest benefits is its flexibility. You can choose Page Setup options for your slides before you begin, while working on a presentation, or after you finish. Whenever you change the slide size or choose a different orientation, PowerPoint changes the current presentation to reflect your selection.

Display the Slide Setup options by choosing File ➤ Page Setup. The Page Setup dialog box appears (see Figure 10.1).

FIGURE 30.23

The Page Setup dialog box

PART

III

Quintessential
PowerPoint

Choosing Page Size

The first option in the Page Setup dialog box is Slides Sized For. You use this option to tell PowerPoint how large an area you've got to work with. You can choose from the following choices:

- On-Screen Show (the default)
- Letter Paper (8.5 x 11 inches)
- A4 Paper (210 x 297mm)
- 35mm Slides
- Overhead
- Banner
- Custom

To choose a page size, click the drop-down arrow to display the list box, and click the page size you want. When will you use the different page sizes? The sizes for 35mm Slides and Overhead are slightly different—Overhead is a bit smaller. With Custom, you can enter the dimensions you want to print. A4 Paper is European letter-sized paper and can be used only if your printer is equipped for it.

 NOTE You may also be able to change the paper size and orientation for your particular printer by using the Options button in the Printers dialog box, but if you plan to use an irregular page size, be sure to specify it by clicking the Custom option in the Page Setup dialog box.

Changing Slide Width and Height

You can also change the width and height yourself, if you're concerned about meeting a particular measurement. When you choose one of the other page sizes, the Width and Height settings change automatically. Change the Width or Height settings by adjusting the values in the box, clicking either the radio buttons, or typing a new value.

 TIP If you make changes and then decide to return to the default settings, open the Slides Sized For box, and click On-Screen Show. The values are returned to normal.

You may never need to worry about the preset size of the slides in your presentation. As a general rule, though, if you use a custom paper size, make sure that for a slide printout you leave at least a one-inch margin all around the edge of the slide to leave room for binding and stapling. If you're planning on printing notes, you don't need to calculate and resize the slide in the Width and Height box; PowerPoint will do that for you at print time.

Choosing Orientation

The Page Setup dialog box gives you two different options for the orientation settings. When printing slides, you might want to use one kind of orientation (slides are typically printed in landscape orientation), but when printing handouts, you might prefer the more traditional portrait.

When you click a different orientation setting, the Width and Height settings are adjusted automatically to reflect the change (see Figure 10.2). The shape of the background will change, but otherwise the slide's appearance on screen will not change.

Changing the orientation

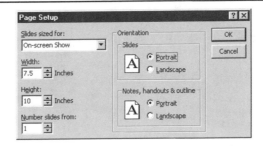

When you're finished with all the Page Setup settings, click OK to return to Slide view. Now you're ready to tackle printing basics.

Numbering Slides

By default, PowerPoint does not put a page number on your presentation slides. To add one, choose View ➤ Header and Footer to add the number to the header or footer of the slide (see Figure 10.3). Click the Slide Number checkbox to add the number to the slide; then click Apply. When you return to Normal view, the page number is displayed in the lower-right corner of the slide (see Figure 10.4).

Add a slide number by displaying the Header and Footer dialog box and choosing the Slide number checkbox.

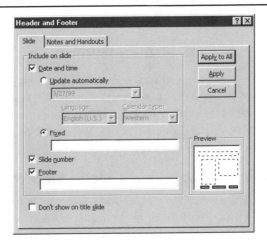

PART

III

Quintessential
PowerPoint

FIGURE 10.4

The slide number is positioned in the lower-right corner of the slide.

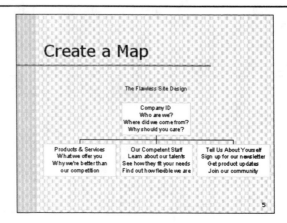

 TIP To insert slide numbers on every slide in the presentation, display the Header and Footer dialog box, click the Slide Number check box, and choose Apply to All.

 TIP I don't like the footer information showing up on the title slide of my presentations, when I'm making my first impression. To tell PowerPoint to skip displaying the slide number on that first slide, click the Don't Show on Title Slide checkbox in the lower-left corner of the Header and Footer dialog box.

Adding Headers and Footers

While you're here, you might as well think about the types of headers and footers you want on your slides and handouts. The header and footer on your slides can give important information about your company, your project, or yourself. You might include your company name or logo, the time and date, the name of the presentation, or other important information in the header or footer.

Adding the Date and Time to Slide Printouts

The first option in the Header and Footer dialog box enables you to add the date and time to your slide. Start by clicking the Date and Time check box. The Update Automatically and Fixed options become available. To add a date that changes to reflect the date of the print presentation, click the Update Automatically option, and choose the date and time style you want from the list that is displayed (see Figure 10.5).

FIGURE 10.5

Select the date and time you want from the Update Automatically list.

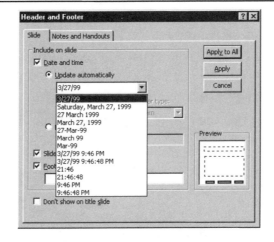

If you want to enter a date that remains the same no matter what the current date is, choose Fixed, and then enter the date you want to appear. The Preview box shows the position in which the date and time will be printed.

Adding a Footer to Slide Printouts

A footer is the information that prints at the bottom of the printed page. In Power-Point, you can add a footer to both your slide printouts and your notes and handouts.

To add a footer, simply click in the Footer check box. The text entry area becomes available, and you can type the information you want to include in the footer.

 WARNING Be sure to include only necessary information in the footer. Cramming too much information into the footer will detract from the effectiveness of your printouts.

When you're finished making choices for the slide printouts, click Apply to All to apply the new settings to the entire presentation, or click Apply to apply them only to the current slide.

PART

III

Quintessential
PowerPoint

Adding Headers and Footers to Notes and Handouts

The second tab of the Header and Footer dialog box enables you to make choices about the way your notes and handouts print (see Figure 10.6).

The Notes and Handouts tab is different than the Slide tab in three basic ways:

- You can enter text to the Header line.

- The Page Number option appears in place of the Slide Number option.

- The Apply button is missing. (You can only apply these settings to the entire presentation.)

Make your choices for the date, time, page number, header, and footer you want on your notes and handouts; then click Apply to All. You won't see the header or footer as you work with the presentation, but they will be there when you print.

FIGURE 10.6

The Notes and Handouts tab of the Header and Footer dialog box

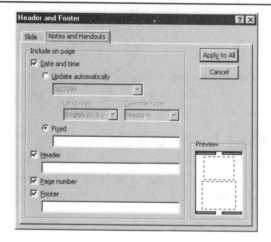

Printing the Presentation

In most cases, printing is a pretty simple process. If you've got all your settings specified and your printer set up, a quick print will probably take nothing more than pressing Ctrl+P and pressing Enter.

First, make sure you've got the right printer selected to receive your PowerPoint file. Choose File ➤ Print, or press Ctrl+P to open the Print dialog box shown in Figure 10.7.

FIGURE 10.7
The Print dialog box

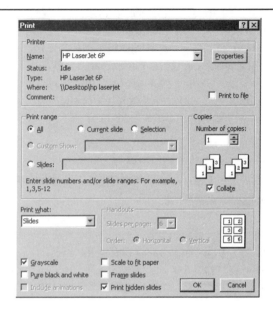

Selecting Your Printer

The first item at the top of the Print dialog box is the Name box, where you should see the name of your printer. If a printer other than the one you plan to use appears in the Name box, click the drop-down arrow beside the box, and choose your printer from the displayed list.

 NOTE If you don't see your printer listed in the Name list, you'll need to use the Windows Control Panel to add the printer driver for your particular printer.

To set options for your particular printer—such as the paper size or orientation—click the Properties button to the right of the Name box in the Print dialog box.

Choosing Print Options

The print options in the Print dialog box are fairly straightforward. Once you make sure you're ready to run with the right printer, you can choose which slides you want to print, select how you want them printed, and specify the number of copies you want.

PART

III

Quintessential
PowerPoint

The Print Range options control which slides in your presentation are printed. The first option, All, prints all the slides (notes, handouts, whatever) in the presentation. The Current Slide option prints only the slide that was selected when you displayed the Print dialog box. If you have created any custom shows for the presentation, the Custom Show box lets you print the materials for the custom show you want. The Slides option lets you choose a range of slides. To print slides 2 through 4, for example, you would enter in the Slides box:

2-4

To print two different ranges of slides, such as pages 2 through 4 and pages 7 and 8, you could enter those specifications in the Slides box like this:

2-4,7-8

 NOTE Don't add spaces before the second range (7–8 in the example above) or around the hyphens.

How Many Copies Do You Want?

You'll also need to decide how many copies of the presentation (or the range of slides you've selected) you want to produce. Type the number in the Copies: box or click the spin button to increase or decrease the quantity.

 TIP The first time you print a presentation or slide, print only one copy. This gives you the opportunity to check what you've done without using a great amount of paper in a first draft. When you've got the slide the way you want it, go ahead and make multiple copies.

If you want PowerPoint to collate—print in order—the multiple copies you've elected to make, be sure that the check mark appears in the Collate box. To copy multiples of the same page (for example, print ten copies of page 3 before you move on to ten copies of page 4), remove the check mark.

What Do You Want to Print?

When you've decided which slides you want to print, you need to think about the format in which you want them printed. You can print your slides four different ways: as slides, as handouts, as notes pages, and as an outline view. Table 10.1 describes each of these different print options.

TABLE 10.1: PRINT OPTIONS	
Option	**Description**
Slides	Prints each slide as it appears in Slide view.
Handouts	Gives you the option of printing up to six slides per page. You can choose whether you want the slides printed in horizontal or vertical order. (These options appear when you choose the Handouts option from the Print What list.)
Notes Pages	Prints the slide at the top of the page and the notes page in the bottom portion.
Outline View	Prints only the text of the presentation in outline form, as it appears in Outline view.

To choose the item you want to print, click the drop-down arrow in the Print What box. The drop-down list shown in Figure 10.8 appears. Scroll through the list, if necessary, and then click the item you want. PowerPoint enters it in the Print What box.

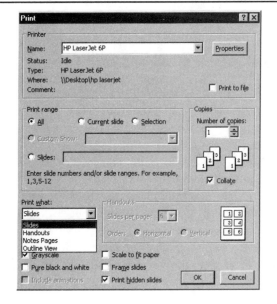

How Do You Want the Page Printed?

The final set of print options controls some of the more subtle print choices you may make concerning the way the slides are printed. Here's a quick overview of when you might use these additional options:

- If you are working with black-and-white slides or you are printing to a single-color printer, select the Grayscale option. This prints hues in shades of gray, giving contrast to your images and text.

- If gray areas make your printouts hard to read, click Pure Black & White to eliminate the gray tones.

- If you have animations placed on your slides, you can click the Include animations check box to include the opening image for the motion clip on your printout.

- If you are working with an irregular page size and are concerned about the size of the slide at print time, click Scale to Fit Paper. PowerPoint adjusts the size of the slide to fit the paper size. If you click Scale to Fit Paper when you're working with a letter-sized page, PowerPoint enlarges the slide to stretch almost to the edges of the page.

- If you are using a black-and-white printout, you may want to frame your slides so readers can easily see where the edge of the slide falls. Click Frame Slides to print the slides enclosed in a thin frame.

- If you've created hidden slides in your presentation (slides that are used as backup—not displayed automatically), PowerPoint enables the Print Hidden Slides option at the bottom right of the dialog box. If you want a printout of the hidden slides, click this check box.

Printing to a File

Another decision you need to make is whether you'll be printing to a printer or a file. You might want, for example, to use the color printer that's only available in the office down the hall. You could print your PowerPoint slides to a file, take them down the hall, and print them on that printer—whether or not that computer has Power-Point. If you want to print to a file, click the Print to File button.

When you click OK to print the file, PowerPoint displays the Print to File dialog box so that you can enter a filename for the resulting file. Enter a name, and click Save. PowerPoint then prints the presentation to the file and saves it with the name you specified.

Finally...Printing!

Once you've got all the options set the way you need them, you can print your presentation by following these simple steps:

1. Display your presentation.
2. Open the File menu.
3. Choose Print.
4. Choose the range and number of copies (and any other options).
5. Click OK.

In a matter of moments (depending on the speed of your printer), you'll have the printouts in your hands.

 TIP The fastest way to print your presentation is to click the Print button On the toolbar. PowerPoint sends the presentation directly to the printer using the current defaults.

How Did It Turn Out?

Once you've got the printed product in your hand, it's a good idea to take a few minutes and review what you've produced. Here are a few questions to help you determine whether your printouts look the way you want them to:

Did you use the right colors? If you printed in color (or even if colored screens were converted to black-and-white output), make sure that the colors you've chosen are not too light. Light blue text will print as very light gray, for example, so against a white background, this isn't the best choice.

Would the slide look better if it were framed? Add frames before the next print by clicking Frame Slides in the Print dialog box.

Is the page cluttered? Remember that open space is as important as the text and graphics on your page. Use it to draw the reader's eye to a certain area on the page.

Would your printed presentation be better for readers if you provided room for notes? You can print Notes Pages so that a reduced version of the slide leaves room for audience notes.

PART

III

Quintessential
PowerPoint

Do the headers and footers contribute to the printout? Perhaps you need to reduce the amount of text in either the header or the footer. Display the Header and Footer dialog box by choosing View ➤ Header and Footer, and then make your changes.

Chapter Summary

In this chapter, you learned the basics of making page setup choices and print decisions. Specifically, you learned how to choose the size of the page, the width and height of the slide, and the orientation. You also found out how to select a printer, choose the number of copies and pages to print, and set additional print options.

CHAPTER 11

Web Publishing and Broadcasting with PowerPoint

A few years ago, the term *Web publishing* didn't exist. The Internet was just becoming known to the masses; the World Wide Web was hot on its heels. But the idea of using the Internet was intimidating enough—who would have thought that just a few years later we would be publishing our own materials and posting them on the Internet, ready for a worldwide audience to view? PowerPoint makes publishing on the Web as easy as creating a presentation. You use all the same tools, templates, and transitions. Multimedia, animation, sound, colors—all the same elements you've been learning to use for presentations through-out the course of this book can be used on your Web pages. This chapter shows you how to turn your presentation into a Web site. But first we'll take a look at some Web basics.

Web Basics

The Internet is a new world—and the World Wide Web is a unique continent in that new world. The Web is a user-friendly way to locate and explore information on the Internet. But there's still a learning curve involved. This section introduces you to some basic information about the Web.

Web Terms

If you are just beginning to learn about the Internet, you may be unfamiliar with some of the terminology you'll see in this chapter. Let's start out by defining a few terms:

Internet   The Internet is a worldwide network of computer networks. More computers are signing on every day.

World Wide Web   The World Wide Web provides a graphical way for Internet users to access information. Users can navigate through pages of information by clicking links that take them to other Web pages with related information. The metaphor of the Web is taken from the effect of the linking from page to page, forming a worldwide web of information channels.

Internet Service Provider (ISP)   Before you can gain access to the World Wide Web, you must have Internet access. You can get an account with an Internet Service Provider in your area or use one of the Internet accounts avail-able through online services, such as CompuServe, America Online, or MSN.

Web Page   A Web page is a screen of information published on the World Wide Web. Individuals or companies may have single pages or multiple pages on their Web sites.

Links   Links are "hot spots" on the Web page that take the user to other pages when clicked.

URL   An acronym for Universal Resource Locator, a URL is the address of a Web page (for example, `http://www.revisionsplus.com/kbm`).

Web Browser   A Web browser is a software program that enables you to view and navigate Web pages. Two examples of popular Web browsers are Internet Explorer (available free from Microsoft) and Netscape Navigator.

What Does a Web Page Look Like?

If you haven't yet begun exploring the World Wide Web, you may be surprised to find that a Web page looks basically like any other computer program on your computer's monitor. Depending on the Web browser you use, you will probably see the familiar Windows interface, so you won't have much trouble finding your way around.

The difference surfing the Web offers over a typical program, however, is how far information can take you. Links can take you all over the world and back again, enabling you to find in a single afternoon information that might otherwise take months to gather. If you were using a program, the information would be finite—you'd have no way to discover information beyond that programmed into the software. The Web offers you the world—and a continually expanding world, at that.

Figure 11.1 shows an example of a Web page. The Web browser being used is Internet Explorer 5. In the toolbar at the top of the window, you see a number of tools that enable you to navigate the Web. The Back button returns you to the last page you visited; the Forward button moves you to forward to another link in the sequence you are traveling. The Stop button stops a page from loading; the Search button opens a search window so you can search for topics, keywords, people, or things. The Favorites button opens a menu of Web pages favorites. (You add Web sites to the Favorites folder yourself, so the contents of this menu will be different for each person.) The toolbar also gives you the means of printing the page, reading your e-mail, and more.

These are the commands for Internet Explorer; Netscape Navigator includes similar buttons and commands in a slightly different interface. Other browsers are modifications on the same theme, but all have the tools to enable you to find, navigate to, and use information on the Web.

PART

III

Quintessential
PowerPoint

FIGURE 11.1

An example of a Web page

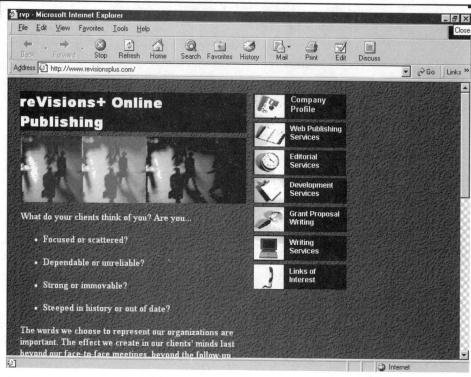

When you click the button on the Web page called *Web Publishing Services,* the action takes you to another page of linked information (see Figure 11.2). Some pages may have links built into photographs, icons, or text phrases. (Linked text is highlighted in a different color, and the pointer will change to a Hand icon when you place the pointer over linked text.)

You can scroll down through the page by pressing PgDn or clicking the down arrow on the scroll bar to the right of the work area. Most Web pages include additional navigation buttons at the bottom of the page so you can easily move among other pages in the site.

NOTE You can download Microsoft's Internet Explorer free of charge by going to Microsoft's Web site at http://www.microsoft.com/downloads.

FIGURE 11.2

The page displayed when you click the Web Publishing Services button on the reVisions+ home page

Working with Web Options

PowerPoint 2000 gives you a greater number of choices than ever for controlling the way you create and work with Web files. Now you can control items such as the way the controls look, how your animation appears, whether graphics are resized, where files are stored, how the page is encoded, what font is used, and more. To get to and work with Web Options, follow these steps:

1. Open the Tools menu and choose Options.

2. Click the General tab.

3. Click the Web Options button. The General tab of the Web Options dialog box appears, as Figure 11.3 shows. Table 11.1 describes each of the tabs in the Web Options dialog box and gives you an idea of what they do.

Use Web Options to control the way navigational controls look, how your browser displays animation and graphics, and how files are stored.

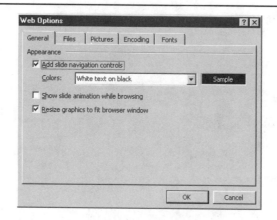

TABLE 11.1: CHECKING OUT WEB OPTIONS

Tab	Description
General	Use the options in this tab to control the way your navigational controls look, whether animation plays while you are browsing the Web, and whether graphics you encounter will be shown as they are or resized to fit your browser window.
Files	These choices enables you to use long filenames, update links automatically, and use Office as the default editor for any Web pages you create using an Office application.
Pictures	These options provide you with a means to accept VML and PNG file formats for displaying and outputting graphics. You also choose the screen size for your display here.
Encoding	This tab gives you the option of saving your Web presentation in one of many international formats.
Fonts	In this tab, you set the character set you want to use in your presentation and choose your proportional and fixed-width fonts of choice.

Creating Links

In order for your Web page visitors to be able to move from one page to another, you must provide links for them. You can create a link using a button, a shape, a picture, or text. First create the item you want to use as the link. For this example, we will use AutoShapes. An entire palette of Action Buttons has been provided in AutoShapes so you can add predrawn buttons to your Web pages (see Figure 11.4).

FIGURE 11.4

AutoShapes include Action Buttons for Web pages, but you can use other shapes, images, or text.

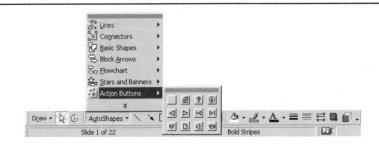

When you choose the button you want to create and then drag the shape on the slide, the Action Settings dialog box appears (see Figure 11.5). PowerPoint wants to know what you want to have happen when the user clicks the button. By default, the mouse click will follow a hyperlink to the next slide. Click OK to establish the link.

NOTE   When you use AutoShapes' Action Buttons, PowerPoint makes guesses about what you want to link to in the Action Settings dialog box. When you create your own buttons or link to clip art or text, however, you must establish the link yourself. In the Action Settings dialog box, click Hyperlink To, and click the down arrow to display a list of choices. Click the one you want, and click OK.

FIGURE 11.5

After you create the button, the Action Settings dialog box appears, ready for you to establish the link.

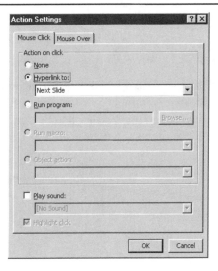

PART

III

Quintessential
PowerPoint

Continue adding buttons as needed to link up the pages in your presentation. When you are finished, preview the presentation by choosing Slide Show ➤ View Show.

Managing Your Links

Now that you've created the links for your presentation-to-Web page, how can you make sure that they will continue working and that the files you need will be where you need them to be? When you save your presentation as HTML files, PowerPoint actually creates a folder to store all the files that go along with the main page. This means that if you use video clips, graphics, and other documents in your presentation, when you save the file as a Web page, all those files are copied to the newly created folder. (The folder is given the same name as the presentation.) All the pieces you need for your links are included.

 TIP If you're interested (or already into) scripting in Visual Studio, you can put your talents to work in PowerPoint. Office 2000 now supports script anchors, so developers can integrate their custom solutions into PowerPoint online presentations.

Displaying the Web Toolbar

While you are working on the presentation and creating your Web pages, it will be helpful to display the Web toolbar. You can do this two different ways:

- You can choose View ➤ Toolbars ➤ Web Toolbar.
- You can click the Web toolbar button in the center of the standard toolbar.

 The Web toolbar then appears beneath the toolbars in your PowerPoint work area (see Figure 11.6). If you prefer, you can suppress all toolbars except the Web toolbar by clicking the Show Only Web Toolbar button in the center of the Web toolbar. The effects of this are shown at left.

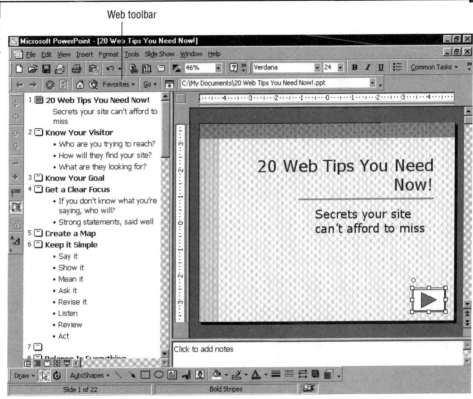

FIGURE 11.6

The Web toolbar gives you additional tools for working with your Web page.

Web toolbar

Saving the Presentation as an HTML File

After you have completed your presentation and made sure all the links work the way you want them to, you are ready to save the presentation as an HTML file.

NOTE What is HTML? HTML is an acronym for HyperText Markup Language, the set of tags that controls the formatting of documents for the World Wide Web. When you save a file as an HTML file, PowerPoint adds the HTML codes necessary to format the pages for the Web.

PART

III

Quintessential
PowerPoint

Begin with your presentation open on the screen. Choose File ➤ Save as HTML. The Internet Assistant begins to lead you through the process of saving your presentation as a Web page.

Saving in Dual Formats

Because the Web is evolving at different rates, it's a good idea to save your HTML files in formats that the most people will be able to view on their browsers. PowerPoint 2000 enables you to save your presentations files in two different HTML formats. One format will be usable with Internet Explorer 4 and Netscape Navigator 3 and later, and another format will support earlier versions of those and other browsers.

To save your Web page in HTML format, complete your presentation, and save it as Normal in a PowerPoint file. Then open the File menu, and choose Save as Web Page. The Save As dialog box appears, as shown in Figure 11.7. Navigate to the drive and folder on which you want to store the file, type a name for the file, and click Save. The presentation is saved as a Web page.

FIGURE 11.7

You can easily save a presentation as a Web page using the Save as Web Page command in the File menu.

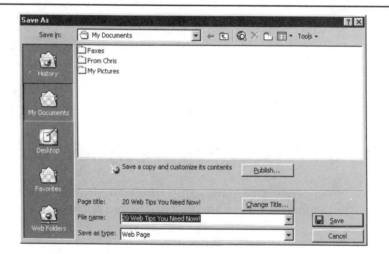

 TIP Another new PowerPoint 2000 feature enables you to open and work with your document even after you save it in HTML mode.

Publishing Your Web Page

PowerPoint 2000 also enables you to do the saving and publishing in one step if you prefer. Display the Save as Web Page dialog box by choosing File ➤ Save as Web Page. When the Save As dialog box appears, move to the drive and folder where you want the Web page stored; enter the filename and title you want, and click Publish. The Publish as Web Page dialog box appears, as shown in Figure 11.8.

You can turn your whole presentation into a Web page, or you can select individual pages to use. If you want the whole thing, leave Complete Presentation selected. If you want a selected portion of the presentation, click the Slide Number radio button, and enter the numbers of the slides you want to include.

 TIP You can go back and change your Web options from this point by clicking the Web Options button in the Publish as Web Page dialog box.

FIGURE 11.8

The Publish as Web Page options enable you to choose which part of the presentation to make into a Web presentation.

Next, you determine whether you want to include speaker notes. If you are creating a Web page for self-directed users and your speaker notes are simply for your use in a presentation, you may want to leave them out of the Web page or incorporate them, if needed, in the body of the presentation.

PART

III

Quintessential
PowerPoint

In the Browser Support area, choose the browser you want your visitors to be able to use in viewing your site. Microsoft Internet Explorer 4 is selected by default, but you can choose whichever option best meets your needs. If you select All Browsers, the files created for your site will be larger than the other two choices, which can mean longer download times for your visitors. Either of the first two choices should work well for most purposes.

Finally, in the Publish a Copy As area, choose the Page Title (you can change the title by clicking the Change button and entering a new one) and the filename. (Click Browse to display a dialog box in which you can navigate to a new location if need be.)

Finally, click Publish to publish your Web page. If you want to see how the page looks after you publish it, click the Open Published Web Page in Browser option, and PowerPoint will open the page in your default browser after it finishes saving files.

Previewing Your Published Page

The Web page created from the 20 Web Tips presentation is shown in Figure 11.9. Notice that PowerPoint creates the frames that look a lot like the frames in Normal view.

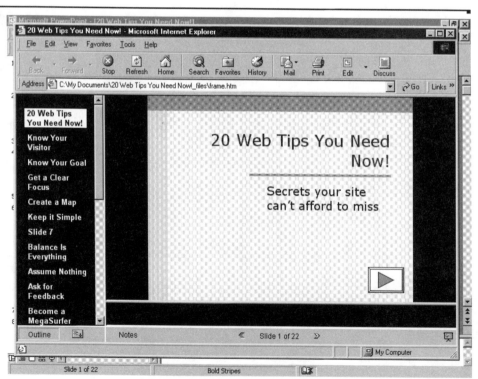

FIGURE 11.9

The published Web page resembles the presentation in Normal view.

The buttons along the top of the window are the standard browser buttons you are used to working with. Beneath the presentation, however, are new buttons specific to your PowerPoint Web page. Table 11.2 lists the various buttons in the Web status bar.

TABLE 11.2: BUTTONS IN THE WEB STATUS BAR

Icon	Name	Description
Outline	Show/Hide Outline	Displays the presentation outline or hides it. When the presentation outline is hidden, the page appears in Slide view.
	Expand/Collapse Outline	Enables you to display or hide the subcategories in the outline.
Notes	Notes	Lets you display the Notes view or hide it.
	Previous Slide	Takes you to the previous slide.
	Next Slide	Takes you to the next slide.
	Full Screen Slide Show	Runs the slide show in a full-screen presentation.

While you are previewing your page, check the following things:

- Test all your links. Do they do what they are supposed to?
- Read through your text. Is it the way you want it? Do you need to edit to make the slides easier to read?
- Check your graphics. Do they appear where you want them to? Are they appropriate to the content? Will they load quickly when a visitor reaches your page?

When you are finished previewing the page, click the Close box, or choose File ➤ Close.

 TIP   Later, if you want to preview the page again, you can do so by opening the File menu and choosing Web Page Preview.

Posting Your Web Page

The way in which you post your Web page to the Internet depends in part on the software your ISP gave you for such things. Before you can upload your Web page, you need to have the following:

- Space on a Web server
- Procedures for uploading Web files
- The software needed for uploading Web files

Some Internet Service Providers give you a set amount of space as part of your monthly subscription. My ISP, for example, gives each subscriber one Web page—with only one graphic (gee, thanks, guys)—for free. If you want to add more than one graphic (by the way, a graphic is a single button, or a piece of clip art, or a line, etc.), you have to pay for extra space. I found it cheaper and less hassle to open an account with a Web service provider, which is a different animal from an ISP. For a set monthly fee, I get many megabytes of Web storage space, which means I can create as many Web pages as I want to, for my own business, for clients, for whoever needs it. Two Web service providers I've worked with are ForSite (`www.forsite.net`) and Netfinity (`www.netfinity.com`).

Next you need to know the procedure for uploading your Web files. Some Web service providers support Microsoft extensions, which means you can use Microsoft's Web Publishing Wizard (you can download this free of charge from Microsoft) to publish your HTML files to the directory on the Internet reserved for your Web page. Other providers require that you use FTP or another utility to place the files where they need to go. Contact your ISP for details.

Finally, you need the software required to upload the files. Again, if you can use the Web Publishing Wizard, you can download it from Microsoft's Web site (`www.microsoft.com`). The first place to start is your service provider, however. If they don't give you the software you need, they can tell you where on the Internet to find it so you can use a program you know is compatible with their software setup.

MASTERING TROUBLESHOOTING

Trouble with the Web Publishing Wizard?

Not all Internet Service Providers enable you to upload Web pages using the Web Site Publishing Wizard from Microsoft. You may have to look for other avenues. One method that I use works faster and more reliably on my system with my ISP than the Web Wizard: I use CuteFTP from `ftp://ftp.cuteftp.com/pub/cuteftp/`. First, I create the presentation for the Web site; then, I choose File ➢ Save as HTML, enter the necessary folder name, and click Save. PowerPoint saves the file to the HTML documents for the pages in the folder I specified.

When the save process is finished, I exit PowerPoint and start CuteFTP. (Note that there are many other FTP utilities available on the Internet or perhaps bundled in with the software provided by your ISP. I use CuteFTP because it's easy to use and reliable.) I then upload all the files from the folder to the folder on the Internet that is reserved for my site. It's a simple process that takes 10 minutes or less for most Web sites I publish.

Broadcasting Your Presentation

A terrific new feature in PowerPoint 2000 enables you to give your presentation to a wide variety of people near and far. As long as your audience members have access to the Web and a Web browser, they can join a presentation you are broadcasting online. Believe it or not, this is as simple a procedure as giving a presentation standing in front of a group of people with a PowerPoint clicker in your hand—except that now you are sitting at your computer and your audience members are sitting at theirs, perhaps scattered all over the world.

What Is Presentation Broadcasting?

Presentation broadcasting is simply the act of giving your presentation online. You set up your presentation with the audience members you want to invite (up to 15 at a time), and they "tune in" to the URL you provide as the address of the broadcast. If your audience members are using Microsoft Outlook, you can broadcast the presentation directly to their monitors at the agreed-upon time; if they use an e-mail client other than Outlook, the invitation to your meeting will appear as a link in an e-mail message, and audience members can tune in by clicking the URL at the appointed time.

What Will You Broadcast?

You can broadcast any presentation you would give in front of a real audience. But even though the technology is in place, there are still some limitations: if you want to have an audience larger than 15 people, for example, or you want to run video within your presentation while Webcasting, you'll need NetShow server support, which is an additional feature your ISP or LAN administrator needs to set up for you.

Here are a few ideas of presentations you might broadcast:

- You might practice with your peers a presentation you plan to give to the board of directors detailing the new sales campaign for 2000.

- A training class for new recruits in online sales techniques.

- A welcome-to-our-school presentation for new students joining your cyber-university.

- An advertisement, infomercial style, detailing key points about your product or service.

Setting Up a Web Broadcast

Here's the process for setting up a Web broadcast of your presentation:

1. Open the Slide Show menu, and choose Online Broadcast. A pop-up menu appears.

2. Choose Set Up and Schedule. The Broadcast Schedule dialog box appears. Click OK to continue.

3. The Schedule a New Broadcast dialog box comes up, as Figure 11.10 shows. PowerPoint already fills in the name of the presentation, the speaker, and the primary contact. The information on this page enables PowerPoint to create the lobby page, which is the first page of the broadcast presentation audience members view when they join the start of a broadcast.

FIGURE 11.10

PowerPoint has a Broadcast Schedule Wizard to help you get your presentation ready to broadcast.

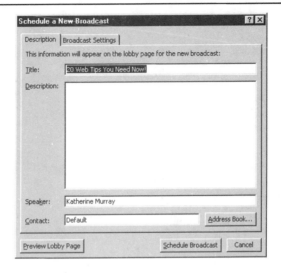

4. Change the information as needed. It's also a good idea to provide a full description of your presentation so participants have an idea what it will be about.

5. After you've entered the information, click Preview Lobby Page so you can see what your audience members will see when you begin the presentation. Figure 11.11 shows you an example. When you're finished reviewing the page, close the browser to return to the Schedule a New Broadcast dialog box.

6. Click Schedule Broadcast. A pop-up message tells you that you must specify a shared location before you can schedule the broadcast. In order to give the presentation, you must have a shared space on a server—either your local LAN or a server provided by an ISP—where you and your participants can meet. Enter a folder location and your screen looks something like the one shown in Figure 11.12.

PART

III

Quintessential
PowerPoint

FIGURE 11.11

Take a look at the Lobby Page to see what your potential participants will see when they first join your broadcast.

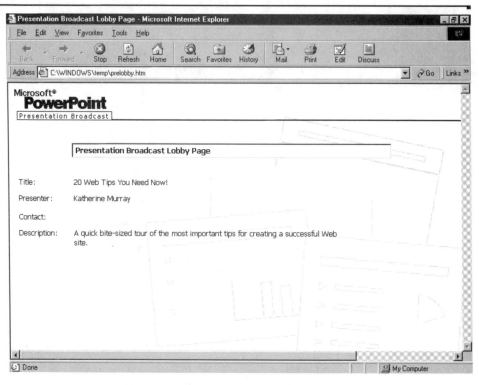

FIGURE 11.12

Specify the shared space where you will give your presentation—either on your LAN or on a server on the Net—and choose whether you want to find out more about NetShow.

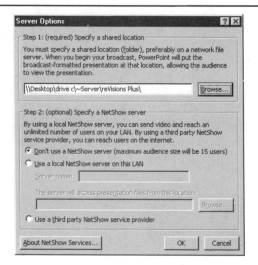

7. PowerPoint will check to make sure your shared space is really out there, and then you can go ahead and set the time and date for your presentation. After checking the space, PowerPoint will alert you that only 15 total users can view the presentation at a time unless you use a NetShow server. If you want to continue without a NetShow server, click Yes. If not, click No and you will be taken back to the Server Options page where you can choose the NetShow settings you want.

TIP If you will have an audience of more than 15 people, you need to use Microsoft NetShow to set up and give the broadcast. This requires a NetShow server or an arrangement with a NetShow service provider. For more information on NetShow and the setup it requires, see your Microsoft Office 2000 Resource Kit.

Scheduling the Broadcast

Once you get the server space settled and determine whether to use NetShow or not, clicking Schedule a Meeting takes you to the Meeting dialog box shown in Figure 11.13. The Appointment tab displays all the pertinent information you need to set for your broadcast, including

- Who you want to send the broadcast to (enter this in the To: box)
- The Subject of the broadcast (this is the title)
- The Location where the broadcast will be given

NOTE If you have elected to use NetShow Services, the Event Address line will show the address where the presentation will be given.

- The Start time and End time
- When you want to schedule a reminder, for yourself and your participants

At the bottom of the Appointment tab you see the text for the Lobby Page. You can edit the text in this window if it's needed.

TIP   To select the people you want to invite to the broadcast, click the Contacts button. The Select Contacts button appears so that you can choose participants from your Outlook Contacts list.

FIGURE 11.13

Scheduling the Broadcast in the Meeting dialog box

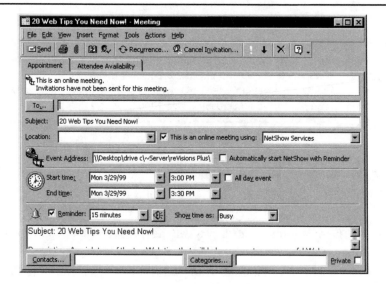

Beginning the Broadcast

Once you have scheduled the broadcast, it will be given automatically at the intended time. You can also start a broadcast manually (so that you can display it yourself for a final check or give it on demand to a few participants) by opening the Slide Show menu, choosing Online Broadcast, and choosing Begin Broadcast.

Joining a Broadcast

If you are using Microsoft Outlook, when you accept the invitation to the broadcast, a reminder message will automatically be sent before the presentation begins. You can join the broadcast by clicking the View Broadcast button in the reminder message.

If you are using an e-mail client other than Microsoft Outlook, you join the broadcast by clicking the URL link at the appointed time.

Chapter Summary

In this chapter, you have learned how to turn your PowerPoint presentation into a Web page. Using the features built into PowerPoint, you can easily add buttons, create links, and come up with a layout that will help readers navigate your site easily. You also learned how to control your Web experience by working with Web options and explored the possibilities of giving your presentation online, in a Web broadcast setting.

The next chapter explains some of the unique challenges of working with sometimes-cumbersome multimedia files. You'll learn how to compress, link, embed, import, export, and prepare your presentations for the road.

CHAPTER 12

Working with Presentation Files

The presentation files you create in PowerPoint—and the graphics, video, sound, and slides they include—will be as diverse as the audiences you present them to. As you begin creating PowerPoint presentations, you'll discover that managing your files as they accumulate and preparing them for use in your office and abroad are important jobs.

In this chapter, you'll learn about the nature of PowerPoint files and find out how to best work with them. You'll learn about the different multimedia files you may work with and find out how to link and embed objects in your PowerPoint presentations. Additionally, you'll discover how to import and export files and how to get ready for a multimedia presentation on the road using the Pack and Go Wizard.

The Big File

Rest assured that your PowerPoint files will be large. Huge, maybe. The basic text won't cause the presentation to take up a lot of room, but the slide backgrounds, graphical elements, and especially the multimedia objects (such as video clips and sound bytes) can push a file into the enormous range. The more multimedia objects you use, the larger your presentation file will be. If your computer has sufficient memory and disk storage space, you may not be worried about file size right now. But once you get a number of files on your system, you may begin feeling the pinch.

Windows 98 Compression

If you are concerned about preserving disk space (or need to copy a large presentation to disk, which can be a pretty challenging endeavor), you may want to use some kind of compression utility. Windows comes with its own compression utility, DriveSpace, which will save you a considerable amount of hard disk space. You start DriveSpace by choosing Programs ➢ Accessories ➢ System Tools ➢ DriveSpace. Figure 12.1 shows the opening screen of DriveSpace.

 WARNING In some cases, file compression can cause irregularities when you're playing back multimedia objects. For example, you may hear slight hitches in the narrator's voice as the computer expands and reads a compressed audio file from disk. If you compress your presentation files, practice the presentation a number of times before you give it live. This way, you'll know what to expect and can determine whether file compression will cause any loss of quality in your presentation.

Windows comes with a compression utility called DriveSpace, which you access from the System Tools menu.

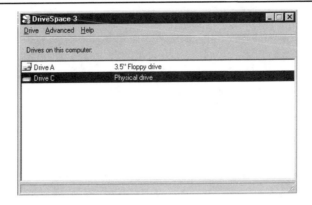

You may already use a different commercial compression program—like Stacker or DoubleSpace—that compresses your hard disk storage space. Whether you use the Windows DriveSpace utility or another one, compressing files saves you valuable storage space on disk. Windows 98 includes Compression Agent, a utility which keeps an eye on your DriveSpace 3-compressed drives and helps you work with compressed files. For more information, display the Windows Help utility and search for Compression Agent.

TIP If you are taking your presentation on the road, you can use PowerPoint's Pack and Go Wizard to gather all the files you've used in the presentation—the basic presentation file as well as all sound, video, and graphics files you have used—and compress them into a package saved on disk. Start the Pack and Go Wizard by choosing File ➤ Pack and Go.

WARNING There are all kinds of commercial compression utilities you can purchase off the shelf or over the Internet. A caveat, however: Be sure to read up on all available compression utilities before you buy. If you have a system administrator or a technical support person handy, ask his or her advice (or permission) before installing such a program. You don't want to try anything untested and unproven, especially with Windows 98—playing Russian roulette with your hard-won data isn't safe.

File Format Compression

When you're working with video, some formats take care of compressing the data for you automatically. When you save an image or video in the JPEG format, the data is compressed by a method that determines which colors are used most in an image file and updates these in each frame. The colors used less frequently are dropped and updated intermittently. This results in a controlled loss of clarity, but this is barely, or not at all, noticeable to the viewer.

MPEG (Motion Picture Experts Group) is another video format that takes the JPEG process a bit further by analyzing the current frame to anticipate what is most likely to be displayed in the next frames. This requires less actual processing of each frame, For example, the background drawn in the current frame is used for the anticipated frames instead of the background being redrawn for every frame.

Massive Storage Options

Yet another option for handling those big files you create by adding media elements is to get more storage capacity—increase the size of your hard disk, for example, or add something called a ZIP drive. A ZIP drive (manufactured by Iomega and available through computer mail order houses like PC Connection) is a piece of hardware that uses 100MB or 200MB removable disks and plugs into your computer's parallel or SCSI port. It shows up on your system as just another usable drive, but it's much, much more. Each ZIP disk stores up to 100MB of information (200MB with the newest drives); your typical 3.5-inch high-density disk stores only 1.4MB.

 NOTE If you're worried about where your printer will attach, don't be—the printer cable plugs right in to the other end of the ZIP drive, giving you the benefit of massive amounts of storage space. It also does not make you choose between disk storage and printing capabilities.

Compressing Many Files into One

Another way to conserve some hard disk space—especially at the "save-it-on-disk" end— involves a zipping utility such as PKZIP or WinZip. These utilities compress a file (or a set of files) so that their size is reduced and they may be easily copied to one or more floppy disks. When the disk arrives at the receiving end, the person using the file simply uses a partner utility (PKUNZIP or WinZip) to expand the file back into its usable form.

Working with Files

All that having been said, you know you're going to have to work with those files, not just compress them and store them away.

Windows 98 changed the terminology of file storage. We no longer use the terms "directory" and "subdirectory" concept at work; now everything follows "folder" and "folder within a folder" terminology. No matter—they are identical in concept. The most important thing about the way you store your files is that it makes sense to you and that you know how to find the files you need with a minimum of toil and trouble.

Here are some guidelines for basic file organization before you get started:

- Don't lump too many different files in one "catch-all" folder. If you have a number of multimedia files for a particular presentation, create a different folder for each object type. For example, have a sound folder, a video folder, an art folder, and a presentation folder.
- If you don't have the folders you need, create them.
- Use nested folders to help organize files clearly.

Planning File Organization

Most likely, you already have some kind of organization system on your computer. You've probably been using Windows Explorer to save, copy, rename, and delete files in various folders. Figure 12.2 shows an example of Windows Explorer.

Take a moment and examine the way you currently organize your files. Hopefully, you'll see some method here. You may be organizing files one of these ways:

- By client
- By application
- By project
- Randomly

FIGURE 12.2

Windows Explorer helps you organize files into folders.

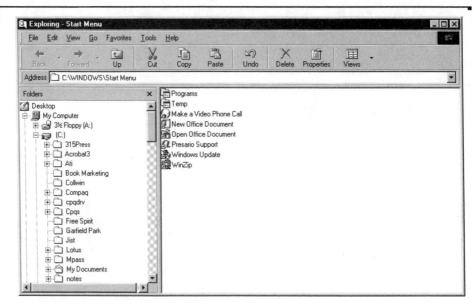

If you are organizing your files by client, you would have a folder named for the client you are working with (for me, a client folder would be SYBEX). Inside the folder, you would store all files related to that client, such as text files, illustrations, outlines, memos, etc. If the number of files inside the folder warrants a subdivision, you can create additional folders inside the CLIENT folder to help organize those files. (I might, for example, create the subfolders TEXT, FIGURES, MEMOS, and OUTLINES.)

If you are organizing folders by application, you might create one folder for your POWERPOINT files, one for your WORD files, and yet another for your EXCEL files.

If you are organizing your files by project, you approach the task from a different angle. When preparing for an annual meeting, for example, you might name a folder MEETING99. Then, everything related to that meeting—PowerPoint presentations, sound files, video clips, and art—would go in the MEETING99 folder. Again, if the file load makes division practical, add folders within MEETING99 to clarify the organization and to make files easier to find.

The one way you don't want to store files is randomly. The temptation to just dump the file in whatever folder comes up when you click File ➢ Save may be great —especially at first, when you haven't created many presentations; but you need to fight it. Get organized from the beginning; it's much easier than cleaning up messes later.

What Kind of Files Will You Use?

The "multi" in multimedia guarantees that you'll be working with a variety of different objects in your presentations. PowerPoint supports a number of files in different formats related to the object with which you're working. Basically, the files you'll be using fall into the following categories:

Text files   Text files you import might include Microsoft Word tables or outlines, text copied from another open Windows application (like Works or Notepad), or a WordPad document you insert as an object on the slide. Figure 12.3 shows a table from a Microsoft Word document used in a PowerPoint presentation.

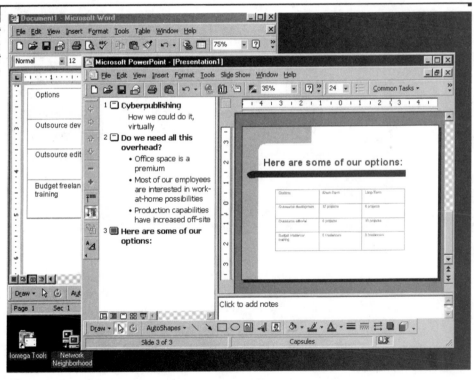

FIGURE 12.3

Using a Microsoft Word table in a PowerPoint presentation

Art files   You might use clip art or custom art files from a variety of sources and in a variety of formats. The format of the art file depends, to a certain extent, on the program that created it—some art programs create bitmapped images (images drawn as a pattern of dots on the screen). Photographs, for example, are bitmapped images. Figure 12.4 shows an example of a bitmapped image.

FIGURE 12.4

A bit-mapped image

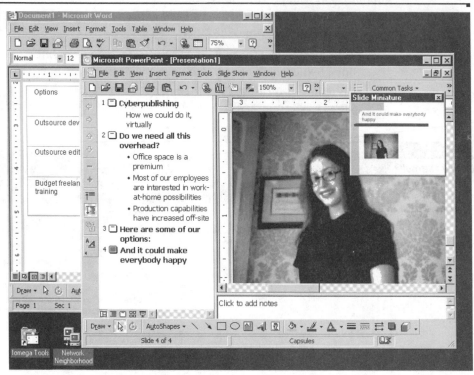

The other type of art file you might work with is a vector image. Instructions in the vector image's file tell the computer how to recreate the object on the screen. As a result, the art is based on mathematical calculations and not on pixels; this gives you a smooth art object that's easy to modify.

Video files   The video formats you'll be working with will most likely be AVI (Audio Video Interleaved), a standard that mixes sound and video; or JPG, a format that compresses video data based on recognizing the patterns of color used in the video file.

Sound files   You'll use either MID or WAV files to record or acquire sound files for use in your presentations. For more information on working with MID and WAV sound files, see Chapter 6, "Adding Sound."

Presentation files   One of the multimedia objects you add to your Power-Point presentation may be another PowerPoint presentation. PowerPoint files end with the extension .ppt, and you use Insert ➤ Object to add the presentation file as an object.

 TIP   You can add a single PowerPoint slide as an object by choosing Insert ➤ Object and selecting Microsoft PowerPoint Slide from the Object Type list.

Linking and Embedding Files

All Windows programs have the capability of linking and embedding objects. OLE (object linking and embedding) is the ability to include objects you create in other programs in your current application, update them from within that application, or have them updated automatically when you change the object. Whether or not this technology works for you can depend on how much memory and disk storage your computer has available. In most cases, linking and embedding won't be a problem—although screens may update slowly.

Linking and embedding objects is particularly important when you're working with presentation graphics because many of the elements you rely on to provide information in your presentation may be created in other programs. For example, you might use a financial report created in Microsoft Works to compare the results of several sales regions, or you might use a logo created in Windows Paint as part of the on-screen demo, or you might incorporate sound into your presentation. All of these items and more can be linked or embedded in your presentation.

Linking vs. Embedding

When you link an object to your PowerPoint file, you create a connection between the object, which you insert in your presentation, and the program in which you created it. Then, when you update the file in the original program, the linked version of the file is updated as well. For example, suppose that you are linking the Microsoft Works spreadsheet to your PowerPoint file. When you make changes to the spreadsheet later, during a Works work session, the changes are automatically updated the next time you start PowerPoint.

TIP You can edit linked objects directly from within the application you are currently using. It isn't necessary to edit the linked object in the originating program. In general, select the object, right-click, and select the command that will enable you to open the object and edit it.

Unlike the linking process, when you embed objects, the data becomes part of the new document, and, if data in the sponsoring program is updated, the changes are not reflected in the embedded object. You can, however, make changes directly to the sponsoring program by double-clicking an embedded object without exiting Power-Point. You saw an example of this in Chapter 7, where you learned about editing video files. When you double-clicked a video object on your PowerPoint slide, you were taken directly to the Media Player, where you could edit the clip as necessary and then return to the PowerPoint presentation.

You can also edit an object in PowerPoint if you choose to embed it rather than linking it. For example, suppose that you insert a section of a Microsoft Word report into PowerPoint as an embedded object. Then, if you wanted to modify it, you would right-click the object and select Document Object ➤ Open. The document would then open in a Word window so that you could make the necessary changes. When you finished making changes, you would click File and choose Close & Return. The Word window closes and the changes are made to the embedded object in your Power-Point presentation.

Linking and embedding objects in your PowerPoint files not only saves you from duplicating effort—you don't have to enter something in one program and then retype it in PowerPoint—but you also cut down on your margin of error. Linking and embedding can help you ensure that you've used the most up-to-date information you have in your PowerPoint files.

Linking Objects

To link an object in PowerPoint, first display the slide on which you want the object to appear. Then open the Insert menu and choose one of the following items:

- Text Box
- Movies and Sounds
- Chart
- Object
- Hyperlink

In this case, because we're talking about inserting objects, select Object on the Insert menu. The Insert Object dialog box appears, as shown in Figure 12.5.

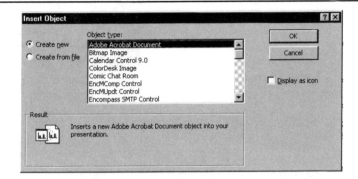

The options in this dialog box are set assuming that you are going to create a new object. To link an existing file to the presentation, click the Create from File option. When this option is active, the Link check box appears to the right of the Browse button, as Figure 12.6 shows. The Link check box controls whether the object is linked or embedded—unchecked, the object will be embedded; checked, the object will be linked.

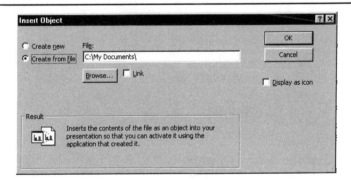

If the file you want to link is not in the open folder, click the Browse button. The Browse dialog box, similar to the File Save dialog box, appears so that you can navigate through folders to locate the file you want.

PART

III

Quintessential
PowerPoint

TIP If you are looking for a specific type of file but don't remember where you've stored it, you can use PowerPoint's search capabilities to locate it. In the Browse dialog box, click the Tools down-arrow; then click Find. The Find dialog box appears. If you know the name of the file you are looking for, type the name in the File Name: box at the bottom of the Browse dialog box, then click Find Now. If you don't know the name, use the search options in the Find dialog box to help you narrow your search. PowerPoint will search the folders you've specified and display the results of the search in the center window of the Find dialog box.

If you've used the Browse command to locate the file, select the file you want, and click OK to return to the Insert Object dialog box. The name of the file you selected now appears in the File text box.

To establish a link between the original file and the object you are inserting in your PowerPoint file (remember, this means that the PowerPoint file will be updated to reflect any changes you make in the original file), click the Link check box. If you want the object to appear as an icon and not as a file or object in itself, click Display As Icon. You might do this, for example, if you are inserting a report in your presentation that you would want to cover in a meeting only if questions were asked. If you linked the report as an icon, you would have the option of displaying it or not, as the situation required.

 TIP You can change the icon used to represent the object. Click Display As Icon; then click the Change Icon button. A small pop-up dialog box gives you the chance to choose the icon you want to use. Click OK to return to the Insert Object dialog box.

When you've made your selections and are ready to return to the presentation, click OK. The Insert Object dialog box closes and the object appears on the current slide.

Embedding Objects

Embedding objects is a similar procedure. Again, you display the Insert Object dialog box by choosing Insert ➤ Object. You can choose either Create New, and select one of the options from the Object Type list, or select Create From File and locate the file you want to embed.

This time, after clicking Create From File, don't select the Link check box. Power-Point will copy the object into the PowerPoint file without maintaining the data links to the original file. This means that when the original object is updated, the changes won't be reflected in the PowerPoint object. You can, however, edit the object you've embedded in PowerPoint by double-clicking the object. This opens a window in which you can make your changes in the application without ever leaving PowerPoint.

Importing and Exporting Files

There will be times when you want to use files created in other applications in your PowerPoint presentations. If you have been working with an earlier version of Power-Point, for example, you may want to use the files you've already created as the basis for your PowerPoint 2000 files.

Importing Presentations

To use a file from an earlier version of PowerPoint, Choose File ➤ Open. Display the folder or drive in which the file is stored. Select the file you want to use, and choose Presentations and Shows from the Files Of Type text box. PowerPoint will automatically convert the file, and when you prepare to save the file, the program will remind you that it was previously saved in a different version and ask for confirmation before continuing.

Exporting Presentations

Exporting a presentation is nothing more than saving it in a format different from the usual PowerPoint 2000 format. To export a file, click File ➤ Save As. When the Save As dialog box appears, choose the drive or folder in which you want to store the file, then enter a file name and choose the format you want in the Save As Type: text box.

PowerPoint allows you to choose between many formats in which to save your presentation, including the following:

- Presentation (the default PowerPoint 2000 format)
- Web Page
- PowerPoint 95
- PowerPoint 97-2000 & 95 Presentation
- PowerPoint 4
- Design Template
- PowerPoint Show

- PowerPoint Add-In
- GIF (.gif graphics file)
- JPEG (.jpg graphics file)
- PNG (Portable Network Graphics Format)
- BMP (Device Independent Bitmap)
- WMF(Windows Metafile)
- Outline/RTF
- Tag Image File Format (TIFF)
- Targa (TGA)

After you've made your choice, click Save. PowerPoint then saves the file in the format you specified.

Running a Presentation on a Computer without PowerPoint

If you need to run your presentation on a computer without PowerPoint, look no further. PowerPoint 2000 includes the Pack and Go Wizard, an automated utility that assembles the different pieces of your presentation into one neat little package that you can then run on another computer, even one without PowerPoint.

 TIP If you don't see Pack and Go as an option in the File menu, click the down-arrows at the bottom of the File menu. The Pack and Go option will appear.

You might run a PowerPoint presentation on a computer without PowerPoint, for example, when you have been working on a presentation for a client and want them to double-check it before the corporate meeting. Or you might send a self-running demo of a new product to a potential client. For any number of purposes, the Pack and Go Wizard can help you get your presentations out and about, where they can communicate your message with or without PowerPoint.

Using the Pack and Go Wizard

To use the Pack and Go Wizard, open the presentation you want to use. Next, open the File menu and choose Pack and Go. The first screen of the Pack and Go Wizard appears, as shown in Figure 12.7.

FIGURE 12.7

The Pack and Go Wizard lets you put the pieces of your presentation together and take them on the road.

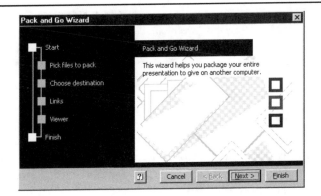

The next screen of the Pack and Go Wizard asks you which presentation (or presentations) you want to pack. The active presentation is shown first. Click Next to continue.

 TIP You can package multiple presentations in one Pack and Go file by clicking Other Presentation(s) and then clicking the Browse button. Choose the files you want to include by pressing Ctrl and clicking the files you want to package.

Next, the Pack and Go Wizard asks you where you want the packaged presentation stored. If you will be sending multiple copies of the packaged presentation to different clients, you may want to keep a copy on your hard disk so you can duplicate it easily. If you are packaging the presentation just this once—perhaps so you can take it home and spend some time reviewing it after the kids go to bed—you can get away with creating a copy on Drive A.

The Pack and Go Wizard will then ask you whether you want to include linked files and/or embedded fonts in the presentation. These will require some extra space—some linked files, especially sound or video files, may take a large amount of space—but if you want your client to see the full impact of the presentation, you should consider packing all elements you included in the PowerPoint file.

PART

III

Quintessential
PowerPoint

You must now determine whether you need to include the PowerPoint Viewer (a utility that enables users who don't have PowerPoint to view the presentations on their computers). The Include PowerPoint Viewer option is checked by default.

The final step is to click Finish. PowerPoint then gathers all the file elements, compresses them, and stores them in the location you specified.

 NOTE Now the PowerPoint Viewer includes password protection for presentations you run on kiosks. You can also hyperlink to other presentations or to an established Web site.

Running the Presentation

When it's time to run the presentation on the remote computer, start Windows, insert the disk containing the presentation in drive A (or other drive letter, depending on the system), and display the drive window. Locate the PowerPoint file produced by the Pack and Go Wizard, and double-click it. After a few moments, your presentation will begin, showing the colors, page layouts, special effects, transitions, and any multimedia features you used in the original.

Chapter Summary

In this chapter, you learned some of the particular challenges you face while working with multimedia files. Although these files can be enormous, you can juggle multiple files gracefully with a little forethought and organization. Additionally, you learned how to link and embed objects in your PowerPoint files, and you learned about the Pack and Go Wizard, which assembles all the different pieces of your presentation into one neat package. The next chapter finishes off the book by taking you right up to the point of no return: a live presentation.

CHAPTER 13

You're On! Giving the Presentation

Throughout the course of this book, you've created a wide variety of elements that fit together to produce an interesting, informative, and effective presentation. Whether your presentation is for a brainstorming group of four or five coworkers or a room full of sales associates from all over the Midwest, the moment of truth comes when you actually step in front of the group and start the show. This chapter helps you double-check the effectiveness of your plan by reminding you of your presentation options, guiding you through a trial run, and suggesting ways for you to evaluate the entire presentation and fine-tune any remaining details. At the close of this chapter, you'll see examples of how different people have used PowerPoint to meet very different presentation needs.

What Is a Finished Presentation?

When you're working on a presentation, and especially when you're up against a tight deadline, you may feel like your presentation will never be done. Like a book, a video, a corporate report, or anything else, there's always room for improvement. Therefore, you may find yourself continually updating and improving your presentation, even after you've given it a couple of times. Just think of all that's gone into it— by the first time you give your presentation, you've done all of the following things:

- You've created the presentation design, by using one of PowerPoint's templates or by starting with a blank presentation and choosing background, text color, and design.
- You've written the basic text for your presentation message, using the Auto-Content Wizard or constructing your own from scratch.
- You've checked for spelling errors in your text with the Spelling Checker.
- You've planned, created, and revised any charts you'll use to illustrate data trends and relationships.
- You've used PowerPoint Central or ValuPack to locate fresh new movies, sound, and art.
- You've incorporated logos, background art, or illustrations, by using Auto-ClipArt to find appropriate clip art or by importing or creating graphics.
- You've added multimedia objects where applicable, including sound, video, and animated objects.
- You've checked for consistency in your presentation's use of visuals, punctuation, and spelling with the Style Checker.
- You've added slide transitions and timed the display of slides.
- You've planned printed materials, including notes pages, handouts, and full slide prints.

What Are Your Options for Presenting?

Many presentations aren't given in the boardroom. They occur on the desk of a prospective client, in the lunchroom, or in the convention hall. Often, you may not be the sole focus of all eyes in the room but must compete with other presentations in other booths, all vying for the same attention.

Perhaps you won't even be face-to-face with the people you're presenting to. You can arrange to give your presentation online, using PowerPoint's conferencing capabilities. When you give your presentation over your company's network, you can elicit direct responses from all participants and control the timing and progression of slides.

 NOTE For information on setting up and giving an online presentation conference, see Chapter 8, "Finishing the Slide Show."

In another scenario, you may simply be creating the presentation, packing it up with the Pack and Go Wizard, and sending the disk off to your client(s) so they can load and review it themselves. You don't have to stand up in front of anyone; you won't even be around to hear the comments from the peanut gallery. The presentation, in this case, must speak for itself.

Finally, rather than standing up with a computer monitor (for small groups) or a large projection screen (for larger groups), you might be using a slide or an overhead projector. In that case, you won't be standing alone with a monitor in front of your audience; instead, you will be working with a slide projector or an overhead and transparencies. Even if you aren't giving a slide show with special transitional effects, the quality, color, and content of your slides will be extremely important. For low-budget presentations, you can create the slides yourself by printing the slides in color on printer-ready transparencies. For higher-budget presentations, you can have slides professionally prepared by a copy center that creates slides.

PowerPoint includes a number of options that help you further customize the way you present your work. Consider using these features for your presentation:

View on two screens Now you can link your computer to two screens so you can see your notes and onscreen tools on one computer monitor while displaying the presentation on the other.

Kiosk presentations If you are planning on setting up your presentation to run continuously as a loop or you want to allow individual users to navigate through the presentation at their own pace, you may want to set up the presentation to run kiosk-style. You can also add voice-over narration that plays continuously during the presentation.

Custom shows You don't need to create a new presentation every time you want to present one, especially not if you already have one that includes slides you'd like to use. You can choose a subset of any set of slides to show in a customized presentation, rearranging them in a new order if necessary and including them with any slides you want to add. Further, even though you may be reordering slides at will and creating multiple custom shows from subsets of various existing presentations, you won't be affecting those original presentations. PowerPoint keeps it all straight for you.

Improved Meeting Minder The new, improved Meeting Minder records your notes and action items as you go through your presentation. You can simply keep the Meeting Minder dialog box open on the screen and add to the notes as needed.

Enhancements to presentation conferencing PowerPoint 95 introduced presentation conferencing, a feature that enables you to give your presentations over the company network or over the Internet and gather feedback from participants. PowerPoint 2000 improves presentation conferencing by giving you the options of giving presentations over Windows NT networks, intranets, Novell networks, and the Internet. A Wizard guides you through the process of setting up the conference and making the connection.

Presentation broadcasting opportunities PowerPoint 2000 enables you to present your slide show to a variety of people in a variety of places. As long as you've got server space somewhere to share, you can invite a select group to come view, comment on, and respond to your presention in real time in cyberspace.

Effective Rehearsal Techniques

When you have all the pieces in place, timed out the slides, and added any transitional effects, you're ready to take a trial run. Here are some pointers.

Even If It's Informal, Practice

If your presentation is one you're giving to coworkers around the lunch table, you may want to practice with one other trusted friend as an advisor. You could do a blind presentation, where you simply give the presentation as you would to any audience member, and ask your friend afterwards a series of questions to see whether she "got the message." Or if you want her to watch for a certain aspect of your presentation, you can tell her what you're trying to accomplish before you begin so that she knows where you're going and can tell you afterward whether your presentation got there.

Choose a Diverse Trial Audience

If you are designing a presentation you will be presenting to a variety of different clients—for example, a corporate ID piece that introduces your training service to large corporations—practice the presentation with many different types of people. Ask people of different age groups and experience levels for their suggestions and observations. Be open to constructive criticism, and be committed to making the best possible representation of your company before you take it on the road.

Include Setup in the Trial Run

Don't forget to practice setting up and arranging your materials. If you will be unpacking a laptop, setting up a docking station and speakers, and laying out printed booklets, brochures, and business cards, practice those things so that you know the whole routine from start to finish.

Go Straight through, from Start to Finish

Even if you forget something or stumble through a transition, keep going. The experience of moving through the entire presentation is more important than doing the same part over and over again until you get it right.

When You're Finished Giving the Trial Presentation, Evaluate

Don't just pack everything away; consider what you've just done. You can use the following questions to help you gather information about your presentation:

What Parts of Your Presentation Need to Change?

Foremost in your mind, once you've finished the trial run, should be what you need to change about your presentation. Avoid the temptation to be overly critical or to tell yourself that the glitches don't matter, that no one will notice. The glitches do matter, and someone is sure to notice. If you resolve to make your presentation the best it can be, the quality will show in your work and in the way you present yourself.

Look clearly at what works and what doesn't in your presentation, and improve it as necessary.

Will Anything Make You More Comfortable Presenting?

Sometimes something as simple as a word change can make a sentence a whole lot easier to say. Think through your trial run and, at any points that you hesitated or lost momentum, ask yourself whether a change would make the presentation clearer. A different word, the addition of clip art, a new chart, a different title—each of these small changes might make a big difference in how easily you present the slide.

What Does Your Audience Think?

If you went through the trial run in front of a group, ask your audience whether anything needs to be clarified. Make a list of any suggestions or changes your audience members suggest. Then, later, when you review your notes, you can decide whether—and how—to implement any of the changes they've suggested. Although input from others is important, you are the one who understands best what you're trying to communicate. Weigh each suggestion against your message, and make sure it fits before you change anything.

Especially if you will give your presentation again and again, any investment you make now in targeting and fine-tuning the presentation will be well worth it in the long run.

PowerPoint Case Studies

As you've seen again and again throughout this book, one of the best features Power-Point offers is its flexibility. Whether you'll be presenting to one person or a party of a hundred, you can create an attention-getting presentation that communicates with vibrant color and vitality the concept you're trying to get across. This section gives you a cross section of examples, showing how PowerPoint can be used in a variety of presentation situations.

The Small Group

Linda is responsible for introducing a new product line at her publishing company. After researching the potential market, Linda has created a presentation to show how her department's brainchild—a new line of instructional videos—is a good risk for budget dollars.

The presentation itself consists of 20 different slides—some bullets and some builds—with charts showing industry trends compared to current statistics on video sales and projections for the future. A sample video clip and voice-over by a celebrity narrator are part of the presentation itself. Animation is used to zoom on the logo, and colors and styles have been chosen to convey an upbeat, modern tone.

Linda will be presenting to a small group of departmental managers in a conference room, so she'll use a large-screen PC monitor to do the actual display. In addition, she has printed handouts with a full-color copy of the opening slide as the front cover, Notes Pages to highlight important points, and handouts including a small reproduction of each slide.

On the Road

Brian works for an insurance company. Part of their new computerized system allows Brian to take his laptop to prospective clients, dial up the home office, and run a professionally made PowerPoint presentation from the company mainframe. This high-quality piece gives the client a taste of what's possible with that insurance provider.

When Brian cannot access the mainframe or when communication lines are busy or slow, he can use a prepackaged version of the presentation to show the client. In this case, he loads the presentation from the disks he created with the Pack and Go to Wizard, show the presentation on his laptop, or if he's included the PowerPoint Viewer on the disk, he can leave the disks with the client to review at his leisure.

To reinforce his message, Brian prepares a printed handout showing all the slides in the presentation, along with notes providing the phone numbers of the various insurance departments at his agency. His name, number, e-mail address, and company Web site are printed as a footer at the bottom of each page so the client can easily find the information to contact him.

The Corporate Meeting

Don has been working on the corporate meeting for almost six months. He's planned the site, polled the prospective attendees to find the most available date, taken care of everything from reservations to catering to parking, and has now inherited the task of overseeing the production of the main presentation. His assistant did much of the assembly work on the presentation, even finding appropriate video in the company archives and digitizing it for use in PowerPoint. Don hired a writer to produce the text, an artist to do custom graphics, a musician to create a piece of music to introduce the presentation, and a camera operator to produce a video of the CEO welcoming everyone to the meeting, superimposed on flashing images of employees at work.

Even though Don won't be presenting himself, it's in his best interest to make sure the presentation is as polished and professional as possible. He has his chosen presenter run through the slide show again and again, looking for possible glitches and practicing until they reach a certain comfort level. With all the video projection and sound equipment in place, Don runs through the presentation the morning before the meeting to note potential hang-ups that he could solve from behind the scenes.

As part of the presentation, the writer has prepared not only a printout of all the slides, along with Notes Pages and an outline, but a corporate report written in Microsoft Word with slides from the PowerPoint presentation illustrating it. A professionally done cover shows the company's logo (used as animation in the slide show), and the document is spiral bound. Once the presentation is completed, they publish it to a folder and upload it to the Internet, so clients worldwide can view the presentation given at the company meeting.

 NOTE Larger meetings require larger plans and larger investments—usually both in terms of time and money. Depending on the size of your meeting, you may be renting a meeting hall, getting the right production equipment, and making sure you're getting a professional-quality sound system. There's lighting—and the control of it—to worry about, as well as where to put the podium, and whether the sound system will carry to the back of the auditorium.

Entrepreneurs in the Cyber Community

Leslie is a co-owner of a small advertising agency that is planning some aggressive moves on the Net. She offers her clients the combined creative power of her experience and her technical insight as well as the how-to practicality of her left-brained techno partner, Evan. Although Leslie and Evan live on separate coasts, they are able to work collaboratively to create effective online marketing solutions for companies wanting to make the Web work for them. They have created a PowerPoint presentation that captures the solid how-to information and showcases their online abilities and creative potential. In groups of six, Leslie and Evan invite prospective online clients in to a shared server space to view their company presentation. When companies see what they can do and find out how easily they can benefit from this type of online exploration, they are hooked. Leslie has printed the outline from her PowerPoint presentation and makes it available on the company Web page (which she also created in PowerPoint). Clients can easily download either the text outline or the entire presentation so they can show other decision-makers in their organizations what's now available on the Web.

Chapter Summary

This chapter completes your journey through *Mastering PowerPoint 2000*. By looking at the various ways people present with PowerPoint, you can get some idea as to what will work best for you, how to evaluate what you've done, and how you can present more effectively in the future. PowerPoint makes it easy to express, review, and revise your ideas, while wowing your audience with color, style, the latest multimedia technology, and professional printouts. One way or another, PowerPoint can help you make sure your message hits home.

PART IV

Appendices

APPENDIX A

Installing PowerPoint 2000

Before you install PowerPoint, take a few minutes to back up your system to tape, floppies, or other media. At the very least, make sure you have copies of all your important files and programs.

The Installation Process

After backing up your system, insert the CD in your CD-ROM drive, and then open the Start menu on the Windows Taskbar and select Run. The Run dialog box appears, as shown in Figure A.1.

 TIP Your CD may be set to AutoRun, meaning that the computer displays the contents of the CD automatically after you insert it. If that's the case, locate the Setup icon and double-click it; then skip to "Installing PowerPoint with Office."

FIGURE A.1

The Run dialog box

In the Open text box of the Run dialog box, type **a:\setup** or **d:\setup** (depending on whether you're installing from a floppy drive or from your CD-ROM drive), and click OK to start installing PowerPoint. If you are installing from a different drive (for example, a second floppy drive that's referred to as b:), substitute the appropriate drive letter and then click OK to start the installation process.

Installing PowerPoint with Office

If you are installing the program for the first time, Office 2000 displays the introduction screen. Click Continue. You are then asked to enter your name and organization. Fill in your information and click OK. A confirmation screen appears, showing you what you have entered. If the information is correct, click OK to continue. If the information is not correct, edit the information as necessary.

NOTE When you run the Setup after the intial time, a different screen will appear. On subsequent uses, you will be given the option of repairing Office, adding or removing features, or removing Office from this first screen.

You will next be asked for your CD-Key. This is the number located on the back of your CD package. (If you are installing from floppy, this step will not appear.)

On the next screen, the install program displays your Product ID. Write down this number for safekeeping; you may need it if you have trouble with Office and need to contact technical support.

 NOTE Once you've installed PowerPoint, your Product ID will also appear in the About PowerPoint dialog box, which you can display any time by choosing Help ➢ About. Having your Product ID written down somewhere outside the program, however, is a good idea in case you experience a program crash and cannot get back into PowerPoint.

The install program then makes sure you have enough storage space on your hard drive and gives you the option of selecting the directory in which your Office 2000 files will be stored. If you want to change the directory where Office 2000 files are stored, click the Change Directory button and, when prompted, enter the name of the directory you want to use for PowerPoint files.

The next screen lets you choose the type of installation, so that you may control how much space the program takes on your hard drive. For most uses, Typical is your best bet. If you want to select which features you install, click Custom and follow the prompts on the screen.

The install procedure will check your hard drive for available space and begin copying the Office files to the specified folders.

NOTE If you are interested in installing only a few Office features—or adding some and omitting others—select Custom. You might use this, for example, if you want to install Word and PowerPoint and leave out Excel.

Installing PowerPoint Later

Even though PowerPoint comes with the Office suite, you may not want to install it until you need it. Suppose that you've been using Word and Excel for some time now and have been asked to do a presentation for the visiting corporate bigwigs tomorrow afternoon. Better install PowerPoint—quick!

To add PowerPoint to the Office suite, insert your first Office CD into the CD-ROM drive. Navigate to the Setup program icon on the CD or use Program ➤ Run and type **setup.exe**. The first install window will appear, as Figure A.2 shows.

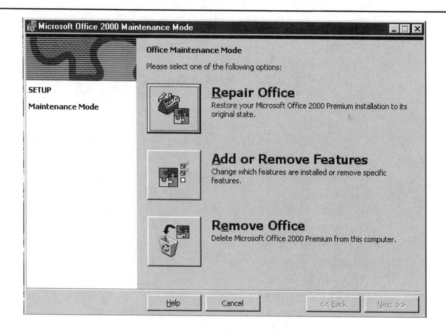

When the first install window appears, click Add or Remove Features. The Microsoft Office 2000: Update Features dialog box appears, as you see in Figure A.3.

FIGURE A.3

The Office 2000: Update Features dialog box enables you to add PowerPoint to installed Office applications.

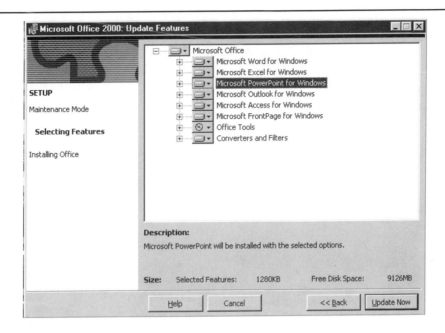

Select Microsoft PowerPoint for Windows and then select Update Now. Follow the prompts to select the features and locations for the files.

Later, if you want to go back to add or remove items, change the installation settings, or reinstall the entire program, you can run Setup again. Running Setup again will not destroy any data files you have created, but it will allow you to reinstall program files or add features you skipped the first time you installed PowerPoint.

NOTE If you are running Setup again and have not previously used PowerPoint's Online Registration option to register your copy of PowerPoint with the Microsoft powers-that-be, you will see the option that suggests you register now. Registering allows you to use Microsoft's customer service operation and to be eligible for discounted upgrades.

APPENDIX B

Modifying Program Defaults

One of PowerPoint's primary goals is to be easy to use right off the bat. For that reason, many options have been preset for you. These options determine, among other things, the way the screen works, how printing is handled, which dialog boxes appear automatically, whether text is replaced or inserted when you type, and how many undos you are allowed to make. As you become proficient with PowerPoint, you may want to change some of the program defaults.

To change the program defaults, go to the Options dialog box (select Tools ➢ Options), which has numerous tabs containing various categories of options, as shown in Figure B.1. This appendix covers each of the options available in this dialog box.

View Options

The View options, shown in Figure B.1, control the elements displayed on the screen during your PowerPoint work session. The following options in the Show area effect the PowerPoint work area:

Startup Dialog Determines whether the Startup window appears when you begin PowerPoint.

New Slide Dialog Displays the New Slide dialog box.

Status Bar Controls whether the status bar appears at the bottom of the PowerPoint work area.

Vertical Ruler   Determines whether the vertical ruler is shown when you select View ➢ Ruler.

Windows in Taskbar   Makes open windows available in the Taskbar.

The following options in the Slide Show area determine what you see during a slide show:

Popup Menu on Right Mouse Click   Controls whether the pop-up menu—which includes Slide Show navigation and enhancement commands—appears when you click the right mouse button during a slide show.

Show Popup Menu Button   Determines whether the menu button appears in the lower-left corner of the Slide Show screen.

End with Black Slide   Displays a black slide at the end of the presentation rather than restarting the presentation at the opening slide.

General Options

The next tab in the Options dialog box is the General tab, shown in Figure B.2. The options on this page control items displayed in dialog boxes and menus. The options in the General Options area include the following:

Provide Feedback with Sound to Screen Elements   This option plays Microsoft Office sounds when PowerPoint performs designated functions or displays certain types of objects. If you don't have Office sounds installed on your system, you can install them from the Office CD or choose Help ➢ Office on the Web ➢ Free Stuff, and click on the Sounds folder.

Recently Used File List   Select this check box to specify the number of files displayed in the Entries box.

Link Sounds with File Size Greater Than *x* Kb   You can reduce the size of the PowerPoint file by having the program link to, rather than embed, large sound files.

In the User Information area, enter your name and initials, if desired. The information you enter will appear in the Properties box or on any printed or broadcast presentations you create.

The Web Options button opens the Web Options dialog box. From this dialog box you can select various options that determine how you use and view the Web.

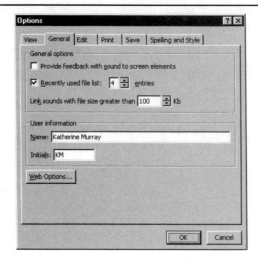

Edit Options

The Edit tab of the Options dialog box, shown in Figure B.3, contains the settings in effect when you're editing the text of your PowerPoint presentation. Here are the basic functions of these different options:

Replace Straight Quotes with Smart Quotes   Automatically replaces straight quotation marks (also called inch marks) with curly quotation marks—open quote marks at the beginning of the word or phrase and close quote marks at the end.

When Selecting, Automatically Select Entire Word   Causes Power-Point to automatically highlight the whole word at the cursor position. This can be really useful or really annoying, depending on what you're trying to accomplish, so remember this feature exists and come back to it to change it as needed.

Use Smart Cut and Paste   This feature, which operates in Slide View and Outline View, removes extra spaces you may have accidentally included at the beginning or end of a phrase or sentence when you swiped the mouse across it to select it for cutting. Additionally, this feature will add any necessary spaces when you paste text into a presentation.

Drag-and-Drop Text Editing   Enables you to select and drag text and graphics from one point to another in your presentation. Without this feature enabled, you are limited to using Cut, Copy, and Paste commands.

Auto-fit Text to Text Placeholder   Lets PowerPoint adjust the text to fit into the text frame.

AutoFormat as You Type   Automatically formats your presentation as you create it.

New Charts Take on PowerPoint Font   Assigns the current PowerPoint font to charts you import.

Maximum Number of Undos   Lets you set the number of operations you can reverse.

FIGURE B.3

The Edit tab

Print Options

The Print options, shown in Figure B.4, enable you to control how PowerPoint handles printing. The options include the following:

Background Printing   Lets you continue working while the document is sent to the printer.

Print TrueType Fonts as Graphics   Prints TrueType fonts as images rather than downloading the fonts to your printer. The only reason you might use this is if you have a presentation with so many fonts that the document won't print at all.

Print Inserted Objects at Printer Resolution   Enables PowerPoint to print objects you place on presentation slides at the printer's default resolution.

Use the Most Recently Used Print Settings   Uses the print selections for the current document when you print the presentation using the toolbar.

Use the Following Default Print Settings   Enables you to select a number of different print settings, such as what you want to print, whether you want to print hidden slides, and more.

The Print tab

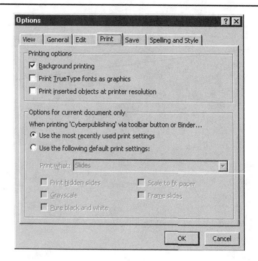

Save Options

The Save options, shown in Figure B.5, control how, when and where your files are saved. The options include the following:

Allow Fast Saves   Saves time because only the changes are recorded whenever you save the presentation during a session; the full file is saved only when you close the presentation or exit the program. (You can override a fast save in specific instances by using the shortcut Ctrl+S to save your presentation. Ctrl+S always saves the full file.)

Prompt for File Properties   Asks for more information about the file during a save.

Save AutoRecover Info Every *x* Minutes Saves the file at the interval you specify.

Convert Charts When Saving as Previous Version Allows you to automatically convert charts to earlier PowerPoint versions when you save the entire presentation in those formats.

Save PowerPoint Files As Enables you to set the default file format for saved files.

Default File Location Enables you to choose the folder in which presentations are saved by default.

FIGURE B.5

The Save tab

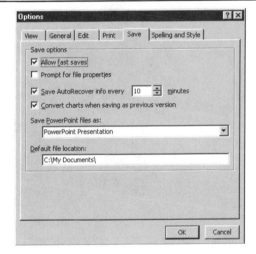

Spelling and Style Options

The Spelling and Style tab, shown in Figure B.6, enables you to specify spelling and style preferences. The options include the following:

Check Spelling as You Type Enables PowerPoint to identify spelling mistakes as you type.

Hide Spelling Errors in This Document Enables you to turn off the auto spelling checker as you work. This option is not enabled by default.

Always Suggest Corrections Activates the spell checker's suggested spelling list. (If not selected, the spell checker will never make suggestions.)

Ignore Words in UPPERCASE   Tells the spell checker whether to flag words in uppercase. (If you use a lot of acronyms, you won't want to be bothered by the spell checker flagging every single one of them.)

Ignore Words with Numbers   Enables you to skip words with numbers. (This uses the same reasoning as the previous option, it's useful for skipping lots of high-tech company names and product names that include numerals.)

Check Style   Automatically checks the style of your presentation.

FIGURE B.6

*The Spelling and
Style tab*

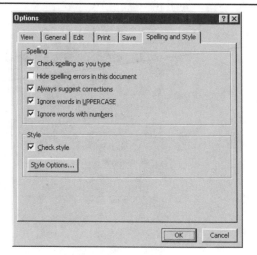

NOTE   You can change the settings for the style checker by clicking the Style Options button in the Options dialog box and choosing the items you want to change. You can modify settings for the way PowerPoint checks the case of your text and the end punctuation. You can also control the visual clarity settings by choosing the number of fonts that can be used, the size of text, the number of bullets, and more.

APPENDIX C

Tips for the First-Time Presenter

Presenting can be a harrowing experience—even if you've been doing it for years. When you are first faced with the prospect of creating and giving a presentation, the experience may seem overwhelming and intimidating. Here are some tips that will help you target, produce, and deliver your first presentation with a reduced level of anxiety:

Ask Questions   When you are first commissioned to do the presentation, ask plenty of questions. Find out who the audience is, what the general age range might be, what the overall tone of the presentation should be, and what the audience most needs to know from your presentation.

Keep a Folder of Styles You Like   Take advantage of opportunities to see presentations done by other people. Keep a notebook or folder of what you liked and what you didn't. Ask yourself what works and why? What would you change if you were doing the presentation? Notice audience reaction and keep samples of the printed materials to see what the presenter felt was most important to include in printed form. Gathering this type of information will help you use what works in your own presentation.

Become an Informed Watcher   You don't have to limit your input to traditional presentations. Even with something as seemingly unrelated as watching television, you can learn something about the presentation you're preparing. What commercials catch your eye and why? What shows hold your interest, and what elements contribute to their success? Make mental notes about what keeps and holds your attention and use them as you craft your own project.

Try a Variety of Styles   If you have time to prepare a couple of samples, try using two or three of PowerPoint's different presentation designs to see what is most effective. Pass the samples around to get the opinions of others in your office or work group. The more feedback you get in the early stages, the better.

Keep it Simple   When preparing the basic content of your presentation, try to keep to a series of simple concepts. The temptation to cram a wide range of information into a 30-minute presentation may be great, but remember that your ultimate goal is to be heard and understood. If you throw too much information at your audience at once, they may not remember the most important points.

Overprepared Is Better Than Underprepared   Practice doesn't necessarily make perfect, but it certainly makes you better. The more time you spend preparing yourself, the better armed you'll feel at the moment of truth. In addition to spending time honing your presentation, double-check to be sure that you have all the equipment, printouts, and space you need. Early in the creation process, make a list of items you'll need the day of the presentation. Several days before you present, review that list to make sure you haven't missed anything.

Make Yourself Comfortable   Remember that jitters are just that—jitters. Once you begin the presentation and see how the audience is responding, much of your stage fright will pass. Taking care to make sure you're comfortable, however, will give you an edge. Wear clothing in which you feel competent and sure of yourself, make sure the conference room or stage is set up so you can move around the way you need to, be yourself as much as possible, and give yourself plenty of time.

When You Discover Something That Works, Use It Again   You don't have to create your next presentation from scratch if you hit on something that works well in your first presentation. Make sure you save the file and, if applicable, use it as a template for future presentations.

INDEX

Note to the Reader: First level entries are in **bold**. Page numbers in **bold** indicate the principal discussion of a topic or the definition of a term. Page numbers in *italic* indicate illustrations.